DUCT TAPE & BALING WIRE

FROM CITY STREETS TO MOUNTAIN PEAKS

Kevin J. Rosenberg

Text copyright © 2021 by Kevin J. Rosenberg

All rights reserved. No part of this publication may be translated, reproduced, stored in a retrieval system or transmitted, in any form or by any means, electronic, mechanical, photocopying, recording or otherwise, for any purpose, without express written permission from the author.

Library of Congress Control Number: 2021910918

ISBN (Paperback) 978-1-7371633-0-5

City of publication: Tucson, AZ

Edited by Tara Yarlagadda

Designed by Annemarie Redmond

To Mom

Thanks for always believing in me, giving me confidence, teaching me bravery, and providing me with a passion for the written word.

TABLE OF CONTENTS

Foreword .... *vii*
Introduction .... *ix*
Chapter 1: The Crucible 1
Chapter 2: 'Field of Dreams' Mentality 7
Chapter 3: Tough Jews 15
Chapter 4: From the Ground Up 25
Chapter 5: Born to Fly 31
Chapter 6: Indoctrination 34
Chapter 7: Spread Your Wings 42
Chapter 8: Top of the Pyramid 56
Chapter 9: The price of Honor 68
Chapter 10: Brick & Mortar 82
Chapter 11: Haze Grey and Underway 103
Chapter 12: "Ever Ready, Ever Fearless" 118
Chapter 13: A Farewell to Arms 128
Chapter 14: Are there Really Angels Among Us? 141
Chapter 15: How Did I End up in Law School? 146
Chapter 16: Breaking Ground, Literally! 152
Chapter 17: "Who's Playing in the Sandbox?" 156
Chapter 18: Living the Dream! 172
Chapter 19: A Sea Change 176
Chapter 20: Civil War 181
Chapter 21: "Cry of the Vultures" 185
Chapter 22: A Rough Transition 190
Chapter 23: Trail Beta – Lessons Learned 198
Chapter 24: "Two roads converged in the woods…" 202
Acknowledgements *205*

FOREWORD

I love gear. I love gear so much that I made an entire TV show dedicated to just how much I love it. And while I played a heightened, asshole version of myself on that show, and while that show was for the most part an aggressively stupid comedy, it was always deeply and firmly grounded in truth: that I love gear.

So on the daily walk to my son's elementary school one morning, when I rounded the normally barren corner of the Chase bank building, only to be confronted by the site of a guy standing behind a small table that was filled with a gear-head's immediate recognition of high quality winter gloves, as well as a colorful, salivating display of Marmot rain jackets, all displayed above a large sign that read GEAR TO GO, my interest was piqued to say the least. Who was this guy and what was his deal and which cool looking jacket was I going to buy even though I didn't need one? A friendship was formed, and here I am almost a decade later, sitting at my dining table, wearing the Marmot rain pants I bought at his first store for inspiration (and perspiration. Not great for indoors), writing the foreword for his book.

I'm kidding about wearing the pants, although now I am tempted to go put them on since they're so cool. But I don't need them. Kevin is a truly inspirational individual. Someone who had a dream, and, from my perspective, took some monstrous chances in pursuing it. Leaving the comfort and security of a steady job to head off into the literal and figurative unknown. I enjoyed seeing something as unique as a street stand with quality gear blossom into a thriving small, local business. Kevin told me that Gear To Go was NYC's only authentic outfitter. Even though I was never able to take advantage, it was great to have that seed planted in my head, knowing this option was right around the corner from my apartment. I popped in often, just to hang out and talk gear, hear about planned trips, just step out of my neighborhood and immerse myself in a small world of gear for a few minutes (or more) of my day. I was saddened and infuriated when I found out Kevin had to close his second, bigger store, just as things seemed to be going so well for him, just as on-line shopping was starting to take its toll on his and many other small businesses. But that's life sometimes, unfortunately. That's adventure. No risk, no reward. Often times heartache. Who knows what's around every corner? And lots of other trite but true platitudes.

    I moved to a different neighborhood a couple years ago. Not too far from the site of the booth where this journey began. And even though it's an absolutely gorgeous, cloudless day that does not require them at all, maybe I'll put on those rain pants, take a stroll to that corner. And maybe some other dad walking his son to school will round that same boring corner, where they see the same boring nothing, every boring morning, only to be confronted by something different on this particular day. The jarring site of a guy sitting on the ground. Wearing some high tech looking rain gear. Crying softly to himself. And when the dad cautiously approaches, keeping his son at bay, and asks if I need help, I'll just gaze up at him and say "I'm okay. I just love gear." Then I'll turn to his son, muster a disarming smile, and add, "And so does Kevin."

— Jon Glaser

INTRODUCTION

This is a modern-day Horatio Alger story that details my life's struggles as an entrepreneur and provides insight into what it takes to build a business in the 21st century. I've included stories from my adventures over the years, which have often forced me to change directions, but also provided the experiences and life lessons needed to take a street stand in Brooklyn and grow it into a nationally recognized business.

Mine is a story of overcoming adversity, dealing with repeated setbacks, finding a way to move forward, and achieving my dreams while also remaining committed to doing the right thing and living a life of adventure. I've fought many battles along the way and even slew a few windmills, while remaining true to my values as I reinvented my life.

On January 7th, 2020, I made national news when I won a landmark legal victory against the student loan industry. Though the case is slowly making its way to the Supreme Court, where it could potentially change the lives of millions, my initial victory has already given hope to those being abused by a heavy-handed, one-sided system.

I was forced to represent myself in this fight because every lawyer I met with told me it was impossible to win. I never believed them. My battle — and subsequent victory — has been covered in countless interviews, articles, journals, and podcasts, but no story has covered the roots of my journey. Until now.

This is the story of how I got there. How a former Naval Officer with an advanced degree and a million-dollar company, ended up in bankruptcy.

Writing this book has been, at times, painful, joyful, and cathartic. It felt like completing this project was a mission that life had assigned me, as if the experiences of the past few decades, the ups and downs, twists and turns, occurred so that I could write this story and share it with the world. It's been a painful process at times, dredging up memories that I had long since buried but never really let go of, but at the same time, it felt good to put this story on paper and share it with the world.

My story has been shaped by adversity, so it seems appropriate that it took the 2020 pandemic to provide me with the time for the personal reflection and solitude I apparently needed to complete this story. Most of it was written during my "solitary confinement" in a rented house on a quiet street in Beacon, NY and a casita in Santa Fe, NM.

If you've ever dreamed of running your own business, I urge you to read my story and learn from my successes and failures. If you're going through a rough time and need to find hope to keep going, I hope you will gain inspiration. If someone in your life has been knocked on their ass, I hope my story will convince you to put out your hand and help them to their feet. If none of these apply to you, I hope you will just enjoy a good story made even better — because it's all true.

LET THE ADVENTURE BEGIN!

CHAPTER ONE

THE CRUCIBLE

August 18, 1998: Naval Air Station Meridian, MS
I suited up in the locker room where we kept our survival gear and walked through the hanger, flight boots stomping on the concrete floor as I rushed to the maintenance window to check out my jet. After several weather cancellations, I was pumped to finally have my first nighttime solo flight.

Pushing open the metal door that led to the flight line, I looked up to see blue sky fading away as darkness quickly advanced. I ran through my preflight checks, making sure all of the control surfaces could move freely and then checked for forgotten tools in the engine intakes before excitedly climbing up the side of my aircraft.

Strapped in with umbilical cords for my oxygen mask and g-suit connected, I lit the fires of both engines, signaled for the plane captain to pull the chocks, and rolled out towards the runway. I met the other solo students in the marshal area where we eagerly waited for the "lead safe" instructor — already airborne — to check out the Military Operating Area (MOA) and clear us to launch, continuously dimming our cockpit lights as our eyes adjusted to the Mississippi night.

Word came in from up above that the skies were clear, and the mission was a go! We taxied out in a staggered column and headed towards runway 1R. I was third to take the runway and couldn't wait to get airborne.

I pressed hard on the brakes as I ran the throttles up to max power, checking the gauges as the engines thundered, the jet shuddering as it fought to be free. I released the brakes and sped down the runway with the roar of a dragster. With no instructor in the seat behind me, I reported the usual checks to myself as the speed rapidly built up. "40 knots, heels on the deck," as the rudder became

1

effective. "75 seat's alive," providing the option to eject from the aircraft if need be and get a swing or two under the silk before I hit the ground.

With about 1,200 feet of runway behind me, I pulled back smoothly on the stick, just as the needle on the airspeed indicator passed 100 knots. Leaping skyward, I immediately checked for a positive rate of climb on the instruments and reached for the landing gear handle when "SLAM!" I felt an impact as the aircraft yawed to the right and then back to center.

"What the fuck was that?" We were always taught to Aviate, Navigate, and then Communicate, so I focused first on keeping the jet in the air.

Confident that I'd be able to stay airborne for at least the next few seconds, I looked down at the instrument panel to troubleshoot, expecting to see "FIRE" lights flashing. Instead, the first thing I noticed was that the Exhaust Gas Temperature on the right engine had reached 850° F (100° above max) and that the RPM on that engine was unwinding past 60 percent.

I'd lost the engine, but I didn't know why.

I followed my training, running through the emergency procedures we were drilled on in order to avoid a catastrophic engine failure. There was a risk that the engine could start to disintegrate, sending compressor blades flying through the aircraft, taking out the left engine — and possibly even me.

My hands followed a well-practiced path through the cockpit, one imprinted on my brain from hours spent studying emergency procedures on homemade flashcards, "chairflying" — mentally preparing for a flight — while waiting in the ready room, and from having instructors pull power on one of the engines while in flight and then calmly announce "simulated."

Following procedure, I pulled back the throttle on the right engine, careful to avoid accidentally pulling back power on the left, which with a full bag of gas onboard was struggling to keep me airborne. I then turned off the master switch for the damaged engine and pulled the 'T' shaped handle that would open the fuel dump valves in the wingtips and lighten my load. Finally, I reached for the transponder and turned the dial to 'EMERGENCY,' lighting me up like a Christmas Tree on air traffic control's radar.

After running through the emergency procedures, I quickly returned my attention to getting back on the ground as soon as possible. I couldn't build up enough airspeed to climb, but wasn't descending either. I knew the runway was 8,000 feet long and that I'd probably gotten airborne in about 1,200 feet, but I also remembered the tall pine trees that lay just beyond the runway, past the collection of trailers we called "WACO." I had just seconds to troubleshoot before I ran out of runway and into the trees.

The instruments were telling a story but I didn't know what it was. I'd completed all of the emergency procedures but the airspeed was stuck at around 120 KIAS, barely above stall speed and only 50 feet off the ground. Since I wasn't able to climb, I couldn't trade altitude for airspeed, and knew from training that many pilots die when they are so focused on pulling away from the ground that they stall the aircraft and crater in.

Time slowed down as I headed straight for the pine trees with just seconds to live. I thought about ejecting and even looked down at the handle which was appropriately placed between my legs. If I pulled that handle I would be out of the aircraft in 0.8 seconds. First the 200-pound canopy would be thrown clear, then the back seat would go, and then finally my seat would go.

By "go," I mean that a nitrogen-filled catapult would violently throw me clear of the aircraft with a force of 32g's — 32 times the force of gravity — then the rocket engine I was sitting on would fire. If pointed skyward my parachute would barely have time to fully deploy before I hit the ground. The forces of an ejection are so powerful that if your legs are just a quarter-inch off the seat, you'll get what's known as "Seat Slap" which will break your legs.

I stared at the handle and thought, "That's gonna hurt!" I wasn't ready to give up and punch out. I focused on the instrument panel, "What was I missing?" Then I saw it, "Fuck, the gear is still down!" I was reaching for the landing gear handle when I felt the impact. Surprised by the jolt, I had pulled my hand back and focused on staying airborne. I quickly threw the gear handle up and moved to the flap handle.

The T-2C Buckeye, or "The Attack Guppy," as we called it, was already an old aircraft by the time I was flying it. Senator John McCain had flown the same aircraft when he went through flight school before I was even born. The jet had a personality, with nuances, charms, and downright dangers that you needed to learn.

One of Buckeye's "charms" was that, occasionally, when you lowered or raised the flaps, one would move, and one would stay in place. This would cause a quick roll to one side that could not be counteracted. "Split Flaps" as it was called, had brought down several aircraft. At least two rusting examples lay in a swamp beyond the runway, which the students had labeled "T-2 Pond." I raised the flaps, and, with my hand ready to reverse the action, I thought, "All I need now is another emergency!"

The flaps retracted without incident and with the aircraft now "clean" my airspeed picked up and I was able to gain some altitude. I needed to get on the ground as fast as possible in case the left engine failed. So, after building up some altitude and airspeed, I began a left turn back towards the field to set up for a landing back on Runway 1R, but also to be in a position for a dead stick landing on 19R — the opposite runway — if I lost the other engine.

One of the first things they taught us in flight school was that you have to sound cool on the radio. If you sounded like you were scared your reputation in the community was over. There would be no chance for redemption.

Turning back towards the field I keyed the mike and in my best airline pilot voice reported, "MERIDIAN DEPARTURE THIS IS STING 919 SOLO DECLARING AN EMERGENCY." Departure immediately replied "ROGER, WHAT'S YOUR EMERGENCY?" In a calm voice I reported, "I LOST AN ENGINE."

I continued my turn and spotted the crash crew leaving their station, racing towards the runway, their red lights sweeping the ground below. I listened as departure kicked everyone else out of the landing pattern. Filled with youth and fighter pilot bravado, I was excited to "own this airfield" despite being barely 25 and with only 136 hours of flight time to my name.

I climbed up to 2,500 feet to reenter the pattern and gain altitude, which I could trade for airspeed if I lost both engines and needed to glide in towards the runway. Switching over to Tower, I repeated that I had declared an emergency and then asked to switch over to my squadron's frequency so that I could run through final checks with the Squadron Duty Officer.

Lieutenant Tooke, the instructor pilot on duty, reviewed the emergency procedures with me. When we confirmed that everything was complete, he wished me luck before handing a phone list to a newly arrived Ensign, telling him, "If anything happens, start dialing!"

Finally, being good NASCAR fans, they shut off the lights in the ready room and scanned the night sky above the runway, waiting to see how this played out.

I entered the landing pattern, set up for a wide approach turn, secured my fuel dump, and ran through the landing checklist:

> *"Fuel transfer off, gear down and locked, ½ flaps, hook up, harness locked, speed brakes out, 14 units angle of attack (AOA), landing light on."*

Reporting "919 solo abeam with the gear full stop," I began my approach turn and set up for landing. Rolling out on final approach, I "called the ball," indicating that I had eyes on the glideslope indicator and was now under the control of the Landing Signals Officer (LSO) stationed alongside the runway.

All of our landings were simulated carrier landings and an emergency landing would be no different, other than the fact that I was coming in a little hot with extra airspeed, since I only had one engine to get out of trouble if I found myself low and slow.

I had no issues with the landing, and safely back on the ground, I taxied back to the flightline. About a dozen maintenance workers rushed out to the jet — not to check on me — but to see what happened to the engine. Though they never even looked up at me, I laughed and jokingly said "I'm fine, guys," as I waved from the cockpit. Turning to my left, I noticed that my plane captain was already alongside, ready to free me from the Buckeye's saddle.

When I climbed down, the plane captain asked, "What was going through your head?" "I can't believe this is happening to me!" was my honest answer. Like anyone that does a dangerous job for a living, I accepted the risks but was also secure in the belief that those risks would never affect me — it was the other guy that had to worry.

It was late on a Tuesday night, so the hangar was empty as I made my way to the locker room. I stowed my survival gear before slowly making my way upstairs to the ready room. Having just toasted an engine, I knew I had a lot of paperwork to do.

Entering the ready room, I was greeted by a standing ovation from the few instructors and students present. It was justifiably a brief celebration as this was only a notable achievement because I was a student with very few hours of flight time. The truth was that if a winged aviator had experienced the same emergency, his handling of it would have gone unnoticed unless he screwed up.

I was proud of what I had accomplished, but mostly for the fact that I had proven to the Naval Aviation community and myself that I could remain calm, think clearly, and make good decisions while under stress and facing a life and death situation. I had been through the crucible and passed the test. Now back to the paperwork.

The mystery surrounding what caused the engine to fail just seconds into flight, was solved when a bat — yes, the flying kind — was found inside the engine's burner section. This meant that the bat's faulty radar had guided him through eight stages of compressor blades, only to lodge himself in the area of the engine where compressed air, fuel, and flame are combined to produce thrust. Using the old aviator justification that "A kill's, a kill," I tried to get them to paint a bat on the side of the aircraft but was unsuccessful.

This incident was just one of the many formative experiences I had while serving in the Navy. Many were good, many were bad, but I'm thankful for all of them, as they taught me some valuable lessons that you can't learn anywhere else. Lessons I would draw upon later in life, including the struggle of starting a small business as a street vendor in Brooklyn at the height of the Great Recession, while already pretty broke, laid off, and on unemployment! Without experiences like the nighttime engine failure, the odds of success might rightly have seemed insurmountable and a sane, rational man would have taken another path in life. I looked at it as, "Okay, I've gone through all the steps, what am I missing?"

CHAPTER TWO

"FIELD OF DREAMS" MENTALITY

In Mrs. Boyle's first grade class, I learned to read while standing on my head. I was also known for watching TV while upside down, so I guess I just needed a different perspective on things. I should clarify that I learned enough to satisfy the educational requirements but not enough to satisfy Mom, who then took it upon herself to work with me using flashcards to make sure I was not just reading at my level, but beyond. I always wanted to send her a photo of me flying upside down with the caption, "See Mom, it paid off!" Sometimes looking at a problem from a different perspective allows you to come up with a new and better solution, sometimes it just results in a headache, and sometimes it's a bit of both.

After briefly practicing law for all of two and a half months, I decided to pursue every man's dream of owning a bar — a Naval Aviation themed bar and restaurant in my case. On job interviews in law school, I was rarely asked what I was studying or what practice area I wanted to focus on after graduation but always, "What was it like to fly jets?"

With the percentage of Americans serving in the military dropping over the decades, I realized there were now generations of successful professionals that envied my experience and wished they had exhibited the testicular fortitude to serve. Though I obviously couldn't strap them into the back of a jet and go cloud surfing, I could give all the lawyers, doctors, and businessmen of New York the social experience of being an aviator.

I started working as a real estate broker, which allowed me the flexibility to work on this project. When that market started to slow down, I took contract jobs as a document review attorney, which paid well and allowed for a flexible schedule. I prepared a business plan to see if my idea made sense and then signed up for a few courses in restaurant management at the New School in Manhattan.

I wanted the bar to be authentic and honor Naval Aviation, so I looked for investors solely within that community. My buddy, Steve Bury, with whom I started flight school, got me started with a $15,000 investment. To build on this investment, I exhibited at Naval Aviation's Tailhook convention in Reno, NV. I had some strong interest and returned the following year as the economy was booming and folks were looking for places to invest.

After the second trip out to Tailhook in 2008, I had commitments totaling around $750,000 from almost 70 investors — all Naval Aviators. I was set; this was going to happen! I returned home on September 7th and sent out the paperwork to finalize the deal and arrange for the funds to be transferred.

I had already started looking at vacant listings when news of Lehman Brother's collapse came on September 15, 2008 as I was working another contract job at a big firm, my last I was certain. At first, I wasn't sure what this meant for me since I didn't own any stock, but the impact would soon become crystal clear as one by one my investors backed out.

I tried to calm their fears, reminding them that people drink during good times and bad and the only thing that changes is what they drink and why. It was no use; it was down to Steve and one other investor. After years of working on this project and just days from having the money I needed to move forward, it was over, up in flames on the tarmac before I even had the chance to taxi to the runway. A week later, I was laid off.

Now on unemployment and with no bar, I wondered what was next. The historic magnitude of the recession quickly became apparent. The only question that remained was how bad it would get? How far would we fall as a nation? As we sank deeper into the 'Bush Depression,' I wrote:

> *"It's after midnight on December 7th, 2008, and I've been thinking about how I will tell my children about the times we now live in and how we got here. I grew up learning about the Great Depression in school, hearing stories from my grandparents about what it was like to live through it and how it affected their lives. They saved whatever they could, never wasted anything, and as a generation, we had all watched as our grandmothers would slip dinner rolls into their purses — a practice they had no doubt learned from when the length of time until their next meal was uncertain.*
>
> *We learned that this could never happen again, that our country had learned better. Laws had been enacted, attitudes had changed, and*

we had learned from our mistakes. Yet, here I sit, out of work for more than ten weeks now with no prospects on the horizon. Things seem so bleak that I don't even know how far away that horizon is. Will the sun rise again in a few weeks, a few months, or even in a few years?

I've thought about how I would dig up the tree in my mother's yard so we could plant crops if things got really bad, or how I feel fortunate that I own a car where the seats fold into beds. I've thought about how lucky I am to be comfortable living in the woods and how tents (I own two) could become a hot commodity.

The one thing I am oddly thankful for is not having a family to support. How do you explain to children that their lives have changed because of the mistakes of people in Washington and on Wall Street? How do you explain that — through no fault of their own — there will be no vacation this year, no more family dinners out, no big birthday party, and hopefully only fewer presents rather than no presents at all?

Of course, being out of work prevents me from even hoping to have a family. Nothing makes a man feel worse than being without a job and the means to support a family. How can I hope to meet the woman of my dreams when I can't even make rent?"

As a young officer, I learned the motto "*Semper Gumby,*" which translates from Military Latin as "Always Flexible." The bar was not going to happen, at least not for the foreseeable future, and the future of the contract attorney industry — already moving to India — was worse than bleak. I knew I had to create my own solution, so I began to reevaluate another business idea I'd developed while daydreaming in law school.

I had formed an outdoor adventure club in law school and led fellow students on trips where we went hiking, sailing, rock climbing, kayaking, and backpacking. For many, this was a new experience and I found that I had a real passion for introducing people to the wilderness and expanding their horizons.

This passion had its roots in the desert southwest. In August 1991, shortly after my 18th birthday, I found myself in Tucson, Arizona, on an Army ROTC scholarship and a new member of the ROTC Ranger Training Program. The rest of the battalion went out into the field once a semester, but we were in the desert almost every weekend practicing small unit tactics such as patrols, movement to contact, and ambushes, under the tutelage of senior Green Beret NCOs and Ranger-qualified officers.

No one in my family hiked or camped, and Boy Scouts in my neighborhood were ridiculed at best and beat up at worst, so I didn't have any real exposure to the outdoors before arriving as a freshman cadet. I suddenly found myself carrying a 75-pound backpack, wearing camouflage greasepaint on my face, and holding an M-16. I loved it, and, eventually, I realized I could just go hiking without the M-16 and an infantry squad behind me.

Organizing the first overnight backpacking trip for my outdoor adventure club, I learned how hard it was for folks to gather the gear they needed for even a simple overnight trip in early fall. A few places rented the basics, such as tents, sleeping bags, sleeping pads, and backpacks, but they didn't even wash their sleeping bags, simply spraying them with a disinfectant like bowling shoes and expecting you to bring a liner. Folks had to either borrow or buy the rest, which meant they were running around the city the day before a trip. I thought, "Wouldn't it be great if there was one place that rented all of the gear you needed and even delivered?"

Guiding was my real passion, and since everyone dreams of turning their passion into a business, I knew that this new venture would also be a guide service. We would provide one-stop shopping for adventure. A customer could come to us and buy or rent everything they needed for a trip. We could even help them plan that trip or guide it for them. It would be the first Full-Service Outfitter in the region. Now, granted, that's a term I invented, but still, the first!

Now, what to call it? I thought about 'Rosenberg Outfitters' but felt that it was a mistake to use your last name in case someone had a bad association with it, or, in my case, maybe they were anti-Semitic. I had heard that it also made it harder to sell a business years later if it bore your name. I thought about 'Brooklyn Outfitters' but dreamed of expanding beyond New York City someday and didn't want to have my growth limited by a geographic name the way Eastern Mountain Sports (EMS) was when it tried to expand out west.

I wanted to let folks know that we were the experts in the region and that we offered guide services, rentals, and sales. I knew that rentals would make us unique; trips would be the most fun; sales would bring in the most revenue. The idea was to make preparing for a weekend adventure as convenient as possible, so we would even deliver.

Building on the military phrase 'Good to go,' I came up with 'Gear To Go' since that incorporated the fact that we delivered but also that we had you covered. 'Gear To Go Outfitters' was the name that fit the concept but now, of course, I needed to find the money to get started. Remember that, I'm still out of work and on unemployment while I'm putting this together.

As part of the recovery from the crash of '08, the SBA launched a special loan program called 'Patriot Express' designed to help Veterans start businesses. The program guaranteed 90 percent of the loan amount and did away with the usual SBA requirements, such as having been in business for two years or putting up real estate collateral to back the loan. I was excited to see the government offer actual help to Veterans looking to start a business rather than simply offering seminars on how to write a business plan or how to network effectively.

Excited about this opportunity, and with business plan in hand, I visited several different banks in New York, but the pushback I faced was disheartening. All of the loan officers refused to even submit the application, often claiming that the program didn't exist. After hearing this claim from Chase Bank — one of the biggest banks in the country — I wondered if maybe they hadn't yet heard of this new program, so I called the local SBA Loan Officer and asked him to please contact the loan officer at my Chase branch and explain the program to him. He agreed, but when I followed up with Chase, the answer was, again, "We're not going to submit this application." The government could bail out these banks when they made risky bets and lost. They could offer a 90 percent guarantee on loans to help Veterans start businesses. But they couldn't force these banks to issue the loans.

With loans unavailable, I reached out to family members, but even those that had the means either refused outright or were too afraid of how far we would plunge into the Bush Depression. I had to scale back the project. What if I started out as an online-only business and opened a brick & mortar location later on? What would I need to get started?

I added up my expected startup costs and figured I could get off the ground with $20,000, but I couldn't find a way to raise the seed money. This is a common problem for those without means looking to start a business and is one of the many fatal flaws in the great American myth of "pulling yourself up by your bootstraps". How can you pull yourself up by your own bootstraps when you can't afford boots?

I was crushed and sank into depression as 2008 came to a close. I didn't have a job, was "living" on unemployment, and going deeper into debt. The bar that I had spent the last few years working on was done with before I even had a chance to open the doors and now it looked like the same thing would happen to my much less expensive idea for an outdoor outfitter. I was running out of ideas and hope at the same time.

On the afternoon of January 15th, 2009 — right around the time that Captain Sully Sullenberger was taking off from LaGuardia airport — I called my buddy Steve Bury from the living room of the Park Slope apartment I was sharing with a roommate I barely knew. I called Steve to catch up, pitch Gear To Go Outfitters, and hopefully get a laugh or two that would lift my spirits.

Steve was still on active duty in the Navy, so he was pretty well insulated from the recession. As a single Lieutenant Commander, he was also at the stage of his career where he would be able to think about investing. I hated to even ask him about a loan since he was my best friend, but he was also my last hope. I'd already asked everyone else I knew and was prepared for him to say no, but I at least had to ask.

Though I totally would have understood if Steve said he couldn't do it, especially since he had already invested $15,000 in a bar that never opened, it wasn't surprising when he said he would help me out and lend me the money. I was confident that the business would be a huge success and wanted to thank him for believing in me and helping me when I was down, so I offered him a share of the profits for the first year on top of his loan and expected that this would reward Steve with a solid return on his investment.

I got to work that night, forming the LLC, hiring a graphic designer, and posting an ad for a web designer. I think all entrepreneurs believe in their hearts that customers have been desperately waiting for them to come along and start their business, to change those customers' lives for the better and to show their respective industries how foolish they've been to overlook this new way of doing things.

In their hearts, entrepreneurs firmly believe that as soon as they open their doors, customer will flood in from the streets and they will become wealthy, admired, visionaries. I call this the "Field of Dreams Mentality," an obvious reference to the 1989 hit movie. Of course, this "If you build it, they will come" mindset rarely works out as planned.

So it was when boxes of gear started arriving at my apartment on 2nd Street in Park Slope. My projections showed that Gear To Go should bring in at least $100,000 in revenue the first year, which would allow me to move into a warehouse — if not a retail storefront — by Spring 2010. Working with the web designer, I created product pages, added trips, and wrote content that described why Gear To Go Outfitters was the business you had been waiting for your whole life.

The website went live on March 3, 2009, and as I waited for orders to come pouring in, I wondered how quickly I could scale up to meet demand as summer approached. I thought about how many employees I would need and whether I should purchase a delivery vehicle, before going back to waiting for those orders to come pouring in. Reality set in after three weeks had gone by and I hadn't received a single order. I was certain that this was just a temporary problem because folks simply hadn't yet heard of Gear To Go Outfitters.

Gear To Go was launched on less than a shoestring budget, which didn't allow for marketing or advertising. Having heard about so many businesses that started online, I figured that those budget items were luxuries I would worry about when I was ready to expand. I wasn't aware of it, but the notion that you could start a business online and have it grow quickly by simply having a website, probably died in the late 90s.

In 2009, my company wasn't even showing up in search results, even though I was the only outfitter in Brooklyn — and certainly the only one focusing on rental gear in the Tri-State Region. You could literally type in "Outfitters in Brooklyn," and I wouldn't show up. I decided to literally shout it from the rooftops! Well, almost, but there was definitely shouting involved.

I knew that once folks learned about my business, it would take off, and I've never shied away from bold actions to achieve my goals. In June 1992, having been denied admission to the Naval Academy twice despite having high scores and recommendations from both New York senators as well as my congressman, I decided to just show up on induction day in hopes that someone would turn down their offer of admission, leaving a space open for me to fill. I'd met all of the admissions requirements so why not? It didn't work out, but as I drove back from Annapolis, I was proud that I had tried and would never have to say "what if?"

This spirit of "fuck it" led me to the farmers market at Grand Army Plaza in Brooklyn, where I strung up a banner with the Gear To Go Outfitters logo on it and handed out flyers while shouting, "Anyone into hiking, backpacking, camping? Sales, rentals, guided trips!" Some folks seemed interested, but there wasn't an overwhelming response, so I figured, let's try Manhattan.

I made a frame for my banner out of conduit pipe and headed to Union Square to try my luck amongst starving artists, wealthy NYU students, and the crazies shouting at strangers whom I hoped to not be confused with, hence the banner, which I thought would give me some legitimacy. I shouted the benefits of my company, handed out flyers, and chatted with the artists and street vendors hawking their wares alongside the spot I had staked out, but again not much interest.

Maybe my field of dreams really was just a cornfield in Kansas after all.

Towards the end of March, I had my first order, two sleeping pads rented for the weekend, which meant $40 and free delivery. Orders did in fact come in, but they were few and far between and by the end of May, sinking deeper into debt, it was clear that I had to cut back on expenses and move out of my apartment. Forced to move back home, I still believed in my idea and knew it would succeed if only I could get the word out. I traveled to the city to set up at different events and attended networking happy hours, but nothing seemed to work.

I had some rental orders coming in and was selling spots on the day hikes I was leading, but there was no real money in that — not enough to make a real living in New York at least. Dispirited but determined, I settled back into my childhood bedroom at the age of 35. Maybe I should have called it then, but that wasn't my personality. I was too stubborn to give up and would work as hard as I needed to in order to make this business a success.

As 2009 drew to a close, I had brought in around $10,000 of revenue — not profit — since the website went live at the beginning of March. I knew that I had to come up with a bold idea to save my business and create a life for myself. It was almost the same thought I had in the cockpit back on that Mississippi night when I looked down at the ejection handle and thought, "That's gonna hurt!"

I wasn't ready to bail out. The solution was out there. I just had to find it.

CHAPTER THREE

TOUGH JEWS

On the night of January 28, 1980, NYPD Officer Cecil Sledge of Brooklyn's 69th Precinct spotted Sal Desarno who was known throughout Canarsie as "Crazy Sal." At 21, Desarno already had a violent criminal history and was a suspect in a recent robbery of a neighborhood donut shop.

As Officer Sledge approached Sal, who was standing beside his Brown Chevy Nova outside of the Nathan's on Flatlands Avenue, he was met by four shots fired from a .38 revolver just feet away. Though wounded, Officer Sledge returned fire, hitting Desarno in the shoulder and thigh before falling to the pavement, his uniform coat catching on the bumper of the Chevy Nova.

Sal then jumped into the driver's seat and took off, speeding down Flatlands Avenue at 80 mph, dragging Officer Sledge by his coat before a collision with a traffic sign set the officer free. It was too late. This hero in blue had already paid the ultimate price at the hands of a violent offender, out on bail after a previous armed robbery conviction. Wounded, and with more officers giving chase, "Crazy Sal" hopped a fence and then jumped through a picture window at 5715 Avenue I.

Inside that home was a 59-year-old woman whose husband was out teaching music lessons that night. She heard a loud noise in her living room and thought maybe a bird had crashed into the window. As she went to investigate, she was surprised by a man in his 20s, holding a pistol and bleeding heavily. The police quickly surrounded, agitating the already scared shooter who was now cornered and desperate.

The woman, Marion Mazur, stood only about five feet tall and had been quietly getting ready for bed when this made-for-TV crime drama literally exploded into her living room. No one would have faulted her if she panicked, cried, or begged for her life, but she didn't. Instead, she calmed down "Crazy Sal," spoke to him like a grandmother, and had him sit on the couch with her. Shen then demanded that he call his mom, which he did, before she talked him into surrendering to the police. That woman was my maternal grandmother. I was only six at the time, but as I watched her being interviewed on all of the local TV stations, I knew that I came from some pretty tough people.

As a kid, I idolized my dad and would ride my bike to the corner of our block in Franklin Square, waiting to see his car on the way home from work or sit on the steps in front of our house so I could be the first to greet him and maybe play catch before dinner. He loved baseball and even had a few Major League players as clients.

My brother and I felt lucky that we got to play running bases with professional ballplayers and even take in Mets and Yankees games from the dugout. The Mets were definitely the family team because we were from Brooklyn, and the Dodgers never really left, they just moved to Queens and changed their name.

The Rosenbergs were doing great through the 1970s. We had a house in the suburbs, two cars, Mom was home taking care of my brother Craig and I, and Dad was home for dinner each night. Life was Little League, block parties, visits to the town pool, and backyard BBQs. We were even able to take a few vacations. Nothing fancy, but we'd maybe take a road trip to Amish Country, a week in New Hampshire to visit my Mom's sister, or my first flight ever, Eastern Airlines to Orlando and Disneyworld, where I was more fascinated by the monorail than Mickey. We were living the American Dream!

One night in 1982, I was awakened by a light being turned on followed by strange voices in the kitchen just across the hall from my bedroom. Through sleep-filled eyes, I saw two strange men in suits, one talking on the kitchen phone, the other talking to Mom. I don't remember how exactly she told me, but I learned that my father was missing and the police were trying to find him. My older brother was awake now, and we were soon being sent to a neighbor's house for the night since there was concern that someone might be looking to hurt us.

It turned out that my father, a compulsive gambler, had borrowed a significant amount of money from the mob. When he couldn't pay it back, the mob threatened his life and ours. Faced with the existential threat he had pondered everything from suicide to robbing a bank and attempted both.

Dad placed a fake bomb in a shoe box and left it inside a bank near his Mineola office. He then called the bank claiming that he'd also planted a bomb in the bank manager's home, and that he would detonate both if they didn't pay up, though I don't know the exact amount or where he was supposed to collect the money. He never showed up at the pickup spot and instead left a suicide note in his office before checking into a nearby motel, where he took a bunch of sleeping pills.

When Dad didn't come home that night, Mom called the police and reported him missing. This was way before cell phones, so they thought maybe he was just working late in his office. The police went to check on him there and found the note. Things quickly escalated, and the police soon connected him to the attempted bank robbery before tracking him down in his motel room. Dad was brought to the hospital to be treated for the pills he had taken and then arrested.

The police believed that our lives were in danger, so we left our neighborhood and hid out at my grandfather's house in Massapequa for a few days. At just 8 years old it was obviously a confusing and scary time for me. After returning to our block so we could get back to school, we again stayed with our neighbors because the police were still afraid that the mob might try to hurt us as a way to get back at our father. I remember walking past our house as bomb-sniffing dogs searched our cars and detectives in suits hovered nearby.

I knew going back to school, third grade at Willow Road Elementary, was going to be tough. News of my father's arrest had been in the papers and had become the hot topic in neighborhood gossip. Always focused on education, our mother told my brother and I that we had to get back to school and get on with life, even if it was hard.

I kept my head down and tried to avoid making eye contact in school that day. I remember sitting on the floor in a corner of the classroom when my friend, Meredyth Otlin, looked at me and said that her mom had seen the article and told her what had happened to my dad. I stared at the ground expecting to be ridiculed or shamed. She said that after hearing about it she went into her room and cried. That moment of empathy meant so much to me and helped me realize that everything would be okay, I would get through this.

Mom went to bat for our dad and advocated on his behalf with the Nassau County District Attorney's office, arguing that he was a good man who was battling addiction and was just scared and trying to provide for his family. She succeeded and the DA dropped the charges. Mom then made sure Dad received the treatment he needed while she took care of us boys on her own.

When Dad returned from treatment, life seemed to be back to normal, but it soon became obvious that things had changed. Our parents fought often, screaming at each other in the kitchen just across the hall from my bedroom door. I peeked out once, only to see my dad take a pot of boiling spaghetti water off of the stove and pour it over my mom's head as she screamed. Fortunately, it had not been on there for long and she was not burned, but it was obviously traumatic to witness and that scene is forever etched on my memory.

Soon afterwards Dad left and took up residence at a motel in West Hempstead. After almost 20 years of marriage, Mom was suddenly dealing with our name being trashed in the news, her husband assaulting her, and then leaving as their marriage fell apart, having to not only care for but also provide for two young boys on her own. Mom showed nothing but courage and tenacity as she stepped up, never letting us see how she must have truly felt — scared, alone, angry, and overwhelmed. Mom was one tough woman!

It turned out that Dad had not only borrowed from the mob, but also from friends, family, and anyone else that would lend him money. He would claim it was to help the family with some unexpected expense, but in reality, it went to bets on horses at Belmont and Aqueduct.

As news spread of my dad's arrest, many of his creditors came calling, demanding that my mom cover her husband's debts as he was nowhere to be found. They assumed that she was in on it somehow — as if they were working together on some scheme to defraud the neighborhood. She pleaded with them that she had nothing to do with it and that she only learned about it after his arrest. With everything else she was dealing with, she was now being accused of being a criminal herself — a co-conspirator. The accumulated weight of all of these burdens and slights would break most people, but not her, she was as tough as they come!

We lost lots of friends, and even many relatives turned their backs on us in our time of greatest need. Most of our neighborhood abandoned us, and I never forgave them for that.

As Mom struggled to adapt to becoming the sole breadwinner — without a job — she often ate cereal or just skipped dinner altogether so that my brother and I would not go hungry. I remember opening the front door to go out and play only to be surprised by a few bags of groceries sitting on the porch, left by caring neighbors wanting to help without embarrassing us. Those that could, helped out by giving us some money to buy food as Mom figured out the next step.

Mom had been an elementary school teacher in Brooklyn before we were born, so she tried to get rehired with the Board of Education, but the only opening was for a special ed teacher at a junior high school in the Rockaways. Teaching special education back then was not held in high regard as it is today, it was a job that no one else wanted. Desperate to provide for us, she was happy to take it. Mom would later go on to earn advanced degrees from Columbia

University, Teachers College, and become one of the first Master Teachers in New York City, guiding educators in her district on the best ways to teach creative writing.

Mom would get us up in the morning, but would have to leave early for the drive into Queens and wouldn't be back until we were already home from school. As we prepared to join the ranks of the "latchkey kids" of the 1980s, she taught us how to use the stove to cook for ourselves, my favorite was Beefaroni, and to tell anyone that rang the bell that Mom was in the shower and couldn't come to the door.

One of the stories that still gets retold at family gatherings happened when my brother was home sick from school one day and it was up to me to get myself ready and off to school on time. I finished breakfast and got dressed but then realized that I still had 30 minutes before I had to leave so I decided to take a nap. My brother woke up midday and wandered towards the kitchen when he noticed me dressed for school asleep on my bed still wearing my coat and backpack. Of course, being a good big brother, he still made me go to school, though I wasn't happy about it at the time.

We also had a whole system in place for when we forgot our keys, which being the smallest, landed on my shoulders. I would climb onto a metal bench on the patio, step onto the adjacent table, climb on top of the air conditioner, pry the window open, climb inside and then open the door for my brother. This of course happened fairly often, and it became a favorite afterschool activity.

If she didn't have meetings or some other obligation, Mom would come home around dinnertime, help us with our homework, put us to bed, and then start grading papers or developing lesson plans until late at night, only getting a few hours of sleep before starting again the next morning. Family dinners around the kitchen table had been the norm before our lives blew up, but now we seemed to be on separate schedules and ate most of our meals alone. In the summer, when she could have gotten some well-deserved rest, Mom took a job at Shibley Day Camp in Roslyn so that we would be able to go to camp for free rather than just hanging out in the neighborhood all summer getting into trouble.

We even took our first vacation as a family — now of just three — on a road trip to Philadelphia for a few days. It was the first time Mom had driven any real distance on her own so she didn't want to go very far, plus money was still an issue. But with Mom at the wheel, Craig navigating in the passenger seat, and me riding in back with the cooler, ready to hand out sandwiches and drinks, we hit the road and had a great time.

As our parents argued, my brother and I became embroiled in a proxy war of sorts. At the time, I wasn't aware of everything that had happened, and was too young to really understand anyway. All I knew was that I wanted my dad home, and I blamed my mom for making him leave. It would take me until college to put everything together and figure out the truth.

We fought often and sometimes violently, leaving holes in the walls that became visual representations of the emotional turmoil we were going through. One night, my dad tried to get into the house after my mom told him to stay away. We were all huddled together in my mom's bedroom when he entered the house. My brother Craig, three years older than me, grabbed a baseball bat and raced to confront him, striking dad in the knee as they struggled.

Determined to hold onto the house and provide some stability for us, Mom reached out to the Mafia loan sharks who had a lien on our house and were threatening to foreclose. This was another of my dad's gambling debts and though obtained under illegal means at usurious rates, it was backed up by a legitimate security instrument that — without action — would result in us losing our home.

Mom set up a meeting with the two gangsters whose cover was owning a restaurant in Lynbrook. She appealed to their sense of family and pleaded with them that, with two young boys to take care of, she could not pay at the rate demanded, nor could she pay the total amount due. Imagine what it must have looked like to these two wiseguys as a five-foot, three-inch schoolteacher tells them that they need to renegotiate the terms of their loan. They agreed, and I think it was because they were impressed by her bravery.

I would spend every other weekend — and the occasional weeknight — with my dad at the room he rented in an apartment just across the tracks from the West Hempstead train station or the basement apartment with the fireplace in Huntington. When we had weekends together, we would spend it in the city visiting dad's friends and relatives, checking out museums, or just walking around different neighborhoods, maybe grabbing a pretzel or knish from a street cart along the way. Occasionally, I would take off from school and spend the day with him. He had an office atop the Paramount Hotel near Times Square, and we would have lunch at the Howard Johnson's on 46th and Broadway, where I was amazed that the waitresses knew him by name.

Soon "nights at dad's" meant sleeping in a strange bedroom at the home of whichever woman he was dating at the time. He bought a Chevy Camaro, which I loved riding in, and would occasionally let me sit on his lap and steer in an empty parking lot. One of the women he dated had two kids my age — a boy and a girl — and we became close friends. They dated for a year or two, and when they broke up, I couldn't understand why that meant I couldn't see my friends anymore.

As I was adapting to what was becoming the new normal for more and more kids growing up in the 80s, I entered 7th grade and my attention turned to music, girls, and trying to be cool. After school, my friends and I would bike over to the arcade or the record store on Hempstead Turnpike and maybe spend a lazy Sunday at the Shopper's Village Flea Market in West Hempstead as the mall was too far away.

I was always bored in Franklin Square and dreamed of living in either the city or the mountains. Though we were living on Long Island, we were too far from the beach to notice and the closest we had to nature was the drainage canal running through town that we called "the creek."

Like most kids in my neighborhood of Franklin Square, just over the border from Queens, my family had moved there from Brooklyn where I was born. Increasing crime rates, better opportunities, and the dream of having a patch of grass for the kids to play on, drove our parents to leave "The Old Country" for a better life in the suburbs. The neighborhood was largely Italian, followed by a good number of Irish families, and then a few of us Jews, though we were a very small minority.

The flavor of the neighborhood, both literally and figuratively, was Italian. There are a lot of similarities between Italians, Irish, and Jews, with our cultures focused around food and family. It also helped that all three groups had emigrated to the US around the same time and shared the immigrant neighborhoods of the Lower East Side for decades, so we were culturally used to each other and mostly got along.

I say mostly because our neighborhood saw a lot more violence than you would expect in suburbia. Sure, there were the shoving matches with the Catholic kids who would claim that "the Jews killed Jesus" when I would point out that it was the Romans — now known as the Italians — or "your people," but that wasn't a big deal. There were rumors about whose dad worked for the mob and what that social club on Hempstead Turnpike was really used for, but there was also the firebombing of two cars on my block while we were having dinner and the gangs that ruled the high school and would spend Friday night looking for someone to beat up, or "jump," just for fun.

Fights in school were broken up, eventually, but overall, there seemed to be a "boys will be boys" sense of tolerance among school administrators. Most of the teachers seemed to have given up and were just counting the days until retirement. With a low percentage of students going on to a four-year college after graduation, maybe most of the students had given up as well. This included one member of our class, who went to jail for manslaughter shortly after graduation, and several more who would be arrested for assault a short time later.

Violence was tolerated and expected. The gangs in our area were known as "fraternities" and each school had their own. At my school, Valley Stream North, the gang was known as Alpha Sigma Phi, or just "Phi" for short. These groups may have originated as actual high school fraternities at some point, but I never met anyone that knew of them as anything other than gangs.

They didn't have assault rifles or pistols but had plenty of knives, clubs, and brass knuckles to make their point and the initiation was rumored to be a gauntlet style beat-in. The school administrators were so inept at maintaining good order and discipline that they even allowed members of "Phi" to wear their distinct black cardigans with red trim — as if they were members of the football team showing off their jerseys on game day.

"North," as we called it, actually combined grades seven to twelve in the same school so you can imagine what it feels like to arrive as an anxious twelve-year-old. I'd gotten into a fair amount of fights in elementary school and had learned the rules of my neighborhood by then. There was no such thing as a "fair fight" in Franklin Square. Being Jewish just about always means you are the minority and at North that meant there were about five of us in a class of a hundred and thirty-five.

The Italian kids always stuck together and looked out for each other, so if you got in a fight with one of them, it was never just you and him — it was you and all of his friends. If it looked like you were gaining the advantage, you might get pushed, tripped, or punched from the group that formed a ring of spectators. Though I never backed down from a fight, and certainly held my own, I can't say I won many either.

I joined the wrestling team in the eighth grade because I enjoyed the competition and like any junior high school boy, I wanted to get stronger, and the rigors of team practice seemed to promise that. I didn't have any friends on the team, but stuck with it and figured that would come in time.

On March 10, 1987, at around 6:30 pm, while on a dark school bus coming back from a match, I sat staring out the window while others roughhoused or bragged about their victories in the day's matches. I sat alone, silently staring out the window, when out of nowhere, a duffel bag came sailing towards me. There were several groups of boys roughhousing, so I assumed that's where it came from and stood up to ask whose bag it was, but no one claimed it. When I didn't receive a response, I figured whoever owned it hadn't even realized that someone was playing a joke on them, so I planned to just turn it in to the coaches as we were exiting the bus.

Seconds later, without warning, someone leaped at me from out of the darkness, slamming my head against the metal wall of the bus and then choking me. The following is an excerpt from the school's investigation that details what happened next.

> "While seated on the returning bus a duffle bag flew in front of him. He stood up and asked, "Who's bag is this?" Suddenly, Joe Dal-Bo jumped on his head, causing his head to strike the side of the bus. Joe then proceeded to choke Kevin.
>
> Kevin then put Joe Dal-Bo in a headlock. Jo Dal-Bo released himself from the head lock and proceeded to throw Kevin against the other side of the bus.
>
> A number of students then jumped on Kevin, while he was laying across the seat. He received numerous blows to his back and his legs.
>
> The fighting stopped and Kevin resumed his seat. Less than a minute later Anthony Bauman approached Kevin's seat and made a verbal remark to him. Anthony proceeded to push Kevin. Kevin then pushed Anthony. Anthony then pulled Kevin to the other side of the bus, resulting in Kevin striking his nose on a seat and also receiving a blow to his head from the side of the bus.
>
> Then a number of students jumped on Kevin again. He received a number of blows to his back and lower extremities.
>
> The fighting abruptly stopped. He stood up with a bloody nose and approached the coaches in the front of the bus."

The coaches treated my bloody nose but showed no concern about any possible head injury — I was later diagnosed with a concussion — before dropping me at home, alone, making no attempt to call my parents or make sure someone would be checking on me in case I passed out.

I was "jumped" on a dark school bus without warning or provocation by another kid on my own team, who was much bigger and stronger than me, yet he still cowardly chose to take me by surprise, relying on the wall of the bus to do most of the work for him. Other members of my same team then jumped in with kicks and punches after I was reeling from a head wound and pinned face down. I tried to fight back but had no chance of doing any real damage.

After suffering the first attack and feeling dizzy from the concussion, an even bigger coward then decided that now was the time to show how "tough" he was by choosing that moment to pick a fight with me. After all that I had endured, I refused to back down, fighting back as once again my head was thrown against the wall of the bus by another "teammate" that was bigger than I was, soon to be joined by other "teammates." No one on that bus came to my defense, not even a kid who lived on my block and whom I had known my entire life. Everyone thought they were tough. I knew they were cowards.

Webster's defines "tough" as being "capable of enduring strain, hardship, or severe labor." I believe that being tough means being able to withstand these cowardly attacks and stand up to bullies by fighting back, showing defiance, and not letting them intimidate you. This idea of what it means to be "tough" — and how I was not going to let them win — was going through my head as I walked to school alone after being out for two weeks recovering from my injuries.

My experiences growing up taught me how to deal with adversity. They taught me to fight back against bullies even when the odds were against me. I learned early how to deal with life's struggles and felt confident that I could accomplish anything as long as I was smart in how I approached it and was willing to endure the challenges that might be in my way. Mom provided a great example of how to be tough, but she also taught me confidence, to believe in myself and not give up. Lessons that would serve me well as I launched a new business in the middle of the Great Recession and struggled to succeed against seemingly insurmountable obstacles.

In line to receive my diploma at high school graduation four years later, I listened to my fellow classmates express fear and anxiety about what lay ahead for them. I smiled knowing that I was finally going to be free from the confines of my neighborhood of small-minded thinking and ambitionless futures. I knew that life would now truly begin and that there was a world out there waiting to be explored. It was time to lace up my boots and get started!

CHAPTER FOUR

FROM THE GROUND UP

My friend, Karen Novick, had suggested I try selling on the street, but I was hesitant. Having grown up in New York, I knew that people viewed street vendors with suspicion, assuming that the goods they were selling were either knockoffs or had "fallen off the back of a truck."

These weren't baseless accusations either. I remember a time in early 80s when the son of one of my dad's business partners came into the office on top of the Paramount in Midtown carrying a brand-new VCR he had just purchased around the corner. He was telling us about what a great deal it was, but when he opened the box, it was filled with rocks. Would anyone trust me enough to buy hiking gear on the sidewalk?

Desperation often disguises itself as boldness, and so it was on the evening of December 23, 2009 when I set up in front of the Szechuan Delight restaurant on 7th Avenue between Garfield Place and Carroll Street in Park Slope. With only two days to go until Christmas, I thought maybe I would get a few bites from busy folks desperate for a gift and running out of time and if I made $50, it was $50 I didn't have before.

My display was nothing but a folding table and some gear roughly displayed alongside a small collection of hats and gloves. Payments were cash only and I handwrote paper receipts if requested. I made $700 that night and celebrated with a dinner of Wendy's chicken nuggets as I drove back to Franklin Square. I set up earlier the next day, Christmas Eve, and brought in over $1,000. "Maybe there was something to this?" I thought, but I also recognized that it could just be the holidays. People were desperate for last minute gifts, and I just happened to be on their way home.

I waited until after the new year to test the waters, setting up in the exact same spot before the restaurant owner told me to not come back. I didn't do as well as Christmas, but I was still bringing in a few hundred each day, which was much more than I was making before I hit the streets. Maybe this was the answer — the solution to building a business in the middle of a recession when banks refused to lend money after bringing down the economy.

Street vending seemed like a possible solution, but there was still the trust issue to overcome. How would I convince folks passing by that my products were legitimate and were exactly the same as the items in one of the big national chain stores in Manhattan? I looked into buying an old bread truck and converting it into a pop-up shop, but I found out that it was illegal to sell anything from a vehicle in the city other than food. I was limited to selling on the street but had to make it look like a store in order to give folks confidence.

I decided to go with slatwall, the grooved, panel-like wall covering that you see in most stores. According to the city regulations, a street stand can be up to eight feet long by five feet high. It can occupy three feet of space extending from the curb, with merchandise displayed at least one foot off the ground. I bought an eight-by-four-foot section of slatwall and had it cut in half so that it would fit in the back of my Honda Element. I then designed a support structure that would fit in the back of my car and conform to city regs while still leaving room for boxes of merchandise. I used carriage bolts to secure the slatwall to the supports and figured I could set up in winds as high as 25 miles per hour without having to worry about the "sail effect" pushing my stand into a parked car or toppling over onto a pedestrian.

I knew that being able to take credit cards would also help to boost confidence in my homeless business, but this was years before you could simply swipe a card on your smartphone. To solve this problem, I bought a cheap point of sale program that I ran on my laptop, which was also hooked up to a cash drawer, barcode scanner, receipt printer, and card reader. To power the whole system, I set up a portable solar panel on top of my car that ran through an inverter and a surge protector before reaching the laptop. To process cards via the internet, I bought a mobile hotspot, which was about the size of a cell phone. I even had shopping bags available and installed battery-operated lights for nighttime browsing.

Sales grew as folks got used to seeing me in the neighborhood. During the winter, most of what I sold were hats, gloves, and traction devices for the ice and snow, and in summer, it was mostly sun hats and backpacks, but I also had strong sales of headlamps, camping stoves, rain jackets, books, and maps.

Each day of street vending began with loading everything into my car and then driving more than an hour to Park Slope, before searching for a parking space. The more difficult it was to find a space, the busier I would be. Once I found a space, it would then take another hour or so to erect the stand, install the hooks, hang the merchandise, and then set up my register and point of sale system.

It was always a rush to open up as fast as possible. I was so focused on setting up in front of the Chase bank on 7th Avenue and Carroll Street, that once I was completely unaware of someone attempting to rob the bank until a swarm of police cars arrived from every direction and an officer asked me what I saw.

Once everything was set, I would generally be out there for eight hours in all kinds of weather, racing to feed the meter every hour while keeping an eye on my stand and making sure nothing went missing. If I was lucky, someone from one of the nearby shops would watch my stand while I ran to the bathroom; other times, I would just have to risk it.

Meals consisted of cold pizza or sandwiches or occasionally hot soup cooked on a backpacking stove when the temperature dropped below freezing. I got to know the other vendors, shop owners, local homeless, and retirees wandering the neighborhood. I'd layer up on the coldest days, but even then, being stuck in one place all day, I'd start to shiver.

I remember standing there, cold and hungry, when a well-dressed businessman — presumably a banker — passed by on his way home from work. I felt a sense of rage wash over me. Why was I stuck out here freezing on the street when I had earned a commission as a Naval Officer, served my country, and then gone on to earn a doctorate degree?

How was it that I couldn't get a loan to open a permanent store indoors? Why was I broke and living in my childhood bedroom when the bankers that destroyed our economy were going home to a family and a brownstone in Brooklyn? How did our economic situation get so bad and collapse so quickly?

It seemed like Banks had become nothing more than legalized gambling operations — not much different than the organized crime figures my Mom was forced to negotiate with. The only distinction was that when they lost, they didn't have to worry about Mafia enforcers threatening harm to them or their families if they didn't pay up. The government covered their bets with our money, yet I couldn't get a loan to open a small shop. Anger can keep you warm on a dark, shivering, Brooklyn night.

When the cold go to be too much, Ezra, one of the owners of Community Bookstore, would let me come in to warm up a bit. I'd keep an eye on my stand from the front door and would only warm up enough to take the edge off. I still had to go back out there at some point, so there was no use getting too comfortable. The coldest days also meant that most folks didn't want to stop and shop on the sidewalk, but I had to be out there to make whatever I could. I just hoped I'd be indoors for the next winter.

The weather wasn't the only challenge of being a street vendor in New York. Technically, you're not allowed to set up within 10 feet of the doorway to a business and 20 feet of the doorway to a residence. Basically, you can't legally set up anywhere in Brooklyn. Not wanting to interfere with another business, I would never choose a spot near a shop selling anything similar to what I sold. There was even some benefit to having me set up across the sidewalk from one's shop. Since my stand was right on the sidewalk, it would actually encourage people to stop and look around, often noticing the nearby shop windows they would have otherwise hurried past.

Most shop owners were sympathetic and supportive, buying from my stand or letting me use their bathroom, but some pushed back aggressively as if I was a threat. Gear To Go was basically a homeless business selling hiking gear, so how could I pose a threat to a grocery store? I didn't but that didn't stop the owner of Back to the Land organic groceries from threatening to call the police if I ever set up in front of his store again.

There was also the shouting match with the owner of JackRabbit running shop, who was incensed that I was selling Clif Bars on the same block as him. But the most humorous interaction I had with an angry shop owner was when I set up across from The-Chair-Man gift shop. I'd chosen that spot because it was next to a Starbucks, and I couldn't get a parking space directly in front so the gift shop next door would have to do. An older woman eyed me suspiciously from the empty store as I set up and then came out to tell me I couldn't be there. I politely told her that I was a Veteran, a legal vendor, and that I was allowed to set up there, hoping she wasn't aware of the 10-foot rule; she wasn't.

She hovered in the doorway of her shop until I was talking to my first customer when, like a cuckoo clock, she shot out of the door yelling, "Pay rent, pay rent, pay rent!" I told her that "I'd love to — are you going to lend me the money to open a store?" She ignored what I said and kept up her chant. My customer looked amused as he took in this encounter that was simultaneously both surreal and so typically Brooklyn.

She wouldn't stop until I asked, "You're a Republican, aren't you?" This set her off even more, and she declared, "You can't ask me that." "You just answered it," I told her as she retreated inside her store. The cops showed up about an hour later and told me I could finish out the day, but I couldn't return to that spot. I wondered if maybe Park Slope wasn't the right neighborhood.

I tried setting up on Smith Street in Cobble Hill, but didn't sell much, and a nearby storeowner called the cops on me almost immediately. I figured I'd try Williamsburg next: "Hipster Central." "Do hipsters hike?" I wondered. I know they like irony and, having roots in Brooklyn, I found it ironic that the neighborhood that represented "Brooklyn" to millennials was considered to no longer be a part of Brooklyn by those that were actually from there. In any event, I decided to give it a try.

I arrived early on a Sunday morning and set up on Bedford Ave, between 6th and 7th Streets, in front of what appeared to be a vacant storefront with its security gate rolled down. Well into setting up my stand, some crazy guy in a beat-up minivan starts screaming, "That's my spot, that's my spot." I didn't even realize he was talking to me at first, and then, I assumed he was referring to the storefront that I thought was vacant. In response, I offered my now oft-repeated mantra: "I'm a Veteran, I'm a legal vendor, I'm allowed to be here," but he just kept on yelling about his spot.

He jumped out, leaving his van in the street blocking traffic, and angrily approached dressed in a dirty tank top and jeans, ordering me to move. I calmly refused, standing my ground without escalating. "You should have gotten here earlier," I told him. I knew this strip was popular, so I'd gotten there extra early to make sure I found a spot. Even then, I'd almost missed out. This was the street vendor version of "the early bird gets the worm!" Seeing that I wasn't going to budge he backed off and focused his anger on another vendor nearby, forcing that guy to move his stand over so that he could slide in next to mine.

He kept yelling and threatening me, but there was no way I was moving. Figuring we might be heading towards a fight, I wanted to cover my ass so I didn't get blamed for starting it, so I called the police to put it all on record. Two officers showed up pretty quickly, and though I didn't expect them to make an arrest, I did expect them to tell the guy to just focus on his own stand and leave me alone.

Instead, the officer in charge told me that I should probably move to avoid him keying my car or something. What made this more outrageous was that she said it with the guy standing right there. This bum looked too stupid to form a sentence on his own, and now she was planting ideas in his head for how best to get back at me. Having done nothing helpful, New York's "finest" left the scene, but I had a feeling that they'd be called back soon.

Things calmed down at first as he focused on setting up his folding tables and unloading filthy crates of used books from his van, but he kept coming over and trying to pick a fight. He would stand behind me, and I would just stare at him and laugh, or he would drop used napkins in open backpacks. He got so frustrated that I wasn't taking the bait that he started yelling things at me as I was working with customers. His low point was calling me a "baby killer" — an insult hurled at returning Vietnam Vets.

Mostly I just laughed it off, but I did decide to give him a taste of his own medicine. When a few customers were browsing the used books he had on display, I yelled, "Be careful, I found bed bugs in a few of his books." They all left and he just stared at me with wide eyes and a shocked look. Seeing that I wasn't going to be intimidated, he soon shut up.

I did okay in Williamsburg, but it was nothing compared to even a slow day in Park Slope. I met some interesting folks and enjoyed people watching but realized that Park Slope was definitely the best neighborhood for my business. There were more families in Park Slope and more folks who owned cars, able to get up to the mountains on a regular basis.

As the day drew to a close, I started to pack up and noticed the drunk book seller was back at it, leaning against my car. It didn't bother me — this was New York after all and if you get worked up about someone leaning up against your car, then you probably shouldn't drive in the city. But as I began to take down the stand, I realized what he was really doing was keying my car — just as the officer had earlier suggested.

I called the police, and again, they refused to do anything about it. I considered retaliating, but his van was in such bad shape that it would actually be an improvement. Most street vendors are supportive of each other, but you do meet the occasional bully out there. Luckily, as in his life apparently, he even failed at his attempt at vandalism as the key barely touched the paint and it only cost about $10 to buff it out with some clay. The biggest disappointment of that day was the NYPD.

Other than setting up at music festivals, such as Pete Seager's Clearwater or Hunter Mountain's Mountain Jam, I focused exclusively on Park Slope. In the weeks before Christmas, the sidewalks were busy with artists and the 'sometimes' vendors trying to make some extra money as folks shopped for last minute gifts but then it would go back to just me alone. I felt like a caretaker of sorts, keeping things going until the other vendors returned in late spring.

After two record-cold winters and one scorching summer, I was beginning to wonder how long I could keep this up. I dreamed of having a floor to sweep and a door to lock. Sales were increasing, and I'd gotten some great press in the *New York Daily News* and *Crain's New York Business*, but banks still weren't lending, and I wasn't bringing in enough to save for the deposit, buildout costs, and inventory expenses needed for a storefront. As the frigid days of February came to a close, I began to think about my bailout point. If I couldn't get a brick & mortar location open by the end of 2011, maybe I should just call it and move on.

CHAPTER FIVE

BORN TO FLY

Ever since I can remember, I had dreamed of becoming a Navy fighter pilot. This dream grew to become the focus of my life, to define my life. I chose the Navy because I felt that flying off of aircraft carriers was the greatest challenge in aviation, and I wanted a challenge. It may have been the old World War II movies that I would watch with my dad and brother, or the time in the late 70s when my dad took me to see an F-14 Tomcat on static display in Eisenhower Park. All I knew was that I was going to fly fighters someday, and I was determined to be the best. I never lost that dream.

    I started my preparation early. In second grade, my mom received a phone call from the elementary school librarian informing her that I was taking out books about the military that were well above my reading level. My mother explained that I would read what I could, study the pictures, and then discuss them with my dad and brother.

    I filled a sketchbook with aircraft designs of my own and soaked up any information I could find on aviation and space travel. My third-grade teacher, Mrs. Rushian, took notice and when NASA sent out information packets about the brand-new space shuttle program, she gave it to me as a gift. I still have it to this day.

    In fourth grade, I went on a class trip to visit the USS Intrepid (CV-11), which had recently been brought to New York City and converted into a museum. I took great pride in my ability to identify most of the aircraft on exhibit and explain to my classmates how an aircraft carrier launched and recovered aircraft. I knew this was where I belonged. I knew I was home.

    I was born to step out onto the flight deck and feel the wind on my face as it swept down the carrier's steel deck. I was born to smell the scent of jet fuel as

I walked confidently towards the F-14 chained to deck with my name stenciled on its side. I was born to fly!

I counted the years until I could head off to flight school and those years seemed to last an eternity. In the meantime, like many other twelve-year old kids in my working-class neighborhood, I got my first job as a paperboy delivering *Newsday* on Long Island. Most kids spent their newfound income on hockey equipment, but I spent mine on books about the military. Wanting to know it all, I studied every book I could get my hands on. I was fascinated. I was hooked.

In ninth grade, I learned about and joined Nassau Composite Squadron II of the Civil Air Patrol (CAP), the United States Air Force Auxiliary. Although it was not the Navy, at least it offered me an opportunity to fly and learn more about the military. When I got my uniforms, I quickly put on my fatigues. It may have only been a youth group, but I was so proud to wear the uniform of my country.

On most Sunday mornings, I would get up early and wait in the high school parking lot for our squadron leader, Captain Canavan, to pick us up and drive out to Republic Airport in Farmingdale, hoping to get a ride in a Cessna 172. The odds of getting a flight were slim, but I enjoyed watching planes take off and land, so I didn't mind spending hours in the terminal just waiting for my chance.

My first flight with CAP was on a chilly, overcast, winter morning. The pilot, Captain Steckard, was a former Marine officer who was probably in his forties and owned a tuxedo shop. He was known amongst the cadets, not only as one of the best pilots, but also the most fun to fly with. He was much more easygoing and relaxed than most, and more importantly, he was not afraid to let you take the controls and actually teach you about flying rather than just give you a ride.

Captain Steckard slowly went through the preflight inspection, taking care to point out individual parts of the aircraft's exterior as he patiently explained the significance of each step on the checklist. We boarded the aircraft, strapped in, and donned our headsets. Captain Steckard informed me that the doors had a tendency to open in flight. If this occurred, he instructed me to remain calm and simply reach over and pull it shut.

A smile ran across my face as I watched the propeller spin to life. I stared up at the clouds we would be joining in the sky, floating effortlessly like sailboats on the waves. I'd always dreamed of playing amongst the clouds and today would be my formal introduction to them.

Captain Steckard allowed me to taxi the Cessna 172, which is controlled on the ground by using differential braking. If you want to turn left, you step on the left brake pedal. I had some initial difficulty maintaining the centerline of the taxiway using this system, especially since I hadn't even learned how to drive yet, but I soon got the hang of it. We took the runway, ran up the engine, and went through the final checks. Steckard released the brakes, and we were soon off the ground and headed into my playground.

I practiced turns through a series of level figure eight patterns over Jones Beach but with the weather worsening we headed back to Republic Airport. I was admiring the scenery below when I noticed a sudden abundance of small white particles whizzing past the aircraft. It was snowing. I had never flown through snow, so it took a second for me to realize what it was. Although it is not a wise idea to intentionally fly through a snowstorm in a Cessna-172, it was truly a beautiful sight. It was as if the clouds were welcoming me.

CHAPTER SIX

INDOCTRINATION

I earned my commission as an Ensign in the U.S. Navy from the University of Arizona NRTOC Unit in December 1996 and received orders to flight school in Pensacola, Florida. Things were backed up in Pensacola due in part to a series of recent accidents, so those of us heading off to be aviators were first assigned to work at the ROTC unit we had just graduated from. I was technically the Assistant Recruiting Officer, but mostly, we just worked out and studied whatever we could find that would help us prepare for flight school.

It was April before I said goodbye to Tucson on a bright desert morning, 23 years old and finally beginning the journey I had dreamed about my entire life. I was headed cross-country to NAS Pensacola and on my way to becoming a Naval Aviator — the only job I ever wanted.

I drove past the Boneyard as I left town — past the rows of F-4 Phantoms from Vietnam and the F-14 Tomcats, the early ones that entered service around the time I was born. I dreamed of revisiting the Boneyard in the future, finding an aircraft that I had flown, and reminiscing about my daring accomplishment in the air. I pressed down hard on the pedal of my brand new 1997 Jeep Wrangler, shifting gears as the engine roared, accelerating onto I-10.

The Interstate may as well have been a rainbow, for I was heading to claim the wings of gold that waited for me in Pensacola. Bidding Tucson goodbye was a bit sad despite the exciting circumstances of my departure. I was headed off to glory but that meant leaving the town that had become part of my identity. I felt more of a connection to "The Old Pueblo" than "The Big Apple."

I may have been raised in New York, but I grew up in Tucson, arriving just days after my 18th birthday in 1991. I came alone then, driving cross country in my 1979 Cutlass Supreme with the Earl Sheib paint job, a case of 20/50 oil, and a dream. I was leaving in a much better vehicle with far less chance of winding up stranded on the side of the road, but I was still chasing that same dream.

Arriving in Pensacola towards the end of a humid Panhandle day, I crossed over the bridge that led to the base and followed the signs to the BOQ (Bachelor Officer Quarters), turning onto the U-shaped driveway lined with white painted tailhooks. It was dark now, warm and humid with mosquitoes circling the streetlights. Walking across the gold wings emblazoned welcome mat that lay at the entrance, I couldn't help but feel a part of something much larger than myself. I thought about all of those students who had come before me and passed through these very same doors, ready to join the ranks of this elite warrior club. I walked through the lobby covered in squadron logo stickers and up to the reception desk, proudly presenting my orders. I was actually here. I was in flight school.

I slept in late the next morning. It was a Friday, and I didn't have to check in until Saturday night. Room 211B was lined with white-painted cinder block walls and featured bland government-issued bedroom furniture, a TV, and a coffee pot. My room shared a common area with the adjacent room, providing us with a refrigerator, kitchen table, microwave, and a couch. I was putting my groceries into the fridge that afternoon when I noticed a light under the door of the connecting room. I figured I would introduce myself after I had finished unpacking, but before I had the chance, out walked Ensign Steve Bury from the University of Florida.

We hit it off immediately, and I was relieved to have met a kindred spirit. We knew we were at the start of a grand adventure, talking about which aircraft we wanted to fly and what flight school would be like. As the son of a Navy helo (helicopter) pilot, Steve was already set on flying Seahawk Helicopters off the deck of an aircraft carrier. He had done his 1st class Midshipman cruise with the Seahawk squadron on the USS George Washington (CVN-73) and that sealed the deal for him. I kept talking about jets. Although he thought they were cool, I could never convince him of the need for speed, though we would both dash outside whenever we heard the roar of the Blue Angels zooming by.

We were assigned to the same class but wouldn't start for another two weeks. We took full advantage of this free time and spent most of it working out in the gym, running on the infamous cross-country course, and practicing on the obstacle course. Due to the high rate of injuries, the cross-country course had been partially moved so that at least half of it was now in an open field marked by a collection of orange cones. The cones were not laid out in a logical, easy-to-understand pattern and seemed instead as if they were just randomly dropped into position.

Dressed in our PT Gear, Steve and I were earnestly applying our liberal arts degrees in a futile attempt to solve the trigonometry problem laid out before us when a fellow SNA (Student Naval Aviator) who had already begun API (Aviation Preflight Indoctrination) happened along and taught us the course. We timed ourselves on the cross-country course; I was worried since I'm not a fast runner, and then headed over the obstacle course. We appreciated having so much time to work out, but being stashed, Ensigns' beer was soon to follow.

If any bar is a legend in Naval Aviation it is Trader Jon's in Pensacola. Trader Jon had been running the bar since his arrival in Pensacola decades before, his bar now filled with parts of aircraft, squadron plaques and memorabilia, as well as pictures of the famous, the notorious, and the rest of Naval Aviation past and present. We grabbed some cold ones, chatted with Trader Jon himself, and toured the walls, examining the history of the brotherhood we were joining.

If Naval Aviation was a religion, this would be its holy place — a shrine to Naval Aviators past and present. A place where retired Vietnam era F-4 Phantom pilots could be seen drinking beer next to brand new Ensigns who had yet to even sit in the cockpit of a real plane. The Tailhook scandal of '91 was still fresh in mind, and business had dropped off significantly as folks worried about getting caught up in the next scandal. Trader's used to be *the* place to go, but it had recently become the place to go *before* you went to Seville Quarter, which, after a couple games of pool, is exactly what we did.

Seville Quarter, aka 'Syphilis Quarter,' was a nice place in its own right. A collection of different bars offering live music ranging from Blues to Pop with an open patio area out back. I actually got 'the wave' going there once while trying to impress a girl from Georgia named Taffy, but mostly, we'd talk about aircraft and hit on girls, usually starting with the waitress to warm up. Steve crashed hard when he found out the waitress serving us was from a small town in Alabama, and opened with a Forest Gump reference, asking her "Is that near Greenbow, it's in the county of Greenbow?" The piercing look in her eyes said more than her Southern manners would allow.

The Deep South was definitely a culture shock at times, and the local bible college added to the entertainment. True believers would stand near the entrance to local bars, often in the way of traffic and with their young children, yelling at patrons to accept their version of religion and forsake that icy cold pint lest they burn in hell.

I usually kept a low profile but was in a sarcastic mood one night as I passed a street preacher, who asked me, "Do you accept the lord Jesus Christ as your savior?" I replied, "No thanks, I'm Jewish." Apparently absent on the day the

Pensacola Christian College taught students about other religions, he forcefully retorted, "You're gonna burn in hell!" Taking the opportunity to educate the man, I reminded him, "Well, we don't believe in hell so I guess I'm all set." This left him confused and verbally disarmed. I wonder if he asked his professors about that.

Dating in Pensacola was a challenge because it seemed like there were the girls that were looking to get married and leave the Panhandle and the ones that were taught to never date a sailor. The ones that were looking to leave town often knew more about your aircraft than you did, knowledge gained by helping countless students before you learn the systems and emergency procedures of the mighty T-34C Mentor aircraft. The notion that girls in Pensacola should stay away from sailors most likely stemmed from the fact that somewhere in their lineage a woman was treated badly by some sailor she had dated and the lesson was passed down through generations.

Of course, not everyone follows these rules, and the Chapel at NAS Pensacola was always kept busy with weddings between a local girl and sailor, and I imagine they proclaim themselves "busiest chapel in the Navy." Undaunted, we would soon expand our stomping ground to include the finer establishments of Pensacola Beach. Places such as Capt Fun's (aka Sgt Sucks), The Dock, and Flounders, gave us some summer options when Seville Quarter played itself out.

One of the first girls I met in Pensacola was Denise, or "Nawlins" as Steve and I called her. We weren't very creative. I met Denise while she was on vacation in Pensacola. She was born and raised in New Orleans, but during the summer, she and her girlfriends made an almost weekly trip to Pensacola Beach. Denise was a slim dirty blonde beauty with a sexy Cajun accent.

The first night we met, we stayed up all night lying next to each other on a lounge chair beside the pool at the condo she and her friends were renting. We kissed under the stars, shared stories, and talked about our lives. New to Florida and having heard stories about gators occasionally finding their way into small lakes and ponds, I cautiously kept one eye on the edge of the duck pond that was not more than 6 feet away from us. I could see the headlines now, "NAVAL OFFICER FROM NEW YORK EATEN BY FLORIDA GATOR WHILE MAKING OUT WITH LOUISIANA GIRL."

I really did enjoy holding Denise in my arms as we watched the sun slowly rise on the horizon. When the sun had taken its place in the sky and morning had officially arrived, we parted ways for a few hours to get some sleep but planned to meet again that night for another evening together.

I woke up in the early afternoon and immediately set to making plans, well that is after I told Steve about Denise. Being a newly commissioned Ensign, which means broke but with a brand new car, I reviewed my limited options and their related costs. Payday wasn't till next week, so any dinner that I could afford would not be all that impressive.

I decided on a blanket, the beach, and a bottle of wine. Sounds romantic enough right? And in a perfect world it would have been great. The bottle of wine was the easy part. I headed over to the base package store and picked up a bottle of their finest ten-dollar Merlot. Then there was the issue of glassware. Although I was now living in the South, paper cups just didn't seem appropriate, so I headed over to Odd-Lot and picked up the closest thing to wine glasses that I could find: a set of four Champagne flute glasses for five dollars. My plan was coming along nicely!

Next, I grabbed the Navy-issued comforter from the bed. It was probably designed to withstand a nuclear blast, so I figured the sands of Pensacola Beach should be no problem. I managed to stuff the queen-size comforter, the bottle of wine, and two champagne flute glasses into my helmet bag, which, as the name clearly states, is only meant to hold an object the size of a helmet. With the top off of my Jeep, I grabbed my helmet bag and confidently headed for certain romance with my Cajun beauty.

On the drive over, I thought that God or the universe was sending me positive vibes when two songs about Louisiana girls came on the radio one after the other. First, there was 'Baton Rouge' by Garth Brooks, followed by 'Adalida' by George Strait. Surely this was a good sign! I picked up Denise at her condo and we headed east to the more secluded areas of Pensacola Beach and Destin.

We pulled over to the side of the road and parked besides the dunes. It was a perfect night with the moon and stars reflecting brightly off the waves as they crashed ashore. The night was warm, but with a gentle breeze rolling in over the water. I swatted away a few mosquitos trying to attack, but felt certain they would go away once we got out from under the streetlamps. We crossed the dunes, found a spot away from everyone else, and I broke out the blanket. Denise and I laid down, holding each other tight as we gently kissed each other's lips while the crashing waves serenaded us. I broke out the wine, uncorked the bottle and poured each of us a glass.

The mosquitos suddenly grew stronger, but surely, they would be gone once the ocean breeze picked up. I kissed Denise' lips, coated with the sweet taste of Merlot, and we both tried to ignore the mosquitos, focused on taking in the beautiful night and each other, but eventually, it became too much. They seemed to have called up reserves!

Although I was determined not to let a few mosquitos ruin my night, a swarm was a different story. Quickly stuffing everything back into the helmet bag, we sprinted across the sands for the safety of the Jeep, which of course, in an effort to improve the romantic quality of the evening, was without its top. As we sped away from the ambush site the itching began in earnest. It quickly got so bad that as soon as we spotted a convenience store, I pulled in for some hydrocortisone cream. We must have used the entire tube. I know what you're thinking, "How romantic." As you probably guessed, Denise asked me to take her home.

And so romance was beaten that warm humid Pensacola evening by a swarm of tiny insects but I'm sure there's a romantic comedy in there somewhere.

Oh, by the way, one of the big differences between Arizona and Florida is the accuracy of the weather forecast. For example, in Arizona you know a week in advance when it is going to rain, but in Florida, you walk past your Jeep — flooded with the top off — as you head off to your first day of flight school.

We filed into the classroom, choosing seats near those we had become acquainted with during our weeks in the stash pool. There were officers from Allied nations joining us for training and as the Germans walked in, we cracked up as someone repeated a line from 'The Simpsons', mimicking Mr. Burns as he whispered, "Oooh, the Germans!" It was the 12th of May 1997 and I'd been on active duty for just a few days shy of six months, but was just now starting my training. "Maybe I should have joined the Air Force!"

Lieutenant Scott Kormis welcomed us and led us through what we could expect in the coming weeks and what was expected of us before giving us our first, and probably most important, lessons of flight school: (1) "Looking cool is everything," and (2) "You have to sound cool on the radio." The six-week syllabus covered meteorology, aerodynamics, engines, navigation, systems, and more subjects I've probably forgotten. Mixed in with classroom time was land and water survival training, physical training, and the obstacle course.

Much of the water survival training involved dealing with worst-case scenarios for landing in the ocean after a bailout, ejection, or crash landing. We'd jump into the pool wearing all of our flight gear and survival equipment and then practice treading water for twenty minutes before "drownproofing" for twenty more, floating underwater to conserve energy until instructed to manually inflate our life vests. This meant catching your breath on the surface and then sinking towards the bottom, as you located the inflation tube of your vest, and emptied your lungs into the tube, before returning to the surface to repeat the process.

We had to demonstrate that we were comfortable in the water, and were challenged with disentangling ourselves from parachutes, swimming a mile in flight suit and boots, and getting hoisted up by our harness for a helicopter rescue. The nose-heavy aircraft we would be flying was expected to pitch over in the event of a water landing, so we practiced riding the rails of the "Dilbert Dunker" into the pool, where our cockpit would flip over once it reached the bottom. You had to wait until everything came to a stop, then calmly release your harness, swim out from the cockpit, and return to the surface.

That was the easy part. The challenging escape came from the 'Helo Dunker,' where there were eight of us strapped into the seats of a large metal tube that vaguely resembled a generic helicopter, or 'helo' in Navy parlance. Once we were all inside, the tube would be dropped about 10 feet, hit the water, and then start to roll over quickly as it sank in the pool. To prepare us for a water landing, where top heavy helicopters quickly roll upside down, we were required to "wait for all violent motion to stop" before releasing our safety belts and evacuating the aircraft. This usually took about 13 seconds, so as soon as the water washed over your face, you'd start counting "1, 1000, 2, 1000, 3, 1000 ..." until it was time to leave. Keep in mind that you're strapped in upside down and underwater, so everything is a blurry, confusing, flipped-upside-down world, where you feel for reference points to find your exit.

On some runs, we'd simply have to find the closest exit, while on others, we'd be blindfolded and required to all exit through the main cabin door. The guidance when releasing your belt was to keep one hand on the seat so that you didn't float away and become even more disoriented. This worked well until once, hanging there upside down after calmly counting down for 13 seconds, I pulled the release and nothing happened. I tugged at it again with the same results. Growing concerned and running low on air, I pulled hard with both hands and managed to free myself but then floated to the floor — now ceiling — and lost my reference point. I spun around and tried to reorient myself, but I could barely see in the water churned up by the other seven students leaving the dunker. I felt along the walls, hoping to find an exit, until I felt a tug at my back as the safety diver pulled me out and brought me to the surface.

When they asked the group how the last run went, I raised my hand and reported that my buckle wouldn't release and that I had to use both hands to force it free. The instructor's sarcastic advice was to "pull harder next time," so with that, we moved on to the next round. When a female Air Force student reported that she had the same problem on that next round, the same instructor said, "We should probably fix that."

Along with the course material we were expected to master, we also learned about how we would be graded once in the actual aircraft. The three main areas were Headwork, Airwork, and Procedures. Headwork was an evaluation of how you thought through problems and came up with a solution. Airwork was your mastery of the monkey skills required to get the aircraft to do what you wanted it to do. Procedures was simply a test of your memory and ability to follow instructions.

Headwork was the most important. You could develop the muscle memory and hand-to-eye coordination required for good Airwork. You could always study a bit more and pay more attention to increase your mastery of Procedures, but good judgment and decision making is hard to teach. Headwork is what really separates those who are able to do the job from those who aren't.

For example, let's say you are required to bring your books with you to class, but you absentmindedly leave them at home, where would you choose to sit? If you said in the back of the class and as far away from the instructor as possible, then you made the right call and exhibited good headwork. Our classmate Bryan did not. Bryan chose to not only sit in the front row but right in front of the Lieutenant teaching the class. The instructor wasn't upset that Bryan forgot his books; he was upset that Bryan forgot his books and chose to sit in the front of the class. Last I heard, Bryan was a physician somewhere in Florida.

Through morning PT, classroom lectures, survival training, evening study sessions, happy hour at the O' Club, and weekends on Pensacola Beach, we really bonded as a class and felt the camaraderie that comes with joining the ranks of an elite group. We expected to fight our country's future battles, flying over an enemy's coast "Feet Dry" supporting Marines on the ground or opening up a pathway for larger bombing runs. Each of us had our unique personalities, but none of that mattered. We were focused on helping each other achieve those sought-after Wings of Gold and the title of "Naval Aviator!"

At the end of API, we were rewarded with our flight suits, leather flight jacket, nylon green flight jacket, and sunglasses. Of course, the Air Force always had more money to spend, so their guys were also issued watches. It was summer in the Panhandle, hot and humid, but I couldn't wait to try on my leather jacket. Perfect fit!

CHAPTER SEVEN

SPREAD YOUR WINGS

I received orders to NAS Whiting Field in Milton, Florida for Primary Flight Training (Primary). This was the phase that would count the most and decide your professional fate. Primary was where you learned how to fly — though many students already had a hundred or more civilian hours — and screened for jets, helicopters, or Maritime Patrol aircraft. Performance in this phase would establish where you wound up in the pyramid of Naval Aviation. Getting jets is a whole lot harder in the Navy than in the Air Force, because we have a lot less of them, and the Fleet needs twice as many helo pilots as jet pilots.

Fair or not, those flying jets were considered to be at the top of the pyramid. Though it is debatable, Maritime Patrol pilots, as well as those flying the carrier-based, airborne early warning and cargo planes, occupied the middle mostly because they were flying fixed-wing aircraft and had a good shot at the airlines after leaving the Navy.

There's definitely an unfair bias in terms of prestige towards fixed-wing pilots in the military but, personally, I think it would be a hell of a lot more fun to be taking off from the deck of a destroyer, pitching and rolling in the North Atlantic, to go rescue a downed pilot or prosecute a submarine contact, than taking off from a land base in Florida in a glorified airliner and running a race-track pattern for 12 hours over empty ocean. But maybe that's just me.

Because helicopters are much slower and can stop and back up if needed, they received the students that maybe weren't catching on as quickly or seemed a bit overwhelmed in the cockpit. They also received some of the stars of their class because assignments were determined weekly by the needs of the Navy. I knew guys that flew helicopters who were ace pilots and some who never should have gotten their wings. If the Navy needed helicopter pilots that week, it didn't matter that you were the greatest pilot ever to fly, you were now a helicopter pilot.

Returning to the Panhandle after visiting family on leave, I checked into the BOQ at NAS Whiting Field in Milton, Florida. Milton was a lot smaller than Pensacola and was located in a dry county, so there wasn't much nightlife. Folks were so desperate for something to do on the weekends that a visit to Walmart often constituted a date. You could definitely drive to Pensacola, but that would require about 45 minutes each way. Most classmates chose to live in Pensacola and just commute to Whiting Field when they had flights, classes, or were scheduled to stand duty.

I was determined to do whatever it took to earn a jet slot and wanted to make sure I was focused, spending my time studying, practicing in the simulator, or working out, rather than laying on the beach. I wasn't exactly an aviator monk and still made it down to Pensacola, often crashing on Steve's couch before driving back home early in the morning, but I definitely missed out on some good times while isolated in Milton. I knew it was largely out of my control, but I wanted to honestly tell myself that I was doing everything I could to earn a jet slot.

I don't consider myself to be religious, but in search of camaraderie and a support network, I decided to attend Shabbat services in Pensacola one Saturday morning. Though we didn't wear uniforms to services, it was obvious who was in the military. Shortly after I sat down, a middle-aged man approached and asked if I was at NAS Pensacola. It turned out that he was a Navy Captain and the Jewish Chaplain for the region. As I said, I'm not very religious, but it was nice to know there was someone who would understand me a bit better than, say, the Southern Baptist preachers that seemed to fill most of the Chaplain billets in the Navy.

I was greeting the Chaplain after services one morning when I was introduced to Jon Sherman from Beverly Hills, California. Jon appeared to be in his mid 20s, so I assumed he was in flight school like me. I asked, "Are you at Pensacola?" "Whiting," he replied. "Which squadron?" I asked. I was happy to hear him say "VT-6." At least I wouldn't be the only Jewish student in the squadron. I followed up with, "What stage are you in?" "Oh no, I'm an instructor." Surprised and knowing that he also outranked me, I said, "Sorry Sir, I thought you were a student."

Our class checked into the VT-6 "Shooters" on the morning of Monday, August 18, 1997. As part of our training, we were each assigned an "on-wing", an instructor pilot who was responsible for getting us to our solo flight, while also serving as a mentor and advisor during our time in VT-6. As they were announcing the assignments, I had a sense of who mine would be. My name was called, and sure enough, I was paired up with Lieutenant Sherman. The Petty

Officer giving out the assignments asked, "He actually requested you. Do you guys know each other or something?" "We've met," I replied with a smile.

To be honest, at first, I wasn't sure if this was a good thing or a bad thing. Sure, it would be great to have someone I could relate to as my adviser and teacher, but it also meant he would probably be pretty hard on me to make sure I performed well above average. When you're in the military with a name like 'Rosenberg,' you represent more than just yourself, you represent your people.

Back in the mid-90s, I was told that Jews represented just over one percent of the US population but made up almost two percent of the military. We served in greater proportion than most ethnic groups, but since that's still a small segment of the military, we were usually the sole representative in our units. For many folks in the military, we were the first and maybe the only Jew they had ever met.

In my time in the Navy I was often presented with questions from young sailors that could have be perceived as antisemitic but were genuine questions from those curious about my cultural beliefs and traditions. Many came from small towns and remote rural areas where there simply were no Jews, and they had been taught some hateful things that they were right to question. I was glad to be there as a "warrior ambassador" of sorts to set the record straight and demonstrate that we were here to fight together for our country.

I did encounter antisemitism in the Navy, but it was always subtle, excused as a joke or simply exclusion from a group as if I was not "one of them." To be Jewish in America means that you're often thought of with suspicion as "the other," so we're often left out. We're viewed as having a secret advantage somehow, when the real secret is hard work and determination. As members of one of the smallest minorities in the country, those of us serving in the military looked out for each other because no one else would.

Instructional flights in Primary were less about learning and more about demonstrating what we'd taught ourselves. Each flight on the syllabus detailed what was expected of you and what maneuvers or tasks you were required to perform. To prepare, you read through the section in the manual, memorized it, and mentally prepared yourself to execute the maneuvers.

The stress to not only keep up with the work, but excel, was demanding and really put your desire and abilities to the test. Everyone there was the best of the best, incredibly smart, well-educated, physically fit, and motivated to succeed. We were on the same team, but we were also competitive with each other, the exact attitude you want in combat aviators.

Those that seemed to have the most difficulty were the ones that had never failed at anything before. In the middle of Primary, I heard the sad news that one of our classmates from API had walked into his squadron to resign from the program after receiving failing grades on two flights, even though students with many more "downs" went on to earn their wings. He then walked to his car and sat down in the driver's seat, before putting a pistol to his head and taking his own life right there in the squadron's parking lot. A tragic reminder of the pressure to succeed.

My first few flights were with Jon, who was California cool, but demanding in a way that made him seem more like an older brother than an authoritarian. Jon would constantly drill me on procedures and force me to continuously improve my Airwork, never settling for "good" because we both knew I had to be better. Of course, there was some good-natured hazing as well, like the time he excitedly told me to look right as he banked hard left, hitting me in the helmet with the canopy.

It's a good thing that Jon was calm, because my first flight didn't start very well. Just two days out of ground school and at the controls for the first time, I was so focused on reviewing the procedures in my head that when we were cleared to take the runway at the midpoint — we only needed half of the runway length — I'd forgotten which direction the tower had told me the winds were coming from. Not wanting to have to ask again, I took a chance and turned left. "I have the controls," Jon announced from the rear cockpit as he spun us around to face in the proper direction. Not a glorious start, but a little humility is good sometimes, especially when someone is there to literally point you in the right direction.

Fortunately, things improved significantly after that. On the next fight, I nailed my first landing and my confidence soared. I worked even harder to prepare for flights with other instructors because I wanted to represent Jon well. I knew that how well I did was a reflection of Jon's performance as an instructor as well as my own abilities as a pilot.

As I got to know each instructor a bit more, I tried to adapt to their personalities. When I flew with the Skipper, Lieutenant Colonel Mills, USMC, I got a fresh haircut and made sure my boots shined brightly. When I flew with Lieutenant Rogaliner, who never seemed to smile, my goal was to keep telling him jokes until he laughed. As we walked back towards the squadron after our flight, I felt defeated as none of my jokes landed.

I perked up when I saw an orange-and-white Coast Guard helicopter on the flight line near our orange-and-white training aircraft. With a smile, I said, "Hey sir, it kind of sucks for those Coasties that they have to fly training aircraft their entire careers." Though not my best material this had to at least cause him to crack a smile. Nope! His deadpan response was, "Well you see, Ensign, their aircraft are orange and white so that they are more visible during search and rescue missions." Finally admitting defeat, I acknowledged his lesson in the obvious and moved on.

I exceled at aerobatics and navigation but had some challenges with formation flying before it finally clicked for me. For me, the challenge was having to react to someone else's flying while acting as a wingman, whereas with aerobatics and navigation, it was all up to me. One of the more satisfying moments of aerobatic flying was when you hit your own propwash at the bottom of a loop — the mark of precision. My skills and confidence were growing daily, and though never "ace of the base," I held my own and ranked near the top of my class.

We didn't have the ability to practice on home computers, so we learned to "chair fly." We would sit down, close our eyes, and visualize ourselves in the cockpit, mentally practicing every step of the upcoming flight, from preflight, performing the required maneuvers, and finally shutting down the engine and climbing out without ever leaving our seat. If the weather conditions were poor and all flights grounded, it was amusing to walk into the student ready room and observe a dozen or so guys sitting there with eyes closed, left hand on the imaginary throttle, right hand on the imaginary stick as they performed maneuvers in their heads. Chairflying is a very effective exercise, and I still use it to this day when getting ready to lead a hike. I run through the landscape and think about what to expect, what the terrain will look like, what can go wrong, and how will I deal with that if it does happen.

Besides going out to the carrier for the first time, the most stressful flight for any student naval aviator was the "safe for solo" check flight, which, once passed would allow us to fly solo for first time. Everything had to be perfect from briefing to shut down. There could be no mistakes — nothing that would cause an instructor to feel the slightest bit uneasy about signing off on your ability to fly solo.

During the brief, you could expect to be asked, "Okay, I'm a drop of oil, take me through the oil system," whereupon you were required to accurately draw all components of the oil system in the proper location and order. The same question could be asked of the hydraulic system or any other component of the aircraft. Steve and I took a trip out New Orleans the weekend before my check flight, and I memorized the oil system for the T-34 on a French Quarter balcony in between visits to Café Du Monde and Bourbon Street.

The briefing for a training flight could often be more stressful than the actual time in the air, so you had to be prepared. I remember wandering into the briefing area with a question for an instructor when I heard a Marine Major correct a student with, "Lieutenant, you best un-fuck yourself!"

"This can wait," I thought as I spun around on my heels and exited the briefing area.

After several days of weather delays, I was excited to see that I was on the schedule the next day for my check flight — until I saw who I was flying with. I'd lucked out so far and gotten my first choice in base and squadron, and even lucked out with Jon as my on-wing, but now I was scheduled to fly the most challenging flight of my young career with the strictest and toughest grader in the squadron, Major Archer.

There was no leeway with Major Archer and no second chances. Everything had to be done right the first time, and most students that flew their safe for solo check flight with him did not pass. I spent the night chair flying, drawing out the aircraft systems, and quizzing myself with emergency procedure flashcards.

November 5, 1997 (31.5 hours of flight time thus far)

The morning of my check flight, I reviewed my procedures and system knowledge before driving over to the squadron. The weather forecast looked good, but that could change quickly. Time for more chair flying in the student ready room before being called down for the briefing. I was confident and nervous at the same time. I felt ready but was ready enough.

I passed through the briefing without incident, and we headed out to the aircraft. On preflight, the Major quizzed me on different parts of the aircraft before we climbed in and strapped on our parachutes. I ran through startup, watched the prop spin to life, and once cleared by ground, taxied to the active runway hold short line.

Cleared for takeoff, I pressed hard on the brakes while I ran the throttle up to max and checked the instruments. With the propeller growling, I released the brakes and we were soon airborne, flying over the base golf course. "Clear, Click, Climb, Call" ran through my head as I raised the landing gear and prepared to depart to the north for our operating area.

I navigated my way up to the Navy Outlying Field (NOLF) in Evergreen, Alabama. Other than night flights and designated radio instruments flights, we practiced Visual Flight Rules (VFR) and navigated by looking for specific checkpoints on the ground, which could be a highway, a unique looking intersection, or an odd-colored roof on a barn.

Along the way, the instructor pulled back the throttle from the rear cockpit and announced, "Simulated." I ran through the procedures for an engine failure and dropped the nose a bit to trade altitude for airspeed as I searched for good place to land. Since we were now a glider, and this was a one-shot deal, I tried to determine wind direction from the trees and any flags that I could make out while looking out for power lines and other obstructions. Setting up to glide into a farmer's field, I quickly noticed that the field was occupied with the farmer driving his tractor in a neat pattern, unaware that above and behind him, we were setting up to make a grand entrance. At 500 feet above the ground, the instructor gave me the power back, and I climbed to continue towards Evergreen.

Landings at the outlying field went well. I wasn't quite ready for the carrier just yet, but I was landing under control without porpoising (bouncing) or landing long. Most importantly, I was landing safe and under control. It was time to head back to Whiting, so I turned south and followed the checkpoints home. The hardest point to find was called "stickman intersection." It literally looked like a stickman from above, but if you were off course a bit, the tall pine trees could easily conceal its location and prevent you from making a critical turn to the Southeast. I scanned the terrain in front of me from left to right, growing increasingly nervous that I had missed it. I rechecked my heading and looked around for familiar landmarks, fearful that all that I had done right up to this point would mean nothing if I missed this turn.

"Bam, there it is" I said to myself as the intersection came into view. After making the turn, I navigated back to home field, contacted tower, and entered the landing pattern. At the "180," abeam the numbers on the runway, "Flop, Chop, Check, and Drop" went through my head as I began my approach with a 30-degree turn to the left while pulling back on the throttle. I checked that the airspeed had come down to where I could safely drop the gear, threw the handle down and confirmed that we had "3 down and locked!" Adjusting my turn to roll out on centerline, I ran through the landing checklist and set up for my final approach, working the controls to keep everything lined up without dropping too fast.

We exited the runway at midfield and taxied back to the line. Walking back to the squadron was uncomfortable. I still didn't know if I had passed or not and didn't want to say anything that would cause him to doubt my confidence or abilities in any way. I'm normally pretty chatty and often took this time to ask the instructor questions about our flight or tell a few jokes, but this time I only spoke when spoken to.

We reached the briefing area, and as I sat down, I held my breath. Major Archer reviewed each phase of the flight, critiquing my performance from notes he taken. All seemed to be going well, but I knew that this could be leading up to "and then you…." I sat poker faced, nodding that I understood what he was saying and acknowledging his advice. I don't remember his exact words, but I not only passed — I earned an above average, the flight school equivalent of an A+. I'm sure my eyes widened with surprise. I was stressed about just passing and was now walking away with an "above" from the hardest grader in the squadron. Even more amazing was what it meant. It meant that I could now take a Navy aircraft up into the sky on my own. I couldn't wait and hoped the weather held so that I could get airborne the next day.

Of course, it being Florida, the weather didn't hold and was below the regulated solo flight minimums for 12 straight days. My "safe for solo" certification expired, and I had to recertify with another tough instructor but on November 18, 1997, I finally left the ground alone and leapt skyward. The only required tasks were to navigate safely to and from the operating area, fly to an outlying field for several touch-and-goes, and then return safely to home field.

I wasn't yet trained in aerobatics, so I flew along the Gulf Coast for a bit before spotting a few ships making their way through the intercoastal waterway towards Mobile. I dove on them, imagining myself as a World War II carrier pilot in the Pacific. As I approached 500 feet, the lowest altitude we were allowed to fly at, I hit the rudder shaker test button, which vibrated the pedals as my imaginary machine guns fired from the wings. Victorious in my mock attack, I headed home to celebrate.

There's a tradition in Naval Aviation that, after you solo for the first time, you get together with your on-wing to celebrate. You wear an old tie, which he then ceremoniously cuts, setting you free to "slip the surly bonds of earth." In return for his advice and tutelage, the young aviator pays his instructor with a bottle of the senior's favorite spirit. I'd heard that Jon liked scotch, so I picked up a bottle of single malt, but having a sense of humor, I also picked up a bottle of Manischewitz Kosher Wine, the overly sweet wine traditionally used at Passover seders. I wrapped up both bottles but hid the scotch.

After he cut my tie, I graciously thanked him for his guidance and instruction as he unwrapped the bottle of purple wine. He suppressed a look of surprise — and probably disappointment — as he enthusiastically thanked me for my gift. This was not the reaction I was expecting, but Jon was apparently just too nice of a guy to say anything. I was expecting him to either laugh or ask "Really?" but there was nothing. I couldn't let it go on any longer so I quickly presented him with his real gift.

I'd still fly with Jon every so often as I completed Primary, but never as much as before my solo flight. Jon continued to mentor to me and honored me as an usher at his wedding. We're still friends to this day, and I imagine that bottle of Manischewitz is still somewhere deep within his liquor cabinet, unopened.

I was excited to begin formation flying and was assigned Ensign Jason Wood (callsign "Hollywood") as my wingman, which obviously spurred a ton of Top Gun quotes. Flying just a few feet from another aircraft made me really feel like I was learning how to be a military aviator. Formation flying was definitely the most challenging phase of Primary and the one where instructors were really teaching rather than just grading us.

December 15, 1997 (55.8 hours of flight time thus far)

Midway through this stage I flew with Lieutenant Craft who had been a P-3 pilot in the fleet. The P-3 is a large maritime patrol aircraft that is based on the same airframe as the Lockheed Electra airliner. It is operated by two pilots, a flight engineer, and a team of system operators and observers on long patrol missions, where they might spend half a day searching the ocean for a submarine or identifying surface contacts, almost never flying in formation with another aircraft.

I was tucked in tight as wingman when I started fighting some turbulence and had difficulty keeping position, getting dangerously close at times to having a midair collision. This was strange because when two aircraft are this close, they usually experience turbulence together and bounce through it as if they were one aircraft. I was really getting nervous that my wing was going to impact the other aircraft, so I told Lieutenant Craft, "I'm fighting a ton of turbulence up here, should I drop back?" "Oh, that's me," he replied. He was on the controls at the same time as me, so we were basically fighting each other and beginning to generate what is known as Pilot Induced Oscillations that were getting bigger and more dangerous.

Aircrew Coordination was stressed from day one of flight school as was the Positive 3-Way Change of Controls, which goes; "I have the controls;" "You have the controls;" "I have the controls." This prevents the exact problem we were now dealing with which has led to fatal accidents in the past. We had executed this procedure throughout the flight, and I had been in control when we joined up alongside the lead aircraft.

The "turbulence" came on after I was in position off 'Hollywood's' right wing, dropped back a bit and stepped down slightly below him, using checkpoints on the lead aircraft as reference points to maintain position. Without taking control of the aircraft, Lieutenant Craft was making inputs to the controls that were either counteracting or exaggerating my own. The result could easily have been catastrophic and cost the lives of four aviators.

A few months later, there was a fatal accident that involved a formation flight of T-34s from Whiting Field. Two aircraft collided over the Gulf of

Mexico with the propeller of one aircraft sawing off the tail of the other. The stricken aircraft was falling out of the sky as the instructor pilot fought to keep it steady, allowing his student bail out. The student's parachute snagged on the damaged fuselage and sadly they both perished in the shallow waters off the coast near Tallahassee.

Lieutenant Craft outranked me so, though outraged, all I could say is "Sir, do I have control of the aircraft?" "Yes, you have the controls" he replied. "I have the controls," I repeated, following the proper procedure. The rest of the formation portion of our flight went on without incident. We then separated from our wingman to perform the remainder of the required maneuvers for the flight, which involved emergency procedures.

Some of the aircraft at Whiting were equipped with NACWS, which stood for Naval Aircraft Collision Warning System — basically a primitive version of the TCAS systems being installed on airliners around this time. If it worked perfectly, it would use the transponder information from a nearby aircraft to alert us that we were close and would also indicate the relative position and altitude of that aircraft. Overall, it functioned properly but was known to occasionally give false positives, indicating an aircraft was dangerously close when, in fact, the sky around was completely empty.

Our aircraft that day was NACWS-equipped. While at the controls, I received a warning that an aircraft was at our 3 o'clock position and 1,000 feet below us. I looked toward the indicated patch of sky and saw nothing. I then dropped the right wing to get a better look but still found nothing. "Sir, I've got a NACWS hit but don't see anything." "Roger, I have the controls" he said as we executed a proper change of controls. Lieutenant Craft then initiated a 145-degree roll to the right and pulled us into a steep inverted dive. We leveled off about 3,000 feet below and he gave me back the controls. "Where was he?" I asked, assuming that Lieutenant Craft had seen the contact and was maneuvering to avoid a midair collision. "I don't know," was the reply, "I never saw him."

"WHAT THE FUCK?" was went through my head. This guy was an instructor pilot who had earned his wings and completed a three-year tour with an operational squadron, yet when faced with a possible collision with an aircraft he could not see, he decides to roll inverted and dive down towards the contact's identified position and altitude. If NACWS had been correct — and thank God it wasn't — Lieutenant Craft's actions would have caused a collision rather than avoided one. Instead of climbing, or turning away to increase separation, Lieutenant Craft — without seeing the aircraft — chose to rapidly close the distance. Talk about below-average headwork!

After two incredibly unsafe incidents in the span of less than an hour, I questioned Lieutenant Craft's judgment as an instructor pilot. Were he flying with another experienced aviator, there would be someone in the cockpit who could push back against these bad decisions. But allowing this man to fly with students with just a few hours of flight time was as reckless as he was.

Since he flew aircraft with large crews, I assume this pattern of behavior was suppressed or unnoticed. As a junior officer, he would have served as copilot for most of his tour, deferring to the senior pilot in command. He was now loose to be as reckless as he pleased, but his actions could cost not only his life, but the life of his student and possibly another aircrew.

We returned to homefield and, as was the procedure at the time, I landed on the centerline, but then maneuvered over to the left side of the runway to make room for my wingman who was landing right behind me. LT Craft objected to this maneuver and demanded that I return to centerline. He then took the controls, brought us to a full stop, and executed a 90-degree turn to the right, followed by another 90-degree turn back to centerline. With 'Hollywood' and his instructor literally hot on my tail, and probably hot on the brakes at this point, LT Craft put our safety in jeopardy for a third time. If my wingman had landed fast or landed long, we would have collided on the runway.

As I left the post-flight briefing, I was furious! How could the Navy let this guy teach students? The command must not know about this, or they'd never let him continue on. I mentioned what happened to some fellow students and learned that just about everyone that had flown with LT Craft had the same view of him as unsafe. Many students had written about their experiences with him in the critiques we were required to fill out, but nothing ever came of it. I felt it was just a matter of time before there was a fatal accident.

Not that safety was the number one priority. In fact, it was during a safety stand-down that I heard those exact words. Just after the Training Wing 5 safety officer had finished telling us that safety was our number one priority, our commanding officer waited for the safety officer to leave and then gave his own thoughts on the matter.

"Fuck that!" he said. "If safety is your number one priority, then you have no business being here!" We laughed and nodded in agreement. Colonel Mills expanded on his statement, explaining that what we signed up for was extremely dangerous and that some of us might die doing our jobs. We were there to be aggressive warriors not airline pilots.

I accepted danger and the risks that go with being a Naval Aviator, but incompetence was something else. The job I signed up for, that I had dreamed of my entire life, had inherent risks but there was no need to add unnecessary ones to an already lengthy list of things that could go wrong.

One of the things that drew me to the military, and to the Navy in particular, was the sense of honor that seemingly enveloped it. Though human, with a history of mistakes and regrets, I've always considered myself a very moral person. I was drawn to the Navy because I saw it as an organization that made honor a core part of its culture. To me, honor meant doing the right thing, even when it wasn't required, even when no one was looking. I had to do the right thing. I had to report Lieutenant Craft to the command.

I figured the best approach would be to give a detailed account of my flight with Lieutenant Craft in my end-of-stage student critique, so on December 19th, after successfully completing the second solo formation flight, I approached the squadron duty officer, Lieutenant Mark Lind, and asked for the formation stage critique that I was required to fill out. Lieutenant Lind had started out in the Navy but transferred to the Coast Guard when, while in flight school, he learned that he would most likely be selected for helicopters. I'm not sure how this transfer was possible, but he did it. He wound up flying the Dassault Falcon 20 aircraft, which is a business jet that the Coast Guard uses for search-and-rescue and surveillance. Not quite an F-18, but I guess he was just focused on flying anything propelled by a jet engine.

Lieutenant Lind couldn't find a copy of the form, so he told me not to worry about it. Because it was required to be filled out, and because I had decided that honor compelled me to fill out the critique in full detail in order to save lives, I told him that I would head over to the Student Control office and pick up a copy. He looked at me strangely, but I didn't think much of it at the time.

I'd flown with Lieutenant Lind for the second flight of the formation stage, so maybe he was concerned that I was going to write something negative about him. That flight didn't go very well. I felt that the helmet I was issued was a bit loose and needed to be adjusted so that my hearing wouldn't be impacted. It was letting in too much noise and was making it difficult for me to hear radio transmissions. On the morning of our flight, I stopped by the survival shop and dropped off my helmet, picking up a loaner for my flight that day. The loaner helmet was definitely a tighter fit, which was what I thought I needed, so problem solved, I headed over to the squadron to wait for my briefing time.

Shortly after takeoff, I realized I'd made a huge mistake. I'd only tried the helmet on for a few seconds but now, having worn it for about 15 or 20 minutes, I felt my head was being crushed like a grape! There was nothing I could do about it in the middle of a flight, so I tried to just deal with it. The pain grew and grew until it was literally foremost in my mind. I was in so much pain that it was hard to think and function.

I brought this to Lieutenant Lind's attention and asked him to take the controls for a bit while I tried to make any adjustment I could — while still wearing it. Taking it off wasn't an option as the helmet provided not only safety from an in-flight head injury, but also contained our microphone and headphones, as well as hearing protection from the extremely loud engine noise. I struggled through the flight and received a grade of average. Given the circumstances, I was fine with that, but I sensed that Lieutenant Lind had made up his mind about me on that flight, believing that the helmet issue was made up as an excuse for my performance. I assume this was the lens he was looking through when he received my critique form.

Aware that many students had previously reported Lieutenant Craft's conduct with no response from the command, I made sure my report included specific details about our flight, as well as my analysis on why his actions were dangerous, and a recommendation as to what should happen next. "He should not be teaching students," I wrote, and should instead be assigned to the ITU (Instructor Training Unit), where he would be teaching experienced aviators how to be instructors rather than teaching fledgling students how to become aviators. An experienced aviator would know when to call out his actions, I reasoned, while a student with a few dozen hours just doesn't have the experience to recognize that a maneuver is dangerous until after the fact and I worried that would eventually be too late.

Though I could have just kept quiet and moved on, relieved that I would never fly with Craft again, I worried how I would feel if he went on to kill someone in a mishap, knowing that I could have done something to prevent it. As Naval Officers, we were trained to do the right thing and have the courage to speak up. I thought back to the letter Admiral Boorda, then Chief of Naval Operations, had written to all midshipmen about the Navy's core values of honor, courage, and commitment. His message meant a lot to me, and I kept a copy which I still have to this day. In it, he encouraged us to "Live instead with the 'Honor Value' for that will be your foundation for service as a Naval Officer." I needed to hold true to the 'Honor Value' and do what was right.

We were also taught that we should stand behind what we say. In API, a Marine Captain instructed us that if we had something to say on a critique, we should sign our names to it. Anonymous complaints were considered cowardly and not taken seriously. I felt that this must be why the command was ignoring so many complaints about Lieutenant Craft, so at the end of my critique I signed my name, ready to stand behind my report if the command had any questions or doubted its veracity.

I returned from leave over the holidays to learn that the squadron had finally taken action. I'll never know if it was the detail I included, that I signed my name, or if I was simply the proverbial straw the broke the camel's back, but Lieutenant Craft was no longer teaching students and had in fact been assigned to the Instructor Training Unit, just as I had recommended. I felt relieved, knowing that I had done what was right and probably saved lives. I had done what was expected of me as an officer in the US Navy.

I flew my last flight with VT-6 on February 11, 1998 and nervously waited for the selection process to play out. Somewhere in the offices of Commander Naval Air Forces (COMNAVAIRFOR), the operational needs of the fleet were projected and then communicated to the office of Chief of Naval Air Training Command (CNATRA). The staff at CNATRA would then rank all of the students that had completed Primary that week according to their grades and then go down the line from top to bottom looking at each student's preferences and the needs of the Navy.

The morning of selection day was spent going back through my flights of the past few months, agonizing over mistakes I had made and wondering what I could have done better. As we were called into the Skipper's office, I remember holding my breath as I waited to learn my professional fate. Where was I headed and what would my career look like?

JETS! Holy shit, I got jets! I could barely contain my excitement and started calling everyone that was waiting for the news, starting with my mom, of course, and then my brother. I called Steve to tell him the news and we made plans to celebrate at McGuire's Pub in Pensacola along with the rest of that week's jet selectees: Nate Dishman, Reid Wiseman, and Ty Bachman. Nate went on to distinguish himself as an F-14 Tomcat pilot, Reid also flew F-14s before joining NASA as an astronaut, and Ty flew AV-8B Harriers in the Marines before becoming a test pilot. Back then, we were just happy to have been selected for jets and to join the ranks at the top of the pyramid.

CHAPTER EIGHT

TOP OF THE PYRAMID

My next assignment was NAS Meridian and the VT-19 "Attack Frogs" of Training Wing 1. I would be flying the North American T-2C Buckeye, which was the aircraft that was causing much of the delays in the training schedule as there were several recent crashes, including at least one fatality.

The most recent problem was a suspected hydraulic system failure that caused the nose of the aircraft to pitch down suddenly, often irretrievably, resulting in what is known as 'runaway trim.' Just a few months before I arrived in Meridian, a student was on final approach when it is suspected that he encountered runaway trim on final approach.

The accident investigation report concluded that he had not locked his harness and was forced up out of his seat by the sudden onset of negative g's — think steep drop on a rollercoaster. He did, in fact, eject but it was determined that he likely pulled the upper handle from under his armpit, which would have caused the metal seat to be projected at him with a force of 32 g's. This latest fatality had grounded the fleet of T-2s for around six months, though they had recently identified and fixed the problem, at least that's what they told us.

The T-2s were old, with the original version having entered service in 1959. They were definitely on their last legs when I arrived at Meridian in April of 1998. NAS Kingsville, Texas had the newer aircraft, the Boeing T-45B Goshawk, and there you flew the same aircraft in both Intermediate and Advanced Strike training. But the program at Meridian had a huge advantage, The Douglas A-4 Skyhawk. Though we flew the two-seat trainer version, the A-4 was a legendary aircraft, having served in Vietnam as well as with the Blue Angels. The chance to fly the A-4 was an amazing opportunity that was made even more enticing knowing that I'd likely be one of the last pilots to train on the Skyhawk.

Located in East-Central Mississippi, Meridian was about as 'Deep South' as you could get. My experience in the Florida Panhandle had already taught me that Southern "hospitality" only exists if you're from the South. If you're not, it's just a way to hide animosity while pretending to be polite. If Southerners were ever treated as coldly or cast as outsiders when visiting Northern cities, I'm sure they would never stop complaining about it, but in their hometowns, it was acceptable to view everyone from different regions as "the other."

I checked into the Wing's Student Control office and joined the pool of students waiting to class up. My start date wasn't for a few weeks, so I was assigned to VT-23 "The Professionals" to stand watch as Squadron Duty Officer. Basically, I manned the phones, kept the logbook, and handled any assigned work from the instructors.

The squadron had just recently received their shiny new T-45C's — the new 'glass cockpit' version with digital displays — and were focused on putting instructor pilots through the curriculum as well as getting the local maintenance team up to speed. Since VT-23 would be an Advanced squadron its mission was to teach students not just how to fly, but fight with their aircraft. As such, the syllabus covered air-to-air combat, bombing, tactical navigation, as well as the ultimate test, landing on the carrier. All of the instructors were fighter pilots direct from the fleet and with extensive experience to help students develop the necessary skills.

In contrast, VT-19, the squadron I was assigned to for Intermediate Strike training, was a mixed bag. With the booming economy of the late 90s, many fighter pilots were leaving the military for lucrative airline jobs, resulting in a shortage at the mid and senior levels. As a result, we had a few Tomcat drivers and Hornet pilots, but they were rare. VT-19 also served as the advanced training squadron for the guys headed off to fly the E-2 Hawkeye or the C-2 Greyhound and as expected, we had a few instructors from their community, but we had an alarmingly high number of instructor pilots coming from the Maritime Patrol/P-3 Orion community and even a good number of instructors from the helicopter community. How was an instructor who had himself just learned how to fly jets a few weeks before me supposed to prepare me for the fleet?

I enjoyed working with the instructors at VT-23. They were laid back, confident, and treated us like kid brothers. We were the next generation, part of the family, and they made us feel like we belonged. In contrast, the attitude at VT-19, especially amongst those that had not come from the fighter community, was a sense that we annoyed them, that we didn't belong and that they should have been the ones training to fly fighters.

I finally classed up for Intermediate and started ground school on Wednesday May 11, 1998. Most of our classroom instructors were retired Naval Aviators that had served in Vietnam and always had great stories to tell. I particularly remember our Systems class instructor, Jack Douglass, who had flown A-7 Corsairs and had ejected three times which immediately made me think of Lloyd Bridges' character in the movie *Hot Shots*, Admiral Benson, when he says, "You know, I've personally flown over 194 missions, and I was shot down on every one. Come to think of it, I've never landed a plane in my life!"

These veteran aviators were also our simulator instructors and though Jack Douglass could be tough, it was Mr. Zeller "The Yeller" whom we feared most. Some of the simulators we had for the T-2 were motion-capable so to reach our "aircraft," we would climb a flight of stairs up to a metal grid deck and brief with our instructor beside the computer console that controlled the simulation. We would then walk out onto a gangway, climb into the cockpit, and the instructor would retract the gangway in order to provide clearance for the motion sim. These weren't visual simulators so we only had the instrument panel to look at, but the motion helped you get a sense of what you would experience in the air.

The instructors also played air traffic control but broke character when frustrated with their students. I was paired up with Mr. Douglass for one of the sim flights where he kept me in a holding pattern for an extended period of time before clearing me to approach the field. As I made my way towards the simulated airfield, "control" called me and asked, "Where the fuck are you going?" "I'm heading towards the airfield," I dutifully replied. "Well where's the final approach fix?" he shouted. "Oh shit, behind me sir!" as I banked hard to reverse course.

The funniest moment in the sims was when I was paired with Zeller "The Yeller." When the simulation was over, I gathered my gear and moved the toggle switch to open the canopy, but nothing happened. I called him on the radio, but he had already removed his headset and couldn't hear me. Stuck in the dark simulator, I wondered if this was some kind of test or part of the harassment package that all students go through. When I didn't appear at his console, he noticed that the canopy on my simulator was still down, got back on his headset and asked what was taking so long.

I told him that canopy wouldn't open and his response was: "Okay, what are you going to do about it?" Confused, I racked my memory for a procedure on how to fix a broken canopy actuator switch and ran through the list of fuses I had memorized. The fuses for the canopy were on the outside of the aircraft so that couldn't be it. With no solution, I replied with a confused "Sir?" He shot back with "What do you do when the canopy won't open and you need to get out?" With that, I pulled the yellow emergency T-handle to jettison the canopy.

In real life, this would have activated a nitrogen-filled catapult that would have thrown the 200-pound canopy clear of the aircraft, but in the simulator, it just released the locking mechanism. Still confused as to what was going on and what was expected of me, I lifted the canopy and stood up in the cockpit as I turned towards the instructor console wondering how far he wanted me to take this "emergency"? Was I supposed to dive out of the cockpit and run away as if the aircraft was on fire? Emergency procedures and options raced through my head until he lowered the gangway and told me to meet him at the console to debrief.

June 11, 1998

After completing ground school and the required simulator hops, it was now time for the real thing. I suited up, checked out the maintenance book, and pre-flighted the aircraft, Side number 918. Climbing into a cockpit with an ejection seat was a new experience, especially getting into the back seat of the Buckeye. The canopy doesn't come up very high, so you have to sort of lean forward as you slide in. I visually confirmed that the safety pins were in place on the ejection seat, but still made sure not to hook the handle with my boot as I angled my way into the rear cockpit. This would be my first time flying a jet, but since it was an instrument flight, I'd be flying from the rear cockpit with my instructor, Lieutenant Raine, in the front.

I clicked in my harness, connected my g-suit and oxygen mask, and then pulled out the ejection seat safety pins. The realization that I was sitting on a rocket hit me just then, and I paused for a second after arming the seat thinking, "Still here!" There was a canvas tent of sorts installed under the canopy of the rear cockpit that we called "the bag," which simulated low visibility/instrument conditions so once the canopy came down, all I could see was the instrument panel as I was "under the bag." Flying a jet for the first time was disorienting enough, doing it without being able to see outside just exacerbated the feeling.

I'd quickly mastered the T-34 and with just a light touch on the controls could lock in altitude, airspeed, and heading, leaving the aircraft perfectly trimmed so that when the instructor in back told me to put my hands up as a test, the aircraft would continue flying straight and level. With just over 80 hours of flight time, I'd suddenly jumped from an aircraft that could fly just over 200 miles per hour to one that could do almost three times that and come close to breaking the sound barrier. The most challenging aspect of learning to fly jets was simply how fast everything happened. Quick reflexes don't make great fighter pilots — thinking ahead of your aircraft does.

I was trying to keep up but noticed I was developing a "helmetfire," where your brain is getting overwhelmed and you're trying to think through the flames. This led to some rough execution of the navigation procedures and even skills I had mastered in Primary, such as point-to-point navigation using the bearing and range from the TACAN beacon, didn't work out well. I was stressed and fighting the urge to vomit.

Thankfully, I regained my focus and suppressed the flames enough to redeem myself and perform a solid Precision Approach Radar (PAR). At the decision height, I executed a missed approach as required, adding power, and climbing away from the runway before transferring control to Lieutenant Raine. With my part of the flight over, I pulled down the bag, breathed a sigh of relief, and then frantically ripped off my oxygen mask searching for the barf bag I had placed on my kneeboard beneath a pile of checklists and approach plates. I'd held out as long as I needed to, but now that I was just a passenger, my body released the accumulated stress into the bright white paper bag.

The flight was a disaster and I wondered if I'd bitten off more than I could chew. Everything happened so fast, and I was reacting most of the time rather than thinking ahead, which I knew was a problem. I grew jealous of the guys that were able to pay for significant hours of private flight time before even arriving in flight school. In my class of eight students, six had over 100 hours of flight time before flight school, and now I understood why it was so hard to get jets without that bonus time. Besides me, the only guy in my class without prior flight time was Russel Girty, a former Rodeo Cowboy from Oklahoma who would go on to fly F-18 Hornets.

It was expected that we would feel "behind" the aircraft at first, reacting to it rather than leading it gracefully through the sky like a tamed Mustang, but I felt like I was an extra in *Blazing Saddles* being dragged through the desert by my horse. When my classmates who had not yet had their first flight asked how it went, I told them, "I wasn't just behind the aircraft, I was hanging on by the tailhook." Fortunately, I had pulled things together at the end of the flight and my performance on the precision approach had saved me. I walked happily away with a grade of "Average."

Average was exactly what it was. Though I was kicking myself for the mistakes I had made and felt overwhelmed by the transition from props to jets, I soon realized: so was everyone else. This was the time to make mistakes and learn from them. To get used to things happening at the "speed of heat" and to get comfortable in an environment where most people would be unable to function. The instructors made sure we knew that it was okay to make mistakes as long as we didn't keep making the same ones.

When we checked into the squadron, we were told "Grades no longer matter," that "You've already proven that you can do this, so just focus on learning." Of course, grades did still matter somewhat, determining which aircraft we would fly after earning our wings. Our options were F-14 Tomcats, F-18 Hornets, EA-6B Prowlers, and S-3B Vikings. My first choice was Tomcats as they were made on Long Island, and I had wanted to fly one ever since seeing one in person at Eisenhower Park back in the 70s. It was just a tough-looking aircraft with lots of raw power and capability. It also required a fair amount of skill to master, whereas the F-18 could literally land itself if needed.

My second choice was the F-18. The cool thing about it was that it was single seat and as arrogant Naval Aviators, we really didn't want someone in the back seat taking part of our glory. Plus, the Super Hornet would be arriving soon which was the future of our community but the F-14 was a legend, a real "tit's machine" as it's called among aviators. There would be time to fly F-18s later in my career.

No one really wanted to fly the EA-6B, aka the "Tactical Station Wagon," because it seats four and your job is to drive three electronic warfare officers around jamming enemy radar as if you were their dad taking them to soccer practice. The job of flying racetrack patterns your entire career didn't appeal to anyone, but if you were really good at landing on the carrier and maybe having problems with air combat maneuvering or bombing, you were likely headed to fly Prowlers.

The S-3, nicknamed the "Hoover" because its engines sounded like a large vacuum cleaner, was the least desirable option since it was slow and tasked with hunting submarines, not shooting aircraft out of the sky, but even that wasn't too bad. You were still a carrier aviator, and that's all that mattered. What separated Aviators from Pilots was the carrier. Among the most difficult challenges in aviation, landing on a carrier at night has been compared to diving into a postage stamp headfirst and trying to lick it.

Of course, I wanted to be at the top of my class and select F-14s, but at this point, I was just focused on holding my own while also playing catchup with those that had prior flight time. I had to work harder than they did, and that was fine. I'd fly the day's mission and come home to study and eat dinner before heading back to the base, hoping to find an empty simulator I could practice in.

I remember driving back to the base one evening on Route 39 feeling tired and just wanting to turn around and watch TV or get some rest. "Did I really need to practice in the sims tonight?" I had the top off of my jeep and the wind in my hair as I sped north along the rural highway with a beautiful orange-red sunset filling up the sky to my left. "What the fuck was I complaining about?" I said to myself. "I'm flying jets! I'm getting paid to fly jets! Life is fucking awesome!"

The more practice I had in the sims, the more comfortable I became in the aircraft and things started to click for me. My grades improved as I recognized the areas where I excelled and where I lagged behind, focusing my efforts on the areas that needed improvement. Still, I had this feeling that I was being judged by a different standard but could never figure out why or what that standard was.

I felt isolated and alone at VT-19. Unlike Lieutenant Sherman in VT-6, who treated me as a younger brother, my class advisor at VT-19 seemed to despise me and it was difficult to even track him down for questions, let alone guidance. Lieutenant Tooke was an E-2C pilot (the airborne early warning radar plane) and was getting married in a few months. He seemed both disinterested and distracted during required meetings, where he was supposed to review my performance and offer guidance and support, and even occasionally skipped these meetings altogether. After going to him for help with a personal problem and being ignored, I requested a change in advisors in early August but was told it wasn't possible.

I never felt like I was truly accepted by the instructors at VT-19. I didn't go out drinking as much as most of the students in the squadron because, first of all it was Meridian, and the nightlife just wasn't very exciting, but I was also focused on studying and being prepared for my flights. I didn't want to show up hungover, sucking down liquid oxygen on the ground trying to regain my senses as I prepared for a flight.

It's been said that being part of a Navy fighter squadron is sort of like being in a motorcycle gang, but your Mom is still proud of you. Drinking to excess is often the norm and a favored activity when on the ground, but it just wasn't my thing. Many of my squadronmates moved into party houses at Dalewood Lake and were joined by our instructors when out on the town in Meridian. I stayed away from the party scene and focused on my studies. I took this opportunity seriously and was focused on becoming a warrior, a man that could be counted on in times of crisis to defend the Nation. The Navy wasn't spending over $2,000,000 on me so that I could get drunk and go waterskiing. It was investing in me so that when the time came, I'd be ready.

We can all sense when we're not accepted so for me it was the reason why that remained a mystery. I wondered if my identity as a Jewish New Yorker had drawn unwanted attention. Though the pilots of the Israeli Air Force are regarded as the best in the world, to the instructors in Meridian, it seemed like I should have become a banker instead as they seemed to feel that I didn't belong in this elite Navy club. My performance in Primary had qualified me for membership in this club, demonstrated that I had the skills and aptitude, but no matter how well I flew, I could never gain their acceptance. Membership in this club within a club wasn't about performance but whether your fit their idea of who should be a Navy fighter pilot.

There was another Jewish student in the squadron, a Marine from New Jersey, who had even served as an infantryman in the Israeli Army, but his last name didn't draw attention the way a name like 'Rosenberg' does. My sense that antisemitism was the cause of my harassment seemed to be confirmed when a Marine Captain openly suggested that my callsign be changed to "Traitor," a reference to the trial of Julius and Ethel Rosenberg. I doubt a student with the last name of Arnold would have drawn the same scrutiny even if his first name was Benedict.

I feel it necessary to add that none of this had anything to do with the fact that we were based in Mississippi. The officers I sensed had an issue with me being Jewish were not Southerners and Meridian was so far 'Deep South' that most locals didn't even know 'Rosenberg' was a Jewish name. They assumed I was German, and I went with it. In fact, one of my favorite instructors, a Marine Harrier pilot, was from Georgia, if I remember correctly.

Antisemitism or not, it wasn't going to stop me, but I also wasn't going to raise the red flag and report what I could sense but not prove. Whatever it was, it didn't matter because this was just a temporary assignment. Just a few months more and I would be in Advanced, where my time stashed with VT-23 had already shown me that there was different attitude, also referred to as the "Command Climate." In the squadrons staffed by actual fighter pilot instructors, I felt welcomed and part of the team. I'd soon leave the disgruntled instructors of the "Attack Frogs" and join the "Eagles" of VT-7 or more appropriately, "The Professionals" of VT-23. I'd just have to put up with having a target on my back until then and not make a mistake.

Out of Control Flight recovery (OCF) was by far my favorite phase of training. I've long been a fan of roller coasters and not even the scariest ride could compare with the thrills of dropping down 10-15,000 feet as you spin and roll while trying to recover. After my first OCF hop, I thought, "Now this is flying." The T-2 was made for OCF and was even used by the Navy's Test Pilot School to offer an advanced course in recovery.

I excelled at OCF and always felt calm when around me earth and sky were tumbling past my visor as we dropped back to earth at 8,000 feet per minute. I led the squadron in OCF with the highest grades of at least the last year and it really seemed like things were coming together. I'd proven that I could not only keep up but excel. Now if only my luck would hold out long enough to allow me to fly the A-4 for Advanced!

One of the 'good deals' of Intermediate was that you got to go on a "road trip" of sorts, knocking out a series of Airway Navigation flights (AIRNAV's) where you fly cross-country navigating on the Interstate Highways of the sky. Most students choose to fly back to their hometown and show off their shiny Navy jet, and I was no different. The biggest challenge was that you had to find an instructor pilot that wanted to go to your hometown since they were in charge of the mission.

There was an instructor in the squadron who was from Queens, callsign "Guido," so I assumed he'd be up for flying home to New York, but he had been on the road a lot over the past few weeks and wanted to stay close to home as the time for my cross-country approached. I asked around, and Lieutenant Kronowit, callsign "Kronowitall," was up for the flight so I set about planning the route we'd take.

August 7, 1998

The plan was to fly from Meridian to Dekalb-Peachtree airport outside of Atlanta for our first refueling stop, and then Chambers Field at Naval Station Norfolk before the final leg up to Long Island, New York. The first two legs would be easy; it was entering the controlled airspace of New York Terminal Radar Approach Control (TRACON) that would be a new challenge. I'd heard stories of pilots getting overwhelmed by fast talking controllers and frequent changes in heading and altitude that needed to be acted on without delay. Having grown up as a fast talker, I figured I had an advantage for once.

We landed at Dekalb-Peachtree and as Lieutenant Kronowit was catching up with a flight school buddy, I filed the flight plan for our next leg and then called my mom to let her know that we were on schedule. It would be a mini airshow, with dozens of extended family members and neighborhood friends headed to Republic airport in Farmingdale to greet me upon arrival. I was hoping they would let us perform a carrier break where we come in at over 500 knots and just 800 feet above the runway but knew that we'd probably have to just fly straight in. Either way, I was flying home in a Navy jet, flying back to the same field where I had my first real flight with the Civil Air Patrol 10 years earlier.

With a full bag of gas for the next leg, we pre-flighted the aircraft and climbed in. The syllabus required a certain amount of the flights be completed from the rear seat, so we arranged that I'd be in back for the first two legs so that I could be in front for our arrival on Long Island. Lieutenant Kronowit gave me the controls immediately after takeoff, and while switching from the Tower to Departure frequency, I received a generator warning light and then noticed an immediate loss of power.

I quickly got on the ICS and asked the LT if he had the same indications and he said, "We hit a bird!" As he took back control of the aircraft and turned towards the field I switched back to Tower and declared an emergency as the fuel dump initiated from the front cockpit released twin streams of white vapor from our wingtips.

I looked down briefly as we banked left and noted the parking lot full of new cars from the adjacent Ford plant we were now flying over, hoping that the fuel we were dumping had time to evaporate before landing on these shiny new vehicles. I pulled out my PCL (Pocket Checklist) and reviewed the emergency procedure with LT Kronowit to make sure we didn't overlook a step. Tower cleared the field for us, and with fire trucks lining the runway, we set up to land as fast as possible just in case we lost the remaining engine.

Back on the ground, we taxied back to the small terminal and shut down the jet. I was standing beside the aircraft as the LT went inside to call back to the squadron and let them know about the bird strike.

The local Sherriff showed up to get some information for his report, and it soon became apparent that he was treating it like a car accident, asking me, "What should I put for the license plate?" I laughed at first, thinking he was making a joke, but when I realized I was the only one laughing, I replied, "I don't know, maybe the aircraft side number?" He then asked me "Who owns the aircraft?" which I thought was obvious given the big US markings and the word "NAVY" stenciled in large letters along the fuselage. I tilted my head like a confused dog and then said, "The Navy!" "Would that be Washington, D.C.?" he asked. "Yep, Washington D.C, just send them the bill," I replied.

Just then LT Kronowit returned and broke the news that we'd be stuck in Atlanta for at least three days as they needed to truck an engine up from Meridian, make the repairs on site, and then perform a functional check flight before we could return home. I broke the news to my family, but hoped the delay would only be temporary, and that I'd be able to make the trip in the next few weeks.

Unfortunately, there was a new wrinkle in the plan. The squadron had been tapped to supply a T-2 for the air show at Ellsworth AFB in Rapid City, SD and since I was ready for my cross-country flight and needed to complete this part of this syllabus, we were drafted for the trip. Guess my triumphant flight home would have to wait for Advanced. "How awesome would it be if I get to fly home in an A-4!"

On the way to South Dakota we stopped at Offutt AFB, just outside of Omaha, NE. Offutt is home to US Strategic Command, which among other things, controls the Air Force's strategic bombers. The runway at Offutt is huge, 300 feet wide and 11,700 feet long, made for scrambling a fleet of heavy bombers and support aircraft, so with a wingspan of just over 38 feet, I felt like a tiny insect landing my Buckeye on the immense runway.

I was in the backseat for the final leg to Ellsworth. We were flying from one beacon to the next using distinct radio signals that gave us bearing and range from the fixed positions on the ground, but looking down, I realized that we were also following the Missouri River and made note of that in case we had any issues with our avionics.

The culture of Naval Aviation is very different from the Air Force, and no matter what we're flying, we're all a bunch of cowboys so as we contacted the tower at Ellsworth, we requested the carrier break. Denied, we were forced to enter at something like 2,500-3,000 feet but were determined to at least come in hot. With field in sight, LT Kronowit pushed up the throttles and lined up for what would be a 7g turn downwind.

I looked down at the field smiling, proud to be here as a representative of Naval Aviation until that smile was washed off my face with the sudden realization that my g-suit umbilical cord had somehow disconnected from the aircraft. Straining to reach the connection behind me and to my left, I struggled to reconnect the hose as the Lieutenant told me to hurry up. Racing alongside the runway, I hooked it in, reporting "Got it!" Before I had a chance to move, I heard "G's coming on!" as we broke left, and I was pinned by seven times the force of gravity, stuck staring at the runway until we leveled off on the downwind leg.

Ellsworth is a B-1 Lancer bomber, or "BONE," base and we were the only Navy aircraft taking part in the show. As such, I of course had to represent all of Naval Aviation and even as an Ensign, with just over 100 hours of flight time, I did my share of trash talking. It was while hanging with one of the BONE squadrons at the Firehouse Brewing Company in Rapid City that I first met Tammy, who I later learned was a reporter for the local ABC affiliate. After going on about the differences between Naval Aviators and Air Force pilots, I invited her to stop by the aircraft at the show the next day for a private tour. "I'll even let you sit in the cockpit," I told her. "Just look for the only orange and white aircraft on the tarmac."

I spent most of the next day standing next to the aircraft talking about the Buckeye, flight school, and carrier operations. I'd brought a ton of squadron stickers with me and was busy handing them out to kids when Tammy walked up. I showed her around the aircraft and kept my word by letting her sit in the front seat while I knelt on the side and explained what all the instruments and buttons were for. I asked if she would have dinner with me that night and was pleasantly surprised when she agreed.

Logistics were a bit of a problem, but I was resourceful. At most airshows, the local car dealership supplies a fleet of demo cars for visiting aviators to use, but since Rapid City is fairly small, that didn't happen. Instead, we were issued Air Force vehicles and only one vehicle per aircrew. Fortunately, the Lieutenant I was flying with was a family man looking forward to a quiet night of rest, so I had our Air Force-blue Chevy Bronco all to myself. I'm not sure if it was youthful ignorance or just a different time, but the idea of picking up a TV reporter in an "official use only" government vehicle never seemed like a problem to me and fortunately not to Tammy either.

We drove up to the old mining town of Deadwood and spent the evening walking the town and literally dancing in the street to the music spilling out of the touristy saloons. We held hands as we sat on hotel porch rocking chairs and talked the night away. We were both at the beginning of our careers and I listened as Tammy spoke with pride about growing up in the same hometown as Tom Brokaw and the challenges of working in a small news market where she had to be both cameraman and reporter. This wasn't the trip I had planned, but I was really starting to enjoy this adventure and didn't want to go back to Mississippi.

CHAPTER NINE

THE PRICE OF HONOR

October 29, 1998

I'm not sure if it was nerves, stress, or just too much coffee, but I couldn't fall asleep the night before and only got about two or three hours of rest before it was time to head in for my flight. I grabbed breakfast on the way to base and met the other members of my Carrier Qualification (CQ) class in a darkened classroom above the hangar.

    Still exhausted and trying to introduce caffeine into my system as fast as possible, I focused on the TV screen as the instructor began the lesson by pressing play on the VCR — never speaking a single word. We watched as a T-2 Buckeye approached the carrier, seeming to almost hover in place before suddenly flipping over and crashing onto the deck as a violent explosion filled the screen. I don't think any of us were familiar with this accident but seeing the exact same aircraft we were about to fly — crash violently onto the deck, left us all silent and reserved as we waited for the instructor to tell us how to avoid a similar fate.

    It was day 1 of Carrier Quals, though the syllabus had changed years ago and we wouldn't go out to the actual carrier until the end of Advanced. Today, we'd be headed up to a Navy Outlying Field (NOLF) near Moscow, Mississippi named Joe Williams Field. All of our landings were flown as carrier landings and we flew the ball down to the deck as if we were landing on the carrier, but today we'd be practicing on a runway, graded to see if we were ready for the real thing.

    It was the final stage of Intermediate Strike training, and we would be moving on to Advanced training next week. We had already received our assignments and some members of our class would in fact be the very last students to train on the A-4 Skyhawk. I was not among them, but the silver lining was that I would be one among the first 20 students to fly the new 'Charlie' version of the T-45 Goshawk. I breathed a sigh of relief, knowing that the harassment I had endured for the past six months would soon be over, and I would now be trained by actual fighter pilots as I prepared to enter the fleet.

It was a bit of a party atmosphere as the hard stuff was over; we'd passed all the major challenges. It felt a bit like a senior class trip, sort of a graduation rite of passage. The Lieutenants in charge of our training were only a few years older than we were, experienced enough to teach us while still learning themselves. They told us they wanted to see "shit hot breaks" as we entered the landing pattern and even dared us to flip them off as we roared past on takeoff.

Half of us would fly up in the morning while the others would drive up in a van, and we would swap out aircraft with the engines running. One of the French Navy pilots that was training with us, Charles Godard or "Chuck," as he was known, had hit a deer with his Chrysler LeBaron convertible, and the local girl he was dating butchered it for him, so when not flying, we feasted on BBQ venison steaks as we watched our classmates perform touch-and-go's. I don't think anyone there was over 30, and we had the airfield to ourselves with no adult supervision in sight.

As I departed Joe Williams as a solo flight on day two, I decided to practice a high-performance takeoff. Upon reaching takeoff speed, I pulled away from the ground but leveled off at about 50 feet. With the throttles up against the firewall, the speed built up quickly as I raced to raise the gear and flaps before they ripped off the aircraft. The Buckeye's wings produced so much lift that I had to point the nose down slightly to keep from climbing until I reached the end of the runway and pulled back hard on the stick, shooting straight up like a rocket. I was climbing so fast and smiling so hard that I almost forgot to level off at my assigned heading and altitude of 10,000 feet, so I rolled upside down and pulled 7g's to land on the mark without busting through my ceiling. What a rush — I can't believe I'm getting paid for this!

November 4, 1998
It was our last day of FCLP and our last day of Intermediate Flight Training. We were all smiles as we suited up and posed for photos with each other before heading out to the flight line. I was last to launch as a solo and made my way north to Joe Williams Field. I wanted to impress the instructors and remembered their challenge to us of "shit hot breaks," so as I approached the field I pushed the throttles up, planning to come into the break somewhere between 450–500 knots and 800 feet above the ground. I pulled back on the throttles and slowed a bit, nervous about coming in this fast for the first time, but then threw them forward again, wanting to prove that I was up to their challenge.

I found my interval — the aircraft I was supposed to fall in behind — and extended a bit so that I would have extra room to bleed off this airspeed. Satisfied that I had left enough room, I rolled left to 90 degrees, pulled the throttles back to idle, and popped the speed brakes out as the g's came on during my descending turn to enter the landing pattern.

As I rolled out in the opposite direction of the runway, known as the downwind leg, I'd slowed to about 180 knots, but needed to slow even further before I could lower the landing gear and flaps, and not close on the aircraft in front of me. Already at idle and with the speedbrakes extended, I followed through on my training and began executing a series of serpentine-like turns to slow down. This maneuver worked as intended, but as I dropped the gear and flaps, the student in front of me, Eric, a Marine who was known to be a bit nervous in the sky, suddenly got on the radio complaining that I was too close to him.

Maybe he had seen me making turns from side to side to slow down, but I had never gotten closer to him than the standard distance in the pattern, so I was confused, surprised, and pissed off. It was typical Marine BS where they thought they were better than everyone because they were Marines, not because they were good pilots. I wasn't sure if he was trying to stab me in the back or if his reputation for airborne anxiety was just proving true, but I hoped the instructors would look up, see our separation distance, and recognize it was the later.

After a series of touch-and-go's, we landed full stop and shut down for a lunch break. One of the instructors, Lieutenant Kevin Lucas, pulled me aside and asked me about the incident. I was honest and told him that I had never come into the break that fast before but wanted to meet the challenge he and the other instructors had thrown at us just days before and that this was my last opportunity to do so. I admitted that I had misjudged when to break and had trouble slowing down, but denied that I had gotten any closer to the other aircraft than the standards set forth in our training manuals. Satisfied, he cautioned me to take it easy and that was the end of it.

It was always a difficult balance in Strike training. We were told to be aggressive and push both the limits of our aircraft and our comfort zone, but were often scolded for doing so. To win in combat you had to be aggressive; while timidity could cost you not only victory, but your life. Navigating the zone between was made even more difficult because almost none of our instructors were fighter pilots. If you came from the E-2/C-2 or P-3 communities, your training was exactly the opposite — it was to fly a stable, predictable pattern and avoid aggressive maneuvers. I was glad this was my last day with these instructors!

We launched for one final round of touch-and-go's, which would close out this phase of training. Since I flew out that day, I would be taking the van back to base and this would be the last time I would ever fly a T-2C Buckeye, but I was too excited about moving on to Advanced to feel nostalgic. Next week, I would begin learning a new aircraft, have actual fighter pilots as instructors, and was now only a few months away from my childhood dream of earning my wings.

The winds had shifted that afternoon, producing an extreme undershooting crosswind unlike anything I had seen before. You're always adjusting your distance from the runway while on the downwind leg to compensate for the winds so that, when you complete your 180-degree-approach turn, you roll out lined up with the runway centerline. If the winds tended to blow you towards the runway, you increased your distance and conversely, if the winds were blowing you away from the runway, you decreased your distance accordingly. With an undershooting crosswind, you are being blown away from the runway and if no corrections are made you will roll out well left of the runway centerline, or "undershoot" the runway.

The conditions encountered that day were so strong that I had to practically fly over the runway and my approach turn felt like I was sort of hovering in one spot, turning in place rather than tracing an arc along the ground. With only 180 hours of flight time at this point, it was a strange sight picture for me, but I figured out the corrections required and managed to roll out on centerline. These conditions were very much out of the ordinary and unlike anything a pilot would encounter while landing on an actual carrier where the ship maneuvers to ensure the wind is in line with the runway.

Rolling out on centerline wasn't the only challenge. Since we were practicing carrier landings, we also had to follow the glideslope down to where the arresting cables ("wires") would be. Still figuring out these new conditions, I would roll out on centerline but was occasionally rolling out a bit above the glideslope ("high") and had to quickly work the controls to get back to "center ball."

Being high is not dangerous, but if left uncorrected, you will land past the wires and will have to go around again. Conversely, being low is extremely dangerous because if left uncorrected, you will crash into the back of the carrier. Since jet engines take time to spool up, you never try to come down from high to a center ball when about to land, because you might take off too much power and not have time to regain your altitude. With this in mind, I made sure I corrected to a center ball as soon as it came into view.

While the conditions that day were extreme, I was glad I had the opportunity to experience them and learn how to adapt should it ever happen again in my flying career. Pleased with my performance and even happier to be done with Intermediate, I climbed down from the aircraft, collected my gear, and took a seat in the van for the ride back to Meridian.

Back in the squadron ready room, I was busy filling out the paperwork for the day's flights when Lieutenant Lucas called me and another student into his office. "Had we left something behind or forgotten to complete some form?" I thought. Lieutenant Lucas closed the door and delivered the shocking news. The other student and I had both received a "down" for the last flight of the day, which meant we had failed the flight. I shook my head in confusion. He then told me that I had been consistently high in my landings.

I was confused because while I had rolled out high a few times, I had always landed with a center ball (on glideslope) and given the extremely unusual conditions, I thought this was understandable. We were supposed to be graded on our ability to land on a carrier, but today, we were dealing with conditions that would never be present on a carrier.

Downs (grades of unsatisfactory) were supposed to be reserved for unsafe conduct or an inability to complete the training requirements, and neither were present. I knew that rolling out a bit high and quickly lining up with the glideslope was not ideal, but it was still very safe, and all of my landings would have resulted in me catching a wire on the carrier. The criteria laid out in the Naval Aviation training instructions backed up my understanding.

CNATRAINST 1500.4E (703)(a)

<u>Unsatisfactory</u> (abbreviation U; numeric grade: 1.0). The student is not ready to progress safely or satisfactorily to the next curriculum event. The student fails to achieve minimum curriculum performance standards or performs in a dangerous manner.

The down made no sense, but we were taught never to argue with an instructor. My facial expressions and body language revealed my sense of shock, confusion, and disagreement, but I kept my mouth shut.

This was my first down in Intermediate training, and I knew of several guys that had received more than five downs before going on to earn their wings. Typically, getting a down meant that you had to fly a few remedial training flights focused on whatever you were downed for, and then fly the graded flight again. Basically, you took the test over again to make sure you could demonstrate the skills required before moving on to the next phase. The down seemed unfair but I accepted it, expecting that I would just go through the remedial flights, demonstrate my skill level, and move on never having to deal with these instructors again.

Though this was in fact the standard procedure, I was quickly informed about the exception for the last stage of Intermediate Strike training. Any downs received during the Carrier Qualification/Field Carrier Landing Practice stage of Intermediate Strike training were to be investigated by a Performance Review Board (PRB). This was an exception to the normal standard where you needed at least two, but in practice, three downs before you were sent to a board. The danger was that any time you went before a Board, you could be attrited — kicked out of the Jet pipeline and sent to fly maritime patrol aircraft or helicopters.

November 9, 1998

Having been lauded for how I handled the engine failure during my first nighttime solo flight, I didn't feel that I had much to worry about, especially since this was my first down. Besides, it was well known that flight grades were subjective and could vary wildly from one instructor to the next. Even the Naval Air Training Command acknowledged this in its instructions:

CNATRAINST 1500.4E (701)

> *There are two basic means of measuring performance and comprehension, depending upon whether judgment is a factor or not. Grades that are awarded based on judgment, whether measured relative to prescribed and explicit criteria or to peer performance, are subjective, i.e., flight grades. Grades that can be assigned without resorting to judgment are objective, i.e., academic and physical training.*

I figured I would stand before the board, acknowledge my mistakes, express my gratitude for the extra training, and promise to do better in the future. I kept to this plan and never argued that the down was unwarranted or that there was nothing unsafe with rolling out of an approach turn a little high but landing with a center ball. I knew there was no point in arguing, so I acknowledged that everything Lieutenant Lucas said was correct and requested a few extra flights so that I could work on the deficiencies outlined before moving on with my training.

I waited in the hallway while the three members of the review board deliberated. It was humiliating to be standing there dressed in khakis while everyone else was in their flight suits. Wearing khakis meant you either had duty or you were in trouble. After about 30 minutes, I was called back in to hear their decision. I wondered how many extra flights I would need to complete before I could retake the last check flight.

I stood at attention and reported to the officer in charge of the review board. After being told to stand at ease, he announced the board's decision. The board had voted 2-1 to attrite, basically to kick me out of flight school. I was completely shocked and speechless. To be attrited from Intermediate Strike training with a single down was completely unprecedented and I'm not sure if it has ever happened before or since.

Still in shock, I asked what my options were and was told that I had none. Since flying jets is considered to be the top of the pyramid, so to speak, and you have to demonstrate above average skills and performance just to get there, students attrited from the Strike program were always given their choice of Helicopter, Maritime Patrol, or Naval Flight Officer programs. Though this had been the standard for everyone previously attrited from the Strike pipeline, they were barring me from continuing on in Naval Aviation and kicking me out with only one down — that was questionable on its merits — after the Navy had already spent almost $1,500,000 to train me.

None of this made sense. I knew a guy that had forgotten to strap into his seat for an aerobatics flight who had gone on to get winged. Another guy flew below the minimum descent altitude of an instrument approach while flying lead with three other aircraft depending on him for their safety, who went on to fly F-18's. Many students received their wings with more than five downs, and I knew of one that had received nine. Just two months earlier, I was being praised as sort of a squadron hero for how I handled the engine failure. Now, with only a single down, I was not only being kicked out of Strike training, I was being kicked out of Naval Aviation!

Decisions like this were supposed to be made in Primary Flight Training, at the beginning, where you demonstrated whether or not you had the basic skills required. There were a fair number of students kicked out in Primary, as the Navy decided whether further investment in very expensive training was worth it or not. Training a Naval Aviator is so expensive that it cost $2,000,000 per pilot in 1998, which is over $3,000,000 in today's dollars. It was so expensive that you were required to serve eight years AFTER you earned your wings. This meant that you were signing up for ten to eleven years instead of the four years owed for a ROTC scholarship. Once you moved on to Intermediate training, the investment was made and barring something extraordinary happening, you were going to be a Naval Aviator. The only question was what aircraft you were going to fly.

I immediately went to see the squadron commanding officer, Commander Devon Goldsmith, and asked him how I could be kicked out with a single down after he himself had publicly praised my skills and abilities. His answer was that he had to support his instructor pilots. The next day, I met with the Chief Staff Officer for Training Wing 1, Commander Edmunds, and requested a meeting with the Commodore, Captain Gene Smith. When Commander Edmunds asked me; "Why are you wearing your flight suit, are you on the schedule?" I angrily replied, "I should be."

I had to wait a week, but on November 18, 1998 I was able to plead my case to the Commodore. He listened patiently, but when I asked if he would review the decision to attrite his response was, "Well, I have to support my Squadron Commanders."

Something was wrong, but I couldn't figure out what it was. After nearly two years of training and an investment of almost $1,500,000 of taxpayer money, why was I suddenly forced out of flight school for rolling out high in an approach turn in truly adverse conditions? I called my buddy, Steve Bury, who had already earned his wings and was now flying helicopters in San Diego. When I told him I had been attrited, he just kept saying "WHAT?, WHAT?, WHAT?, WHAT?...." I felt the same way.

As I mentioned earlier, it seemed like I was being graded against a different standard and I felt like I was generally unwelcome in the squadron but could never figure out why. Whatever it was, I just accepted it as the harassment I had to put up with until I reached Advanced training, where all of the instructors would be fleet fighter pilots. It had just been something to endure, but now it had cost me my career and my dreams. I wondered how and why this could happen and now, with nothing but free time on my hands, I began to look into things.

First, there was the issue of the down on my last flight. As I said earlier, you don't go to a board with just one down except for this very last stage of training. This very last stage of training takes place at an outlying field where the highest-ranking officer was a Lieutenant, and no one was over 30. I went through training without a single down but then on the last flight — the last opportunity there is to kick me out, and the only time when a single down will bring you before a board — suddenly, I get a down for what would normally be considered, at worst, average performance.

I'm then brought before a board and counseled not to argue and just agree with everything they say if I want to avoid trouble. The board is split and votes 2-1 to not only kick me out of Strike Training, but out of Naval Aviation completely. This is unusual because the standard for attrition is three downs, and as I've pointed out, many students have been allowed to earn their wings with far more. It is even more unusual because the board refused to allow me to move on to fly helicopters, P-3s, or even take a back seater job as a Naval Flight

Officer. This wasn't professional judgment, this was personal. It seemed like a well-planned hit job executed by closely knit junior officers.

I began looking into things and started to review Squadron, Wing, and Training Command regulations and instructions. This was still the early days of the internet so none of it was online; I had to conduct my research in person at the squadron. Basically, I had to use the offices of the organization I was investigating in order to investigate their misconduct.

On November 5, 1998, the day after I had received my down, my grades for the air-to-air gunnery stage of training were retroactively changed to marginal. On November 16, the day I was scheduled to meet with the Commodore, my grades for formation flying and radio instrument stages of training were retroactively changed to marginal. This was 55 days after I had completed formation training and 145 days after I had completed radio instruments. Even after my grades were lowered, my overall flight grade point average was 3.014, which is considered average in flight school, just as it is in college.

CNATRAINST 1500.4E (703)(c)
Average (abbreviation: A; numeric grade 3.0). The student is ready to progress safely and satisfactorily to the next curriculum event. The student's progress is equal to curriculum performance standards for satisfactorily completion of the curriculum requirement.

Convinced I was onto something, I ignored the dirty looks I got while conducting my research in the squadron's offices and simply smirked in response. My research produced evidence that the squadron and wing staff had violated Training Wing One Instructions, Commander Naval Air Training Command Instructions, and even the Uniform Code of Military Justice. This was wrong and just like dealing with bullies in high school, I was going to fight back, the question was: how?

The easiest thing to do would have been to contact my congressman or senator. What happened was not only personally outrageous, it was also a waste of a taxpayer dollars. I'm confident this would have worked and that I would have been back flying jets again in a matter of weeks or months but there was a high price to pay if I went this route.

Back in Primary, I was in the same squadron as an African American female student who was legitimately attrited. She just couldn't perform up to the standards required despite instructors offering her extra help and even fellow students working with her in the simulator to help get her to where she needed to be. She threw out the racism flag, complained to her congressman, and was back in training just a few months later. She was back, but the way she had gone about it meant that she was now a pariah, an outsider and no longer on the same team.

She continued to fail to meet the training standards, received a record number of downs, and was finally attrited for a second time. I knew of a few stories like this, and the lesson was clear: whether right or wrong, if you go outside the fold, you'll never be able to get back in. I planned to make the Navy my career and truly believed that Navy leadership would set things right. I just had to find a way to let them know what happened.

November 23, 1998

I checked out of the squadron and also formally requested a meeting with the Admiral in charge of Naval Air Training, submitting a request for Admiral's Mast. I had no choice but to leave the squadron, but I would not go quietly.

My request for Admiral's Mast was accepted but because it wasn't required; I was forced to pay my own travel expenses. I left Meridian early on the morning of January 5, 1999 to begin the 12-hour drive from Meridian to NAS Corpus Christi, Texas. I left Meridian hoping that the faith I had placed in the Navy's leadership was well-deserved and barring that, I prayed for a miracle.

January 6, 1999

As I prepared for my meeting with Rear Admiral Mike Bucchi, I laid out my service dress blue uniform to make sure everything was perfect and that I had covered every detail. Having been promoted to Lieutenant Junior Grade just a few weeks earlier, this was the first time I would be wearing my black uniform jacket with the newly sewn thin gold strip placed above the thicker one I'd worn as an Ensign. I'd been on active duty for just over two years now and had barely begun my Navy career, yet my future lay in the hands of a man who was nearing the end of his.

I showed up early and was met by the Admiral's Flag Lieutenant. I had expected a one-on-one meeting with Admiral Bucchi, so I was surprised to find around a dozen senior officers were joining us in the Admiral's office. I thought, "He's a two-star Admiral, why does he need so many Captains and Commanders with him to address my concerns?"

I tried to tell my story, but whenever I spoke up, the other officers in the room would chew me out. I was intimidated into silence and prevented from fully telling my story. Admiral Bucchi asked a few good questions but never let me answer them. He tried to justify his position, telling me a similar version of the line that I had been hearing all the way up the chain of command, "I have to support my wing commanders." It was obvious that there was never any intention to hear me out or address the issues I had raised. Admiral Bucchi ended the meeting by telling me, "What happened to you was wrong; it never should have happened, but I'm not putting you back into flight school."

If he could acknowledge it was wrong, why couldn't he take corrective action? Again, he was a two-star Admiral after all, not some deck Seaman. I was crushed and defeated. I had put so much hope into this meeting and that included hoping for a chance to tell my story, but I was denied even that. I lost faith not only in the Navy's leadership that day, but in the Navy as an organization. It was as if a part of me died that day.

I felt pretty dead inside overall as I stood in the offices of the Naval Air Training Command. My despair must have been apparent on my face and in my demeanor as the Flag Lieutenant tried unsuccessfully to lift my spirits and then cautioned me, "Don't do anything stupid." I don't even remember walking out of the office, collecting my things from the Bachelor Officers Quarters, or getting in my car and leaving for the trip back to Meridian. What I do remember is driving over a bridge and just staring at the water thinking, "What if I just turned the wheel to the right and ended it all."

I developed sort of a death wish on that long ride "home." Was it even "home" anymore? There was nothing appealing about living in Meridian other than the fact the I was flying jets and now I wasn't even a part of that community, knocked completely off the pyramid. I committed to volunteer for whatever dangerous assignment I could and really felt like I had nothing to live for.

Several times during that long ride home, I looked at a ditch or a stand of trees and thought about just driving into them, but I couldn't do it. I'd lost the career I had dreamed of since I was a boy, and I'd lost membership in an exclusive club that I loved. I'd lost faith in, and reverence for, the organization I had always admired and whose stated values I'd tried to emulate. I'd lost my sense of who I was. Who knew that my commitment to the Navy's core values would cost me so much! I thought of ending it all, but I couldn't give that satisfaction to those who had wronged me. I was too tough for that and I would not take the easy way out. I was going to fight back!

Immediately upon my return to Meridian, I began researching charges against Admiral Bucchi under Article 138 of the Uniform Code of Military Justice, known as a 'Complaint of Wrongs.' I dove into the regulations violated by those that had booted me from the flight program and wanted to point out the inconsistencies in their application, especially when Admiral Bucchi refused to enforce the very same regulations he had put in place. The Navy was supposed to be an organization governed by rules and not the whims of those in power. Again, my eyes were opened wider as to how the Navy actually operated.

My interest in the law developed during this period. I saw how the weak could fight back against the strong through research and a well-thought-out argument. Having seen how Navy leadership was handling my case I should have gone to Congress immediately, but again, I thought that the next level of command, the Chief of Naval Education and Training, or even the Secretary of the Navy would set things right, and I wanted to be able to return to Naval Aviation having remained faithful to the organization. I wanted to fight from within the organization so that I would not become a pariah once I was readmitted to the fold.

The problem I kept encountering was that everyone with the power to investigate and overturn the decision to attrite me was dependent on the subordinate I was complaining about for their own job performance. There was no option to ask a disinterested third party to investigate whether what happened to me was fair, just, or even in accordance with Navy Regulations. I kept hearing versions of "Well, I have to support my …". There was never a thought of supporting me since what happened to me didn't affect whether they got promoted or not. Still, I held out hope. This was admittedly naïve, but I desperately wanted to have my faith in the Navy restored as much as my pilot slot.

I was now involved in an appeals process that would take at least a year, if not longer, so I had to figure out what to do next in my Naval career. The major options were Surface Warfare, Intelligence, Supply, or Aviation Support. Of those options, only Surface Warfare (Cruisers, Destroyers, Frigates, etc.) would allow me to remain a 'Line' or combat arms officer. I may have been disillusioned with the Navy, but I still wanted to be a warfighter and not serve in a support role. Besides, if I was restored to my rightful spot in Naval Aviation, it would be a bonus to be qualified in two warfare communities and might even improve my chances of command someday.

I asked to leave Meridian as soon as possible and transfer to Naval Station Newport, Rhode Island for training in Surface Warfare. The staff at Training Wing 1 were eager to see me go, so I received orders to class up just a few weeks later. While still in Meridian, I continued my research and prepared my complaint.

Despite having kept my grievances within the Navy, I had already become an outcast and was made to feel like a leper that everyone tried to avoid contact with. Only two of my friends at Meridian would even talk to me, Nate Dishman and Martin Hill. It was from them that I learned that an instructor from Whiting Field had come to Meridian and complained that I had screwed over an instructor at VT-6, insisting that they should find a way to kick me out.

I have no way of knowing exactly who that was, but Lieutenant Mark Lind, the instructor who tried to get me to skip filling out my formation stage critique back in Primary, did visit Meridian during the time in question and was accompanied by Lieutenant Colonel Mills, my former squadron commander. If you remember, Lieutenant Lind had transferred to the Coast Guard when it looked like he would receive orders to fly helicopters in the Navy, but now he was trying to switch back to the Navy and fly jets. As part of the application process, he was required to complete a jet familiarization flight with an instructor in Meridian.

Shortly after their arrival in Meridian Captain Dunn, USMC, the Wing's Student Control Officer, went searching for me in pool of stashed ensigns and second lieutenants asking, "Who's this fuck Rosenberg?" This happened before I had checked into Meridian and while I was on leave after completing Primary, so I never knew about it. I was never even told about it until after I had been attrited — not until Nate and Martin asked if maybe the two events were related.

Nate and Martin had both heard details of the critique I had filed back in Primary and told me that most students knew about it. This had a chilling effect throughout flight school where students would now simply report that everything was perfect when asked to fill out a critique or report any unsafe conduct.

Nate's wife, Sandra, told me that my personal information, obtained during a Human Factors Board conducted by the squadron after their Performance Review Board, was being widely shared throughout the squadron and that Instructor's wives were cautioning the wives of students to make sure their husbands stayed away from me because "associating with me would surely damage their husband's careers," warning that I was "unstable and might do something crazy!"

I was abandoned by longtime friends like Kevin, a Marine I had gone to college with and known for years, who blew me off and refused to even lend a sympathetic ear. I reached out to my friend Matt, who had been a Surface Warfare Officer (SWO) before transferring to Naval Aviation, wanting advice on serving as a SWO. We spoke for a few minutes the first time I called, but then he stopped answering my calls or returning my messages. One instructor almost made me laugh when he told me, "You just don't have the right stuff," a reference to the Tom Wolfe book by the same name. I laughed unintentionally thinking he was making a joke, especially since I was being kicked out with higher flight grades than many that went on to earn their wings.

I was left crushed by how unfairly my career as a fighter pilot had ended and was now also abandoned by a community that prides itself on taking care of one another. For some it was the fear that if it could happen to Kevin Rosenberg, it could happen to me. For others, my attrition served to boost their egos, to give them the false notion that they were somehow better than me. For most, I think they were just scared and followed the advice of the instructors warning them to stay away from me. Nothing would keep me from fighting back, and I would not be intimidated. I knew I would be back someday and wondered what they would say when I outperformed them in the sky.

With the help of Nate and Martin, I packed up a Ryder truck and left for Newport. I got a late start and only made it to Tennessee that first night, but it felt so good to be out of Meridian and heading North. I'd stop at my mom's house in New York for a few days before making the short drive up to Rhode Island. Not the way I wanted to return home, but after being abandoned by my Navy family, it was nice to be around my actual family — people that cared for and supported me no matter what.

CHAPTER TEN

BRICK & MORTAR

March 2011

I was striking out in my effort to find a permanent home for Gear To Go and wasn't sure how much longer I wanted to live the arduous life of a street vendor. I'd noticed a small shop on Garfield Place east of 7th Avenue but had dismissed it as too far from the main shopping streets with barely any foot traffic. There was no "For Rent" sign posted, but since the security gate had been down for months, it was obviously vacant. Desperate, I figured I'd at least find out how much the rent was so with no contact information available, I threw my business card under the security gate, where it mixed in with the pile of leaves that had collected under the narrow opening.

Weeks went by with no response, so I stopped in at the adjacent drug store, hoping they knew who owned the vacant space. Peter, the white-haired gentleman at the counter, told me that he knew the owner and would pass on my request, but added that he thought the owners were looking to get $2,500 per month. "Wow, that's more than I expected," I said as I looked down at the floor figuring this was once again a lost cause. Nevertheless, he told me he would pass on my info and ask the landlord to contact me.

A few days later, I heard from Peter and it turns out he was the landlord. Peter was a widower who had inherited his interest in the building and now owned the property in partnership with his two brothers in law. We set up a time for me to check out the space. It was small, just over 200 square feet, but it had two large display windows and a finished basement. Far from ideal and somewhat out of sight, I wondered if I was making a mistake but decided to make an offer. At this point, it was really a question of trying to make this small space work or give up on the idea forever.

We discussed my plans for the space, and since I couldn't come up with a large deposit or high rent, I offered a share of the profits in exchange for reduced rent. I'd been denied so many times so I wasn't very optimistic and kept my focus on the street stand. I hadn't told anyone, but I had decided to shut down after the upcoming summer since street vending wasn't going anywhere and it looked like I'd never be able to afford a physical storefront.

Still barely getting by and living at home, I was catching up on email in my childhood bedroom when Peter called. This was it, my final rejection before shutting down Gear To Go Outfitters.

We exchanged pleasantries and then he said, "We discussed it." Here it comes, I thought, "And we're going to give you the shop." I sat at the desk I had last used as a high school student in a stunned silence that lasted until Peter said, "That's a good thing!" Now awake from my trance, I said, "Yes, that's a very good thing, thank you! I was just thinking of what I need to do to get started."

Peter and "The Brothers" as I called them, weren't interested in a profit-sharing arrangement but offered me a plan where the rent would start at $1,500 per month and go up over time to $2,500. I would also have to pay a one-month deposit but could make payments during the first year. I accepted and immediately got to work planning the buildout and figuring out how to make the best use of this tiny space. More stunned than excited I walked out of my room and told my Mom "I got a space!"

April 2011

I had an address now, not just a P.O. Box. The shop at 217 Garfield Place was now Gear To Go Outfitters, New York's only full-service outfitter! The next step was to hire a staff. I already had a few part-time guides helping me with the trips but needed more folks to cover the shop.

Their backgrounds were diverse and ranged from Asa: a playwright and one of my guides; Lou: an Eagle Scout and private school teacher; Evan: a wilderness skills enthusiast and knife-making aficionado; and Avi: who went on to win the first season of 'Survivor New Zealand.' I was committed to paying a living wage and paid my employees $14 and hour while billion-dollar corporations like REI were paying $10.

I interviewed them in the empty store with bare walls and promised them that the job was real. I was looking for folks with significant outdoor experience and unique backgrounds. Of particular importance was whether they had experience leading trips, whether that meant as a professional guide, a college outing club, or even just among their friends. I was looking for experts that could really help folks find the best gear for whatever they were planning.

One of the questions I would ask was why they wanted to work in my shop. The most surprising answer I received was from an applicant that told me that he also wanted to open a gear shop in Brooklyn and figured it would help to get some experience working for me first. He didn't get the job. Happy with the staff I had found and hopeful that I could give them the hours they were looking for, I brought them in for training.

Sitting in a circle of wooden folding chairs, I explained that we would distinguish ourselves from other outdoor stores by providing expert advice and guidance rather than just trying to push customers into buying what we had to get rid of, or what was the most expensive item. We would ask questions, listen to their answers, and then offer a range of options within their budget.

I covered the standard issues and procedures that are involved with running a retail shop such as return policy, opening and closing procedures, when the schedule would come out, and when they would be paid. When I got to what to do if we were robbed, I went into the standard line of "Just give them what they want and don't try to be a hero." There was silence as a few of the guys looked at each other and one said, "We're all pretty big guys. I think we can handle it if he doesn't have a gun." Amused, I said, "Yeah that works but just remember that you don't have to — though I will certainly reward you if you do!"

The rest of the training would have to be done on the job and to do that, I needed to build out the space. I measured the shop and created an architectural style diagram to help me maximize every square foot while also considering what the customer should see both as they walked by and when they entered the shop. An outfitter should make folks long for the outdoors — to see a wall of backpacks and dream of adventures to come. Convinced I had a solid plan, I moved on to the next step.

I borrowed a ladder and used paracord to hang the vinyl logo banner I had been using when I set up at music festivals. I planned for this to be temporary, just until I could afford a proper sign but later realized that no one could really see the sign except for my neighbors across the street so why waste the money? Later my justification became, "If Hurricanes Irene and Sandy didn't take the sign down, why should I?"

Shortly after hanging the sign, my next-door neighbor came by and seemed disturbed. I introduced myself and wondered why the interaction seemed tense. She said that her daughter had told her I was opening up a tattoo parlor next to her house. I laughed, pointed to the banner, and told her that no, it was in fact an outdoor outfitter, a camping store. I guess the logo had caught the girl's imagination and she ran with it to an unexpected place.

My brother, Craig, was a huge help with the buildout, providing knowledge, tools, and labor. Hanging the slatwall was challenging because the walls were uneven, the plaster seeming to warp in some areas, while another wall was solid concrete. Because of the condition of the walls, I figured it would take another two days to finish up, but Craig had to get back to work, so I hired a pair of local homeless guys I knew from being a street vendor. Standing in one spot on 7th Ave for hours each day over one and half years meant that I knew just about everyone in the neighborhood.

The four-by-eight-foot slatwall panels weighed 90 pounds each, so I really just needed someone to hold them in place while I drilled the holes, replaced the drill bit with a screwdriver, and then sank in the screws to secure the panels in place. At the end of that second day, I knew we were almost done but needed the guys to come back the next morning in order to finish hanging the panels before cleaning up all of the leftover sawdust and debris. Since I'd been acquainted with these guys for more than a year and sympathized with their struggle, I paid them for the day's work and then paid them for the next day in advance.

They never showed up on that third morning, and I couldn't find them at their local hangouts, so I chalked it up as a lesson learned. I did see them in the neighborhood a year later as they ducked down a side street to avoid me. With no one to help out, I set about completing the job on my own. Fortunately, we had completed the lower sections the day before, which also included the panels where I needed to cut openings for light switches and electrical outlets. I balanced the 90-pound panels on top of the lower section and held it against the wall with one hand while drilling holes with the other. The challenge was when I had to swap out the bits with just one hand free, careful not to drop anything.

Now with the floor swept free of sawdust and mopped clean, I was ready to start setting up the merchandise. It was a tiny shop, but would do for now, and at least I didn't have to build it every morning and take it apart every night. I had backpacks prominently displayed along one wall so that as you walked by, your eyes would be drawn to a wall of color. Towards the back was the staircase to the basement, which left only about a foot of floorspace between the bannister and the wall. I had to utilize every inch of space, so this would be where I would hang the sleeping bags, which required us to balance over the stairwell in order to grab bags for customers. Wanting to draw in both outdoorsy and city folk, I displayed a range of colorful water bottles up front because hey, everyone loves a good water bottle!

We opened our doors on Saturday, April 16th, 2011 and my first customer was a German diplomat who lived in the neighborhood and had passed by earlier that morning. His daughter was taking part in a summer adventure camp and needed a good backpack so I went through the options, fit her for a pack, and had my first indoor sale. Folks came in but it was definitely slow, and I wondered if I'd made a mistake. In any event, I truly enjoyed having a floor to sweep at the end of the day.

I made as much, if not less, than I would have with the street stand that weekend and the week that followed was even slower. On a day where I'd been in the shop for hours and only sold two bandanas, I noticed a father walking by with his young son stop to check out the window display. I had the door open and walked outside to chat with them and was reinvigorated when he looked at his son, pointed at me and said, "This is what you call persistence!" I almost cried. I'd been struggling so hard to make this dream a success and had overcome so many obstacles and challenges. To hear someone else acknowledge that and show respect for what I had achieved was overwhelming — like I had won an award.

Several of the local business owners I had met while street vending offered advice and support. The biggest help came from Ezra of Community Bookstore, and Tony Fanning, a local realtor. Both offered their old A-frame chalkboard signs that they were replacing. With my landlord's permission, I placed one of the signs in front of Palma Chemists on the corner of 7th Ave and Garfield Place, which not only increased business it also led to some confusing encounters when folks would wander into the pharmacy asking about camping gear rentals.

I was still living at home that June, trying to save up money to move back to Brooklyn, when an acquaintance let me know that she would be out of town through the end of August and needed to sublet her apartment which was just around the corner from my shop. I immediately agreed and was thankful to have my own place again even if it was just for two months. The apartment was located on 7th Avenue, just above a psychic's office, so every night as I walked up the stairs and passed below the pink neon sign, it looked like I was searching for clues about what lay ahead. Who knows, maybe I was.

I tried all through August to find a place I could afford, but the neighborhood was getting more popular than ever, and I was getting priced out. With my friend returning to Brooklyn at the end of the month, I was faced with the possibility that I would have to once again move home into my childhood bedroom. I viewed this as a defeat and refused to be defeated, so I made plans to move into the shop basement until I could find an apartment.

I bought a set of truck bed tie down rings, which I anchored into a brick support column and the brick wall of the basement. This allowed me to rig up a hammock at night and still have room to move around during the day. I bought a mini fridge for groceries, brought over a microwave I had in storage, and since the light switch for the basement was upstairs, I used one of the rental camping lanterns for light. The security gate was powered by an electronic motor so I kept it up at night lest I be trapped like a sardine in a tin can should there be a fire.

The first night went well, and I woke up early so that no one would figure I out I was living in the basement. First of all, it was illegal. Second, it violated my lease. Third, it just looked bad, and I didn't want my customers to know how hard I was struggling just to get by. I'd throw a ballcap on and then head to the gym to work out and shower before returning to the store. On my second night of camping out in a camping store, I woke up cold and without a blanket. I worried that I wouldn't sleep much that night until I remembered that I was sleeping in an outfitter and had dozens of rental sleeping bags behind me.

Fortunately, this arrangement only lasted for about six weeks as my realtor friend, Tony Fanning, found me a small apartment I could afford that was just blocks from the shop. The neighbors were noisy and it was on the first floor facing the street, but I was thrilled to finally have an apartment back in Brooklyn.

In addition to those that had become regulars at the street stand, new customers started coming in due in large part to the chalk board sign on the corner and some good press I'd been getting. I paid attention to what they were asking for and if I didn't have it, I'd try to order it for them. As a way to gauge interest, I'd stock a new product if at least three customers came in asking for it. This ranged from little things like frisbees, travel adapters, and kid's backpacks, to shade tents and luggage.

I learned to adapt to what the neighborhood was looking for rather than what I wanted to sell and realized that I had to sell a lot of water bottles in order to sell a single pair of snowshoes or crampons. I was really becoming a part of the neighborhood and enjoyed folks waving on their way home from work or stopping in to tell me about their latest adventure. Since I also lived in the same neighborhood, I'd run into folks at the grocery store or one of the local bars. When they couldn't remember my name, they'd say, "Hey, you're the gear guy!" I've been called worse.

Folks from the neighborhood loved to come by and browse the new products we carried, talk about their latest adventure or ask for tips on where to go hiking. I referred to the shop as an 'Adult Toy Store' until someone politely reminded me that it might be taken the wrong way, so I changed it to 'the OTHER Adult

Toy Store.' There were lots of shops in the city to make you *look* outdoorsy — to make you like you were headed off to get dirty — but we were the ones that could actually help you get dirty!

When one of the local moms came in asking if I could put together a wilderness skills afterschool program, I jumped at the chance. I remember hearing a computer entrepreneur from the 80s being interviewed about how he learned his trade. His advice was, "You never say no to new business!" He said that he would listen to what the client needed and would then go home and figure out how to do it. I'd never taught kids before, but I could figure it out, and I looked forward to passing on the skills I had learned over the years.

I started out with second graders and endeavored to teach them the basics of map and compass skills, shelter building, flora and fauna, wilderness medicine, fishing, primitive fire, and what to do if they got lost. I was eager to make sure they got their money's worth, so after picking them up and marching them over to Prospect Park like the Pied Piper, I wanted to get down to business and start teaching.

The first lesson was mine. I learned that you can't take a bunch of second graders that just got out of school and expect them to sit down and focus on learning. Snacks and play time must be the first priority! I also learned that it is in fact possible to get six fishing lines tangled up in mid-air. I really enjoyed working with the kids and it also furthered my ties with the community as I watched them grow up.

The summer of 2011 marked my first visit to the Outdoor Retailer (OR) trade show in Salt Lake City. OR is more than just a trade show; it's where the outdoor industry comes together to form bonds, plan new partnerships, and share ideas. It's part trade show, part convention, and part reunion, where business stops at around 3 p.m. as booths roll out the kegs. I'd heard about OR since I started my company in '09, but couldn't afford the trip when I was a street vendor. Now with a brick & mortar shop in the most competitive retail market on earth, I knew I had to step up my game and make sure my shop was stocked with the latest and greatest in outdoor gear.

Walking the floor of the Salt Palace convention center, I felt like I was with my people, but it was also pretty intimidating. I was there by myself, shopping for a store that was arguably 225-square feet depending on how you measured it, while other retailers had multiple locations and came to OR with teams of buyers. Everyone seemed to know each other, and it felt a bit like the first day at a new school. I overheard a few buyers discussing how many units of a new product they were ordering, and I knew that I could never sell that much in a decade. Did I really belong here or was I out of my league?

The sheer size of the show was a bit overwhelming, and I never did get to see everything, but I found some new products to carry, including a few that I was the first to bring to market. I also made some great connections and started building a reputation for Gear To Go in the outdoor industry. I left Salt Lake City that year inspired. Inspired to work even harder to grow my business and come back to the show in a few years with my own team of buyers, telling stories about my days of street vending over beers on the show floor.

As the summer ended, I was making a living but barely. The rent for the shop was edging up towards $2,500 and sales were slowing as folks got back to the routines of school and work. I'd always done well selling warm hats and gloves on the street, but now indoors, I wanted to stock up on the warm jackets and fleece I knew customers would soon be looking for. Banks were just starting to lend money again, but now I had another problem: student loans.

Though my federally guaranteed loans had been in a series of deferments and forbearances since I was laid off during the recession, my private loans were with Access Group and they kept "losing" applications for the same programs. I kept applying until they finally told me outright that since it was a private loan they didn't have to work with me on any arrangements regardless of what was going on in my life or with the economy as a whole. Instead of working with me and accepting what I could pay at the time, Access Group threw me into default and obtained a judgment against me, threatening to seize my assets.

With a judgment on my credit report, there was no way I was going to get a loan, and without a loan to grow my business, there was no way I was going to be able to repay my student loans. I reinvested everything I could to keep the business alive and growing, but this caused a problem as sales slowed dramatically in the fall, just as my sales tax bill for the busy summer season was coming due and I couldn't make the payment.

Each day as I walked up Garfield Place to open the shop, I worried that I would see a seizure notice taped to the gate. I wondered who would do it first, Access Group or the State? I knew that the State would simply sell off the company assets until the tax bill was paid, but what would Access Group do? The value of the company was nowhere near the amount I owed in student loan debt so would they try to take over and run the shop? That option didn't make sense, but neither did telling a debtor that was having problems keeping up with the monthly payments that the entire loan amount was now due immediately.

New York State was easy enough to work with, especially since I had reached out to them and not the other way around. I worked out a payment plan, got caught up, and learned to put away money from the summer so that I could pay my tax bill on time. Access Group was another story. It took several years to convince them that I had no assets other than Gear To Go and that it was in their interest to work with me. In the end, we worked out a payment plan which was the same result they would have achieved if they had worked with me in the beginning, but at least I no longer had to worry about the shop being seized.

From the beginning, Gear To Go was almost literally being held together by duct tape and baling wire. I did just about everything myself, from building my own store fixtures, working to drum up press interest, designing advertisements, and ordering new products. It was a struggle just to get by, and I was often delaying some vendor payments to pay those that were either further past due or from whom I needed new products. Rent for the shop was often past due, which meant I couldn't afford to pay myself, so I occasionally fell behind on rent for my apartment as well.

We offered so much more to our customers in terms of knowledge and experience, but I couldn't seem to get the word out. Our existing customers were extremely loyal, waiting weeks, if need be, to buy a product from us rather than the national chains, but the scale at which we were operating wasn't enough to ensure long-term viability. Every day was a struggle, but at least I finally had a shop. I knew that if I kept at it, things would eventually work out, so maybe it was time to pursue other life goals as well.

I met Tiffany on Jdate and we met up for drinks at Shade Bar on West 3rd and Sullivan. I waited for her on the corner and recognized her right away as she walked up. She was a lawyer and had worked for a few big firms, but was now starting an in-house counsel position, which paid less but provided a better quality of life.

As we sat across from each other, separated by candles and wine glasses, I wasn't sure we were a match. I was really attracted to her, but she was almost too much of a lawyer — like she couldn't leave that side of her at the office. As she questioned me about my life, my goals, my philosophies, and ideas, it felt like just that, questioning, like she was interrogating me. New York is a tough city, so I can understand a woman wanting to be careful, but it seemed a bit excessive.

She asked me, "So what do you believe in?" I immediately thought of the epic speech from 'Bull Durham,' — one of my favorites — and briefly thought about reciting it from memory. Instead, I started talking about politics and my philosophical views on life before quickly abandoning my answer, calmly moving the candle out of the way and setting aside her wine glass. Reaching over, I said "This is what I believe in" as I gently pulled her towards me. I'm not sure how long the fireworks lasted but as I pulled away, her eyes were still closed. We moved in together a few weeks later.

It seemed like everything was coming together for me. I was madly in love with Tiffany and was passionate about what I was doing for a living, but after the Christmas season ended, sales plummeted. I just didn't have the access to capital needed to stock up on winter jackets and boots — things people were coming into the shop for. I was stressed about losing the business, putting in long hours, and once I told Tiffany about my student loan debt and the judgment, like many couples, we started to fight over money.

She said that "I didn't fight well," meaning that I quickly escalated things, which looking back was probably true, but I resented that she was focused on my finances and really just needed her to be supportive as I struggled to grow my business. I made some attempts to start over, but it was too late. In April, while we were relaxing in the Long Meadow of Prospect Park, out of the blue, she said "I'm moving out." We'd fought so much that I knew it wasn't even worth trying to save things now, it was over. I threw myself back into trying to make Gear To Go Outfitters a success and hoped that maybe, with time, we might be able to start over.

I've always tried to innovate, to find creative solutions and new ideas. When I realized that most of the people signing up for my trips to the Hudson Highlands, Shawangunks, and Catskill Mountains, didn't really need a guide, but were just looking for a way to get to the wilderness, I decided to look into offering a shuttle service. Sure, for some a guide in the Catskills makes sense, but for most folks with even a few hikes under their belt, it's simply an unnecessary expense. These hikes can be strenuous, with steep climbs over rock filled trails carved out by the glaciers, but they are well-marked, well maintained, and if you need help, it's not far away.

What if I could just give folks what they wanted, a ride up to the mountains in the morning and guaranteed pickup that night. I looked into the costs and regulations that would govern such an operation and decided to give it a go. I called it 'Trail Taxi,' and offered a specific route each day where customers would have a range of trailheads to choose from and could even choose to be dropped off at one and picked up at another.

Customers really seemed to love the idea, and I began to offer more routes and hire a few drivers as interest in the new service continued to grow. Even the Outdoor Industry Association (OIA) took note of what we were offering and acknowledged Gear To Go with an award for innovation. Now we could sell or rent you the gear you needed for your trip, help you plan that trip, and even take care of transportation to and from the trailhead. This brought the notion of a full-service outfitter to the next level.

The only problem was New York State. We were using a 15-passenger van to shuttle would-be hikers out of the city and into the mountains, the same 15 passenger van we used for our guided hikes, but if were dropping folks off and not guiding them, the State categorized us as a bus company. This meant that every driver had to obtain a commercial driver's license, the van itself had to undergo frequent inspections by hard-to-find state inspectors, and there was a whole new level of paperwork required.

It didn't make sense that we could take the same customer from the same pickup spot in Manhattan and drive them up to the same trailhead without any of this burden as long as we hiked with them, but if we dropped them off, all of a sudden we were in regulatory hell. Being the only one in charge of essentially three businesses already — a Retail Shop, Rental Outfitter, and Guide Service — it was simply too much to manage, and I had to shut it down. I thought it might do well as a standalone business but owning a bus company was never one of my dreams.

Despite all of the struggles and challenges, I really loved owning my little shop. It may have been a tiny kingdom, but it was my kingdom, my vision. When I found a great new product that I wanted to bring in, I didn't need to go through a lengthy approval process, I just placed the order. If I wanted to teach a new class or offer a new hike I just did it. And when I decided that I wanted to move out of the minor league of guiding day hikes in the Catskills and start offering international adventure travel vacations, beginning with a trip to Iceland, I just did it.

In July 2013, I traveled to Reykjavik with one of my guides to scout out the Laugavegur trek. Though definitely on the map as a tourist destination ever since the eruption of Eyjafjallajökull in 2010 disrupted air travel to and from Europe, few Americans had actually been to Iceland and it was a unique offering at the time.

We camped out on the scouting trip, but I made sure to check out the huts along the way. It was obvious that the huts were the way to go when we brought clients the next year. My philosophy on accommodations is to always go with the most comfortable option that allows you to get to where you want to go. If that's a tent, great. If it's a three-sided lean-to, great. And if it's a geothermally heated hut with mattresses, gas stoves, and pay-per-use hot showers, even better!

Walking amongst this spectacular scenery that changed dramatically each day, I knew this was why I started my company in the first place. I wanted to help folks experience a true adventure in the outdoors and provide them with the gear, knowledge, and guidance to make sure they ventured out safely. It was adventures like Iceland that spurred me to open my shop, and I couldn't wait to share this special place with my clients.

When I started Gear To Go, with my new entrepreneur optimism I figured I'd only need to be the guy running the shop for the first year or two and then I could focus on guiding. Of course, reality wasn't even close to my vision, best laid plans and all, and I soon found myself in the shop almost every day of the week so that not only was I not guiding, I was barely getting out on the trail myself. Scouting this trip in Iceland really brought me back to why I had become a guide in the first place. It really made me question where I was, where I wanted to be, and what I needed to do to get there.

I brought a group of 11 clients to Iceland the following year and shared the adventures of the Laugavegur Trek with them. Gear To Go was now officially an international adventure company and the only question was: where our next adventure would be? Looking at the map, the answer for me was obvious: Greenland!

I knew I didn't want to live out my years as a shopkeeper in Brooklyn. An outdoorsman may find himself living in a city like New York, brought there by circumstances encountered on the road of life, but a true outdoorsman soon begins to plot his escape from the city for life in the mountains. The mountains are just in your soul and in my case, also in my surname, Rosenberg, which translates as 'Mountain of Roses.'

I began to plot my exit strategy and figured I needed to either sell or grow. I was open to either and didn't have a preference one way or the other, but I needed a change and I needed to get out of New York. Growing meant capital, and after Access Group put my private student loan debt into default, bank loans were not an option. This left an angel investor as the only option, but without a background in finance, I didn't know how to find one to pitch my idea. I tried crowdfunding at one point, but the results were disappointing, as marketing has always been a weak point for me.

I reached out to other guide services and outfitters in the area, as well as the few outdoor brands that were based in New York. There was definite interest, but most either wanted to buy pieces of the business rather than the company as a whole, or their timeframe for a new store was two or three years out.

I was interviewed regularly for local newspapers and magazines and had even been on TV a few times — first on ABC's Nightline and later the Science Channel. Recognized as the local outdoor expert in New York, I figured this would translate into increased brand value, but I soon realized that my personal brand was what had increased in value, so without me coming along as part of the sale, there was little interest in a tiny outdoor shop on a side street in Brooklyn. I didn't want to work for someone else so maybe it was time to shut down, to cut my losses, and get out of the city.

With my brother and mom in NYC (1970s)

First jet solo flight (July 1998)

With Steve Bury after his winging ceremony (August 1998)

Shooting straight up in a T-2C Buckeye (1998)

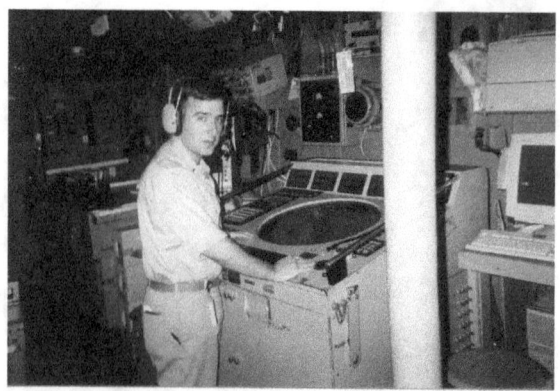
Hunting submarines on USS Hawes (FFG-53) (1999)

Boarding Officer - Persian Gulf (Summer 2000)

Aden, Yemen (August 2000)

NS Norfolk, VA (December 2000)

Global War on Terror deployment (Winter 2003)

Street vending (January 2011)

Opening day of the first brick & mortar shop (April 16, 2011)

First International Adventure - Iceland (July 2014)

Patterson's Pellet in the Shawangunks, NY (October 2014)

Interior of the first shop on Garfield Place in Brooklyn (Winter 2014)

View from the summit of Mount Killington, VT (May 2015)

Garfield Place wall of the new shop (2016)

New shop (Spring 2016)

On the rim of Markarfljot Canyon, Iceland (July 2016)

In front of the larger shop (Fall 2016)

Happy to show off the new shop (Fall 2016)

Cover of 'Outdoor Retailer' Magazine (Winter 2017)

Kaaterskill Falls, Catskill Mountains, NY
(February 2019)

Appalachian Trail (2019)

CHAPTER ELEVEN

HAZE GREY AND UNDERWAY

I checked onboard USS Hawes (FFG-53) as the Anti-Submarine Warfare Officer (ASWO) on July 22, 1999, exactly one year after my first jet solo and the day before the ship was due to get underway to hunt subs in the Bahamas as part of Submarine Force Atlantic's (SUBLANT) first dual Submarine Training and Readiness Evaluation (SUBTRE). We would play the Opposing Force (OPFOR), so this meant that just weeks out of ASWO school, and having been onboard for less than 24 hours, I was now in the spotlight, sailing south to hunt, not one, but two fast attack submarines.

Getting underway to perform the mission I was in charge of was a great opportunity to work with my sonar team and identify strengths and weaknesses as I worked to improve our Anti-Submarine Warfare (ASW) capability. One thing I noticed on Hawes was that much of the focus of the overall combat team was centered around the Mark 13 missile launcher, nicknamed "the one-armed bandit."

The Oliver Hazard Perry class Frigates typically carried 4 RGM-84 Harpoon anti-ship missiles and 36 SM-1 surface-to-air missiles. The SM-1 was already outdated by the 1990s and the newer, more air defense-capable ships of the fleet, were employing the SM-2 with greater range, better accuracy, and with vertical launch systems, a quicker response time. Air defense was not our primary mission and we weren't very capable at it to begin with. The SM-1 was sort of a last-ditch effort if we had a missile or aircraft inbound that hadn't been taken out by the rest of the battlegroup. We were an ASW platform and that's what the fleet expected of us. I worked to point this out to those in our Combat Systems and Operations departments and tried to refocus their attention on our primary mission.

Within my own team, I was determined to dramatically increase the level of training. Chances were that we would be headed to the Persian Gulf on our upcoming deployment and the Iranians had been increasing their harassment of both military and civilian shipping in the Straits of Hormuz and the Gulf in general. Though they mostly used small boats in their operations, they did have very capable Russian-built Kilo class diesel submarines and the Iranian Navy had engaged the US Navy with conventional naval forces just over 10 years earlier during 'Operation Praying Mantis.' That battle was an overwhelming defeat for the Iranians, but that didn't mean they hadn't learned from their mistakes and I knew better than to underestimate an adversary.

Since much of the damage inflicted on the Iranians came from US Navy attack aircraft, it would make sense for them to turn to their submarine force for future engagements. I wanted my team to be ready should it come to that. I was not going to let Iranians score a "CNN moment" showing an American warship listing to one side with smoke billowing from its open wounds. We were good, but I wanted us to be the best. I thought of the character 'Joker' from the film *Full Metal Jacket* and said, "I want to be the first kid on my block with a confirmed kill."

The most dangerous job on the ship was that of Boarding Officer, in charge of the Visit, Board, Search, and Seizure (VBSS) teams that would be used to board ships in the Persian Gulf and inspect for violations of the UN Embargo against Iraq. The job had been traditionally assigned to the Ordinance Officer (ORDO), but he had a wife and young son and was looking to get out of it. I remember being present as he discussed the matter with our Department Head and before ORDO could finish his sentence, I jumped in and said, "I'll do it!" "Are you sure?" they asked. "Absolutely, and besides, I'm single and don't have any kids." The job was mine.

For the enlisted sailors on Hawes, VBSS was a volunteer job, and we had a mix of sailors from all departments on both twelve-man teams. I was responsible for both teams, and since there wasn't a lot of guidance or tactics in existence at the time, we were largely tasked with developing our own training program and procedures. We even had to pick our own uniforms with the only guidance being that it should give the impression of law enforcement rather than military force. I was proud to be the point man on the mission that would occupy most of our time in the Gulf and worked to develop a training program that would get our teams ready to perform the mission when called upon.

Since we would be in port for a few months, I looked for training opportunities wherever I could find them. We were tied up alongside our sister ship USS Simpson (FFG-56), the only other Frigate in our squadron (Destroyer Squadron 22), and since our equipment was being overhauled, I had made arrangements with the ASWO on the Simpson to use their Sonar equipment to train on and run computer-generated Onboard Training (OBT) scenarios. Excited about the ability to keep training even though our gear was out of commission, I proudly announced my new plan at division quarters in the ship's torpedo magazine.

My Chief Petty Officer, "Sonar Bob," looked shocked, then hurt, then angry, and I couldn't understand why. I hadn't mentioned this to him but figured he would be pleasantly surprised at this opportunity, since he was as motivated as I was to improve the ship's ASW capabilities. Instead, he objected, and did so in front of the men; which was not the way these things were usually handled and bordered on insubordination. I firmly instructed the Chief that this is what we will be doing while our equipment is being worked on. Sonar Bob walked out of the magazine.

I was stunned and angry but finished quarters and then tracked down the Chief to find out what had set him off. This wasn't characteristic of him and we had become a great team, so I felt it was more that I was missing something than that he just decided he didn't have to listen to me. Sitting across from each other over mugs of coffee, Sonar Bob explained that sailors did not train on other sailor's ships; it was a pride thing.

Sonar Techs don't only operate their equipment — they also repair and maintain it — so announcing to another ship that we needed to borrow their Sonar Control Room ("Sonar") and Combat Information Center (CIC), was an embarrassment. To me it didn't matter and I just wanted to get the job done, but I recognized that this might be due to my origins in aviation, where we flew whichever aircraft was up and ready.

I recognized that this was my error — that it was my mistake in not discussing it with my senior enlisted man who was there to advise me. Sure, I was in command and could have ordered the training to take place regardless of how the Chief felt about it, but it wasn't urgent. Balanced against the need to keep up unit pride/esprit de corps, it would have been a compound error to do so. There would be other training opportunities.

One opportunity that did come up was the Fleet ASW Course at Naval Station Mayport in Jacksonville, Florida. We were able to get slots for Sonar Bob and myself, as well as the Hawes' primary Antisubmarine Tactical Air Controller (ASTAC), who was my liaison with any supporting aircraft helping out with the hunt. Hurricane Floyd had been in the news in recent days, so it was no surprise that the base was beginning to board up as we arrived for the course.

Unsure of the storm's path, or if we'd be able to finish the course before having to evacuate, we sped up the pace and lengthened the days in an attempt to cover the required material. As predictions about Floyd's path reached a consensus, it became obvious that the Jacksonville area would be hit but also that the storm would then continue up the East Coast, rather than making the originally predicted right turn out to sea. It's actually safer, though by no means comfortable, for a ship to be at sea avoiding a hurricane rather than tied up in port crashing into the dock and breaking its mooring lines, so the Navy ordered all ships in the forecast area to prepare for sea.

The order came down as we arrived for the final day of class. I called the ship and told them that it was my intention to fly back to Norfolk as soon as possible so that we wouldn't miss the sortie. To be honest, I was excited about the opportunity to sail into stormy seas. I'd come to enjoy the rocking and rolling that a Frigate — roughly 450 feet long but only about 45 feet wide — experiences in rough weather. I looked at it as a new adventure. Sonar Bob and the ASTAC were not as enthused, so when we arrived at the airport amidst a crowd of worried travelers looking to flee the storm's path, they were happy to be bumped as I pleaded our case with the gate agent that we were in the Navy and had to get back to our ship in Norfolk.

As we prepared to get underway from Naval Station Norfolk early on the morning of September 15, 1999, I marveled at the sight of every single ship at the largest Naval base in the world heading out to sea. It seemed like we were rushing off to fight World War III as we passed the Chesapeake Bay Bridge-Tunnel and made our way to our assigned location.

Soon, our 4,000-ton warship would be rocked by 40-foot seas on an ocean of nothing but white foam as we struggled to keep the bow pointed towards the waves and hoped to avoid capsizing. When your ship is rolling up to 45 degrees, it's a bit hard to get any work done, so I headed up to the bridge to take in the view. As I climbed the ladder, I noticed the Executive Officer (XO), Lieutenant Commander Tim Mahan, ducking a wave on the bridge wing with one of the lookouts. A surfer, the XO wore a huge smile; he was dreaming of riding these waves not avoiding them. The Captain on the other hand looked tense. It was his ship after all, and he was responsible for getting it back in one piece.

I held on as we crested another wave and felt nearly weightless as we dropped down into the trough, water overtaking the warship and plunging us under the waves like a submarine. "That was awesome," I whispered to the sailor standing next to me.

The roller coaster continued and as we came to the top of another building-sized wave, I had that same feeling you get when you hear the "clink, clink, clink..." of the chain slowing down right before the epic drop.

"Yeehaa" I yelled out, enjoying the ride as we plunged beneath the waves once again.

My grin was short lived as Commander Dixon turned in his chair, locked his gaze upon me and shouted, "Mr. Rosenberg, this is not funny!" Inside my head, I was thinking: "What are you talking about, we're underwater and riding the ultimate roller coaster?" but what I said was, "Yes Sir!" I know when I've worn out my welcome, so I decided it was a good time to leave the bridge.

I stopped by my stateroom to grab something out of my locker when I noticed Dave, one of my fellow Junior Officers (JOs), in the bottom rack by my feet. He opened up his blue curtains, and I saw that he was well on his way to growing a beard. Dave was basically a prisoner to his stomach at this point, trapped in his rack except for brief adventures to the nearby head. I grabbed him some saltines and water so that at least he'd have something in his stomach since there was no sign things would let up anytime soon. We'd been in the storm for a few days now, and the movement was constant. What hell he must be going through! I hoped he'd be able to get a larger ship for his next assignment.

On watch, we would keep an eye on the clinometer, which indicated how much of a roll we were taking. Rolls of over 40 degrees had become routine, and we were often hitting 45 degrees, but we were told that the mast was supposed to fall off at 47.5 degrees to keep us from capsizing. The bridge watch team was all in their teens and twenties, so we practically took bets with youthful enthusiasm as we rolled closer to that magic number, collectively shouting "Oh, oh, ahh!" with excitement and then disappointment as we came close but never reached the magic number.

Regular daily activities become challenges when the floor below you drops away and you're left to walk on the walls instead. Meals in the wardroom, usually something to look forward to, grew more "interesting". Arriving for dinner, I found a vacant seat at the opposite end of the Captain's table and asked the Skipper for permission to join him. Behind Commander Dixon was the single porthole in the Wardroom, and through its small window I watched the view suddenly change from sea, to sky, and quickly back to sea again.

The china had been replaced with paper plates, but the cooks seemed to have had a sense of humor that night as they were serving what they called "Beef-Corn Pie," a misguided ode to Shephard's Pie that consisted of not even beef, but ground turkey, corn, peas, and mashed potatoes. It looked like vomit on a plate and didn't taste much better.

Still, I was hungry and my only other option was a cheese sandwich or a Lipton Cup-o-soup I had stored in my locker. As I waited to be served, I heard "click, click, click" as the silverware drawers behind me popped open and sprung towards me. Envisioning a cartoon-style onslaught of knives and forks, I ducked forward and covered the back of my head with my hands. I paused for a second, preparing for impact and then looked up to be met with laughter, an outcome I much preferred over a barrage of sharp objects which had thankfully remained inside the open drawers.

Soon, the storm moved on, the waves calmed, and seasick sailors emerged from their racks to clean up and rejoin the crew. The adventure was over and the '*Groundhog Day*' routine of life at sea reemerged. Back to Norfolk and paperwork. We'd be in port for the better part of the next 30 days before heading back out with the other five ships of our squadron to start working on fighting and operating as a group, rather than as individual ships.

Departing on October 14th for Destroyer Squadron 22's Group Sail, we sailed down to the Caribbean to begin training for our deployment the next summer. The highlight for me was taking part in what is known as 'PCO Ops,' where soon-to-be sub-commanders are put through their graduation exercise, taking turns in command of a fast-attack submarine during simulated wargames. Having built up a reputation for skill and aggressiveness, I was often put in charge of the squadron's ASW team, giving orders to not only my ship but also to four destroyers and our sister Frigate, as well as aircraft that were operating in support.

Once contact is acquired, there's a tendency for all of the ships to swarm towards the target like kids going after a soccer ball. This not only makes for a confusing situation, it also puts a ton of noise into the water that can create a sound veil of sorts, giving the submarine a chance to escape and disappear into the deep. As such, my biggest challenge wasn't finding the submarine; it was keeping the rest of our team from letting her get away.

I recognized that aggressive Sub Captains had a weakness. They wanted their kills to be against the latest, greatest, most high-tech warships on the planet, the Arleigh Burke Destroyers. I didn't think they'd spend much time searching for a Frigate, so I worked to mask our sound with nearby merchant ships while our towed array sonar was deployed well below the noise we were making. With the bright shiny new destroyers creating a tempting target, I analyzed bottom contour charts and though, "What would I do if I wanted to plot a stealthy attack?"

Far away from the destroyers and with our sensors in prime position, we lay in wait. Patience was key, and since we had helo's embarked, I had them drop sonobuoys — active and passive listening devices — alongside nearby merchant ships to make sure there wasn't a submarine hiding underneath. We soon had passive contact and used the sonobuoys to triangulate the sub's position. Sure enough, they seemed ignorant of our presence and were headed straight towards the higher value targets. As we vectored in our helo for a weapon drop — an exercise torpedo without a warhead — I hoped it was a lesson learned for the new Sub Skippers, a warning to not get cocky and ignore the low-tech warship — with a highly skilled crew — as they listened to the high-frequency pings of the torpedo's sonar closing in for the kill. Simulated, of course!

My efforts to refocus the warfighting efforts of the crew to ASW paid off during this exercise. We'd lost contact on one the subs we were tracking, and I was racking my brain trying to determine where best to search, when a sailor manning the console for the ship's fire control radar noticed a tiny blip regularly appearing on his radar and moving very slowly. Intrigued, I maneuvered the ship to give our sensors a better look and had the ASTAC vector in our helo to drop some sonobuoys. Sure enough, it was our missing sub! This observant sailor had picked up the radar hits off of the sub's periscope as she was closing in to attack. Another hard kill and proof that my efforts were paying off.

Even though in wartime, an over-the-side torpedo shot from our deck would put us dangerously close to an enemy submarine, we still had to practice it to maintain proficiency. This meant maneuvering close to one of our OPFOR submarines in order to take the shot. Having scored numerous sub kills over the last few days, I'd gotten a bit cocky. Down in the dim blue lights of CIC, I was staring at the contact on my screen while issuing commands to the bridge crew one deck above. I'd been kicking ass with ASW since I arrived onboard three months ago and wanted to show off with what was an easy exercise.

I came in hot — sort of the surface ship equivalent of my "shit hot break". Getting within range I ran through my procedures and then realized I'd lost my situational awareness. This submarine wasn't submerged; it was on the surface and I was charging towards her at 30 knots. I quickly realized that I hadn't considered that she would not be submerged so her course and speed were now critically important. Not wanting to admit my mistake, I tried to quickly work out a solution as we droned ahead at full speed.

The Captain called down to ask what my intentions were while I was still working out a solution, so I replied that I intended to close on the target. As we prepared to launch the weapon, my headphones filled with the voices of sailors asking me for information. My sonar techs fed me target information. My torpedomen got the weapon ready for launch. The bridge crew asked where to steer. Meanwhile, I was also coordinating the launch with the Battle Group watch team, our ship's Tactical Action Officer, and the staff at the weapons range who would be recording data from the weapon once launched. In the middle of this chaos, a sailor approached me from behind to ask a question. I didn't have the mental bandwidth to talk to another person, so without even looking, I put out my hand to signal: "Stop talking!"

Of course, it wasn't a sailor, it was the Captain. I was the newest officer on the ship and I had just "stiff armed" the commanding officer! Appropriately infuriated, he yelled so loud the submarine crew probably heard him as he jumped up and down and pounded on my console before storming out. I felt like Maverick in 'Top Gun' after getting chewed out for buzzing the tower with Goose telling me, "Nice move Mav, real slick!" There was silence in CIC and I wasn't sure if I was even still the ASWO.

I was still trying to process what just happened when the bridge watch team called down and asked what I wanted them to do. I responded with, "Well, I want to go kill the submarine but I'm not sure what the Captain wants to do!" Of course the Captain was on the bridge now, so he jumped on the circuit and warned me that I if I fucked up one more time I was fired! I calmly asked the Captain, "Am I still in charge of this operation and do I have your permission to complete the exercise?" I received a gruff "Affirmative" as we finally got into position and launched the torpedo right over the side like a scene out of a World War II movie.

The exercise was over, but I still had another hour or two on watch as I tried to hide in my corner of CIC, laughing a bit at myself but also wondering how it all went south so fast. With my watch over, I left CIC and as soon as I stepped out into the passageway, a sailor gave me the 'stiff arm' with his palm adorned with a smiley face. "Ha," I thought, "That was clever, I wonder how long he was waiting there for me." As I made my way back towards officer's country, it was obvious that the entire ship was now in on it as I was greeted by a never-ending stream of 'stiff armed' smiley faces. Gotta hand it to sailors to find the humor in anything!

I found the Captain and profusely apologized, explaining that of course I didn't realize it was him and would never disrespect him like that. He'd had time to cool down and aware of how I had at least provided comic relief for the entire crew and improved unit morale, accepted my apology, and even laughed about the incident. I'm not sure, but I seem to remember that he also drew a smiley face on his palm.

Despite what became known as the "talk to the hand" incident, things were going well on the Hawes. The command was beginning to take note of my performance, which, in the Navy — like many organizations — means you just get more jobs. In addition to serving as the ASWO and Boarding Officer, I was soon designated as the Mine Warfare Officer, Wardroom Mess Treasurer, and when the XO realized I could write, Public Affairs Officer. This was of course in addition to standing watch as Conning Officer and later Junior Officer of the Deck, as I worked towards qualifying as Officer of the Deck and earning my Surface Warfare Officer pin.

Though only onboard the Hawes for four months, I had already made my mark and demonstrated what I was capable of when not accidentally insulting the Captain. In an early fitness report, written in November 1999 as Commander Charles Dixon was leaving for his next assignment and Commander Jeffrey Scott Jones was taking over command, Dixon noted:

> "LTJG Rosenberg is an outstanding junior officer who quickly demonstrated superior performance. His level of enthusiasm, professional skill, initiative and pride have already been noticed by seniors and peers. LTJG Rosenberg's abilities are well ahead of his level of training and he is constantly looking for new challenges.
> -Exceptional knowledge of ASW. In his first week on board, LTJG Rosenberg proved to be an outstanding ASWE during SUBLANT's first dual SUB TRE holding passive contact on both 688 Class Submarines. Qualified OOD inport the first week after returning from U/W period. Immediately recognized for his excellent shiphandling ability.
> -Always goes the extra mile in assigned tasks and ensures they are accomplished well ahead of schedule. Flawless execution of ASW Battle Plan during 3-99 Submarine PCO-OPS. HAWES had numerous hard kills during hot war scenarios. Assistance to CO was commendable.
> -LTJG Rosenberg demonstrates extreme commitment to the Navy's Core Values in everyday leadership practices. His appearance sets an example for others to follow.
> -Dramatically increased the level of training within his division and has developed his men into an outstanding ASW Team. He develops his subordinates as leaders and is always looking out for their welfare. Potential for increased responsibility and professional growth is noteworthy despite a very short time on board."

I enjoyed serving under Commander Dixon and viewed him as a solid leader who knew how to delegate and develop his team. I was rethinking my plans to get out of the Navy if I didn't win my appeal, but a lot of that would depend on the next CO, Commander Jones. The Executive Officer, Lieutenant Commander Tim Mahan, would remain onboard until shortly before we left for deployment in June of 2000. If I decided to stay in the Navy, it was going to be because of Tim Mahan. I liked his style of leadership, laid back but making sure the job was done. He focused on developing his junior officers (JOs) and served as a mentor to us all.

Having spent two years in flight school and just now beginning my career as a Surface Warfare Officer, I was behind my colleagues in terms of checking the boxes for advancement. The XO recognized this and after observing me for a few months, saw what I was capable of and talked to me about my intentions, letting me know that he planned to recommend that I skip the second division officer tour that is the normal career path. I'd head straight to department head school after completing my tour on the Hawes — the Navy equivalent of skipping a grade in high school. He even spoke about setting me up to command a Patrol Craft or a Minesweeper early on. It felt good to be welcomed into the SWO community and not made to feel like an outsider as I was in the Strike training. I wasn't convinced yet, but I was coming around.

Of course, not everything was rosy with the XO. There was the time my sailors and I forgot to send off a required message. It was a minor mistake, but it made the command look bad, so I was called into the XO's office along with my Department Head and my Chief, but at first I didn't know why we were there.

The screaming began immediately, but I still didn't know what it was about until he referenced the message. As the revelation that we had forgotten about it washed over me, I thought, "Well, at least I didn't 'stiff arm' anyone this time!" In the middle of his tirade, the XO walked out of his own stateroom, leaving the three of us standing there silently at attention.

Confused, I leaned over to my Chief and whispered, "Is he coming back, or can we leave?" "No sir, he'll be back," was Chief's anxious response. And he did return to spew more fire at us. I acknowledged that the fault was mine and promised to never let it happen again.

I was fired up at getting chewed out for such a minor thing, so with the fire still burning, I assembled my sailors in the torpedo magazine and spewed fire at them just as the XO had at me. They didn't speak but their faces said it all. "Why are you yelling at us? We just kicked ass hunting the most sophisticated submarines in the world and then forgot to send a message that no one reads anyway!"

I dismissed them and then realized that the big mistake I had made was not forgetting about the message, but yelling at my sailors for no worthy reason. I wanted to apologize but couldn't because that would show indecisiveness. After that incident I vowed that I would be a heat shield, taking heat from above but never passing it on to those below. I'd never respected officers who were "yellers" while in ROTC, and I wasn't going to become one now. I just needed to find a bunch of aluminum foil.

Commander Jeffrey Scott Jones joined us in Miami and rode back with us as he and Commander Dixon reviewed turnover items and prepared for their change of command ceremony. My first impression of Commander Jones was disappointing; he didn't seem anything like the skilled warrior I was hoping for. He seemed goofy and reminded me of the cartoon character 'Mr. Magoo' or for a more recent reference, President George W. Bush.

He seemed to sort of wander through life avoiding a series of potentially catastrophic accidents through the wisdom of others or just plain luck, which he'd obviously had in abundance to get this far in his career. I hoped I was wrong, but when speaking with him, I often felt like I was explaining things to a child. This might be a very long tour, but at least I could get out in just over a year if I wanted to and thankfully, Lieutenant Commander Mahan was still onboard as XO, so at least we had some stable leadership for a while.

The realities of the Surface Warfare Community were coming to light. I'd been fortunate to have briefly served under a commanding officer I admired and respected and an Executive Officer whom I saw as a mentor. I had been leaning towards staying in the Navy even if my appeal was unsuccessful, but now I was quickly rethinking that decision.

I had come in as a career man, a "Lifer," and initially loved everything about the Navy, but being booted out of flight school for holding true to the Navy's core values had made me question my career plans. This was a huge 180 for me since all I had ever wanted to do was serve in the Navy. I hoped I'd find inspiration somewhere, but as I looked up at the chain of command on Hawes, I found quite the opposite.

The new XO, Lieutenant Commander Kevin Hill, met with each of us JOs and asked us about our career plans. Did we intend to stay in the Navy or where we set on getting out? I told him that I was a "fence sitter," that I wasn't sure. I was still angry about what happened to me in aviation, but Commander Dixon and Lieutenant Commander Mahan had started to convince me that a career as a SWO might be pretty rewarding. I was giving Lieutenant Commander Hill the opportunity to convince me why I should stay in the Navy, but I think he took my statement as a threat to his performance evaluation. He already saw me as negative mark on his record and wrote me off, rather than try to show me why I should stay in.

My faith in the new leadership on the HAWES continued to evaporate as time went by. At a battle group meeting we learned that we would be joining the Fifth Fleet in the Persian Gulf after a series of port visits in the Mediterranean. During a break, I was standing in the hallway outside the auditorium with a few of our department heads when Commander Jones approached and told me that my reputation for hunting submarines had spread; the COs of the two submarines in our battle group wanted to come onboard and learn more about how we conducted ASW.

"Roger that sir, I'll just run them through an OBT Scenario."

He replied, "Hey Kevin, why don't you run them through an OBT Scenario?"

"Roger that," I said as he walked away.

Turning to the nearby department heads, I waved my hand and said, "These are not the droids you're looking for."

Our reputation as aggressive warriors took a hit once Jones took over. We were back out at sea in March 2000, operating off the coast of North Carolina and Virginia in an area known as VACAPES for COMPTUEX (Composite Training Unit Exercise). This was the first time our Destroyer Squadron would be working with our aircraft carrier, USS George Washington (CVN-73), and her cruiser escorts. It was also the first time we would be observed by the Admiral and his battle group staff.

With USS Albany (SSN-753) and USS Providence (SSN-719) serving as the OPFOR attempting to attack the carrier, the fight was on. USS Cole (DDG-67) gained contact on one of the subs and was in charge of prosecuting that contact. We were pretty far away, so rather than charge in full speed and make the situation worse, I was keeping my distance, scanning the area so that if we picked up contact, we could help to triangulate the enemy's position, while also searching for the second submarine that was still out there.

Commander Jones came down into CIC and walked up to my console, a large box with a round screen displaying tactical information, such as the position of ships and aircraft as well as where contact on the sub was last gained. It was a rather large device that you stood at and was known as "the washing machine."

I gave the CO an update on the tactical situation, informed him of my plan, and explained why I thought it was the best course of action. Looking at the screen, he noticed that our helicopter was flying nearby and this drew his curiosity. He ordered me to have the helo lay a line of sonobuoys between us and the last known position of the submarine, so that we would pick her up if she made a beeline for us. At the time, we were about 60 nautical miles or so away from where the sub was last detected.

I explained that, while that would be a reasonable option if we had a P-3 supporting us — loaded with almost 100 buoys — we only had one helo in the air with just over a dozen. Besides, I explained, we were so far away that even if the sub was steaming at us full speed, the geometry would change over time and the sub wouldn't even come near the buoys. He wasn't convinced. Frustrated and aiming to make him understand that I knew what I was doing, I said,

"Roger that Sir, what types of buoys do you want and what settings?"

"Well, what are my options?" he replied.

As I explained the settings for the buoys, I knew he didn't understand how to deploy them and was just going to go with the middle range, which is of course what he did. I listened as the ASTAC gave the instructions to the helo pilots. I heard them point out the futility of the plan, but after being told that it was the Captain's orders, they had no choice but to waste the buoys. I hope at least the dolphins got a kick out of them, because that's probably about the largest underwater object that came anywhere near.

We were soon left out of the fight, stationed away from the action where Jones couldn't get into trouble. Barely maintaining steerage at 3-5 knots, we were relegated to protecting the USS Supply (AOE-6) off the coast of North Carolina. It was frustrating and humiliating. We were getting ready to deploy, which meant we had to be ready for war, but because of our CO's incompetence, we weren't getting the training we needed.

We had no contact and weren't anywhere near where the rest of the battle-group had been tracking the opposing submarines, but the CO insisted that we man a full battle watch as if we were in the fight. After 16 hours of nothing I asked the TAO (Tactical Action Officer), who was in charge of fighting the ship, if we could secure the watch and get some rest. We'd still have sonar techs listening for contact, but there was no reason to be manned up with a full team that would be burned out if we ever actually did gain contact. He agreed and I returned to my rack, looking forward to getting the only sleep I'd had had in well over 24 hours.

Twenty minutes later, I woke up to the ship wide announcement to man ASW battle stations. Assuming we'd gained contact, I rushed back to Combat, only to find out that situation was the same, no contact. The TAO looked apologetic as he told my team and I that the Captain had simply ordered ASW stations manned at all times.

I thought to myself, "I really hope we don't go to war with this Captain!"

The next day, the situation was the same as I came on watch at 0200 and relieved Sonar Bob. We were astern of the SUPPLY, cruising slowly off the coast of North Carolina and probably 70-100 miles from where the action was. I'd grabbed a cup of coffee in the Wardroom before coming on watch but after days of six hours on and six hours off with no action, boredom and sleep deprivation were taking their toll. Sonar had nothing to report, and we had no information that a submarine was anywhere near us. We were, as usual now, out of the fight.

Chief stuck around and we were making small talk as I stared at the screen with sleep-deprived eyes, hoping to just stay awake in the dim blue light of CIC with six hours to go on watch. There was nothing happening that involved us, not on the surface side, not on the air side, and not even any nearby civilian shipping traffic to be aware of. It was the middle of the night and the only thing going on was a team effort to stay awake. How come they don't show moments like this in the recruiting commercials?

About 15 minutes into the watch, while I was still in the process of waking up, Sonar reported broadband contact astern of us, which meant that they were listening to manmade noise, but couldn't yet identify its source. To get a better idea of the location of the noise, I'd have to maneuver the ship so that we could triangulate the target and fix its position. I keyed up the encrypted transmit button and broadcast a report to the Squadron duty officer, but the signal seemed to drop off, and I wasn't sure if it went through.

I ordered a turn to port so that we could better listen for the target and figure out where she was, but the bridge refused to follow my orders. I reminded them that I controlled the ship's maneuvers while hunting submarines and repeated my command. Just then, Sonar got back on the circuit with a report of narrowband contact, identifying the source as one of our Los Angeles Class Attack Submarines. Shit! I repeated my orders to the bridge with more urgency now and asked the TAO to instruct the bridge to follow my commands. I then immediately jumped back on the secure net to update the squadron:

"FLASH, FLASH, FLASH, ALPHA-XRAY THIS IS HAWES."

Clearing the circuit and letting everyone know that I had an urgent transmission. I then reported that we had definite contact with one of the OPFOR subs and gave the approximate position. The encryption sync seemed to drop off, so it seemed like, on top of everything else going wrong just 15 minutes into the watch, we were now also having comms problems. I continued on in case the transmission had gone through, and requested permission to go active with my sonar, followed by a request for weapons release authority to engage the target.

I didn't have time to wait for the response as Sonar jumped back on and reported: "Weapon in the water!" The submarine had fired an exercise torpedo at us. With my undefeated record about to be shredded, I ordered the bridge to execute a torpedo evasion maneuver, but the Conning Officer replied with questions on how to do to that. This was something taught back in the schoolhouse so, though frustrated, I gave him specific instructions, but he wasn't following them.

I ripped off my headset and started towards the door, intending to fly up to the bridge and supervise the maneuver directly. Sonar Bob got in front of me and reminded me that I had to stay in Combat and couldn't leave my station. Frustrated, I walked back to my console and put my headphones back on. I couldn't believe it! I'd been on watch for 15 minutes and was now going to be responsible for the ship being taken out. As anger and frustration washed over me, Sonar came back on the circuit with a message: "April Fools!"

I'm not sure if I felt shock first or relief, but it was definitely a mixture of both. The prank was epic and had taken hours to coordinate, with all of the watchstanders in CIC and on the Bridge in on the joke. I was impressed! Only sailors would have the sense of humor and dedication required to have pulled this off. There was only one problem, most of my transmissions had actually gone through and the now the staff at Destroyer Squadron 22 were urgently asking for an update as they prepared to divert assets our way.

Sonar Bob had slyly been releasing the encryption button but not before parts of my report had made it across the net. Given that it was the middle of the night, I figured the watch officer was another junior officer, so I took a gamble.

Instead of making up an excuse, I just told them, "Sorry, it was apparently an epic April Fool's joke."

"Roger that," came the reply with a chuckle.

CHAPTER TWELVE

"EVER READY, EVER FEARLESS"

We left for deployment on June 21, 2000, but headed first to the Puerto Rico Operating Area, so the battle group could complete several required training exercises that bad weather and rough seas had prevented back in May. The schedule was already intense, but with the focus already on wargames, I figured this was good time to address what I saw as a potential deficiency before we were busy with other tasking in the Med or the Gulf.

With the increasing threat of a small boat swarm attack from the Iranian Republican Guard, we had been outfitted with a 25-millimeter chain gun on our starboard side, just behind the torpedo tubes. The problem was that these weapons had been known to fail and we really hadn't had the opportunity to test ours, so I put together a plan to run it through its paces in a simulated small boat attack exercise.

Eight months into my first division officer tour, I was tapped to "fleet up" to a second division officer tour position, taking over as Ordinance Officer, which meant I would be in charge of the ship's missiles, guns, and small arms. Basically anything that went "boom" would be mine, including the chain gun. The message went out to Naval Personnel Command on July 3rd, informing them of the Captain's decision, which stated:

> "LTJG ROSENBERG WILL ASSUME DUTIES AS ORDO MID-DEPLOY. LTJG ROSENBERG IS FLT ATTRITE AND RAPIDLY BECOMING OUTSTANDING SURFACE DIVO. FLEETING HIM UP TO 2ND TOUR DIVO JOB (ORDO) WILL CATCH HIM UP TO HIS SWO PEERS."

After running my plan up the chain, I brought it to the Captain for approval. "But it might fail," he said to me.

"Yes, sir, that's the point, I want to find out if it will fail."

"But then we'll look bad if we have to CASREP (Casualty Report) it to the fleet," he said.

I replied, "Well sir, we'll look even worse if it fails in combat."

"Sorry, I can't sign off on this," was his response and the last word on the issue.

I saw this as another side effect of the Navy's practice of having officers with an engineering background go on to command warships. Unlike the Brits, who separate Engineering and "Topside" officers, the US Navy allows "Snipes," — as Engineers are called — to bounce back and forth. Responsible for the ship's engines, electrical generators, and auxiliary systems, engineering officers learn to be cautious by necessity, but you don't win battles by being cautious. With many officers spending much of their early careers focused on maintenance and repairs before moving on to command, this culture of cautiousness has spread wildly amongst the officer corps in the years since World War II — a time with no major naval combat action. Officers are now judged not by taking risks and preparing for war, but by playing it safe and creating more paperwork.

The culture of risk avoidance didn't always characterize the Navy. Admiral Chester Nimitz, Commander in Chief of the Pacific during WWII and one of the most revered officers ever to serve in the US Navy, actually ran his ship aground as a young Ensign. In today's Navy, he would be forced out, never given a chance to learn from his mistakes in peacetime, but for the sake of our nation that was, thankfully a different time.

As we neared the coast of Portugal, I was finally given the Officer of the Deck (OOD) board I had been waiting for which, if passed, would authorize me to be in charge of the ship when the Captain was off the bridge. I'd completed the requirements months earlier and had been endorsed by the officers I stood watch with, but the Captain and XO just never seemed to have time for their JOs and often put training and advancement on the backburner.

It was July 2, 2000, and I'd been ready for this since March. I confidently answered all the questions thrown at me; I knew my stuff cold. There was an uncomfortable moment when Commander Jones presented me with a question that didn't make any sense, forcing me to try to interpret what I thought he meant to ask. I wanted to make it clear that I knew what I was doing and that I could be I trusted with the watch, so I corrected him and then offered an answer to the question I thought he intended to ask. There was nervous laughter from the other officers, and "Oh, yeah, that's what I meant," from the Captain as I wondered if by being right, I'd once again shot myself in the foot.

I passed, and in private, the board members joked with me about having to correct the Captain during my OOD board. I stood watch that night and took pride in the fact that I had achieved this milestone faster than any officer on the ship, and in spite of the delays from the CO and XO. I enjoyed the responsibility as well as the opportunity to conduct the watch in accordance with my leadership style.

After two weeks of intense wargames, the crew was ready for liberty as we arrived in Gibraltar, the gateway to the Mediterranean, on July 5th. We could have pulled in on the 4th but were ordered to cruise slowly off the coast for an extra day. We would be pulling into the Royal Navy Base at Gibraltar, so I assumed the battle group staff were concerned that some young sailor would get drunk and start a fight with the Brits over the Revolutionary War. No matter the date, we were more than ready to let off some steam.

I'd grown increasingly frustrated with the incompetency and lack of professionalism in my chain of command but kept those feelings to myself. I knew that you should only complain up the chain — never down — but I also knew that the upper part of that chain wouldn't listen. After dinner with a few of my fellow JOs, we wandered into a bar where a bunch of my Sonar Techs and most of my boarding team members were hanging out.

I bought a round for my guys and thanked them for all the hard work they'd been putting in, grateful that we had a few days in port to relax. I don't know why, but Tony, one of my best sailors, then decided to spill his beer on a local guy, but as the guy turned around, ready to fight, Tony just grinned and put his hands up as if it was an accident. I didn't want Tony to get in trouble and felt bad for the other guy, so I intervened, apologized on Tony's behalf, and bought the man a beer to diffuse the situation.

Soon it was me that needed help. The frustrations of the past few months, of dealing with a Combat Systems Officer that didn't understand Combat Systems, of working for an XO who was an arrogant prick, and of serving under a Captain who never should have been allowed to enlist, let alone command a ship, came to a boil as I traded my frustrations for beer and whiskey. I was stumbling drunk, but fortunately, two sailors from my boarding team came to my aid, practically carrying me through the streets of Gibraltar as if they were helping me off the battlefield.

The rule was that as long as you could walk up the gangway you were sober enough to avoid getting into trouble. I paused as we reached the pier and slowly made my way up the ramp with the encouragement of the sailors nearby. That should have been the end of the night, but as I reached the quarterdeck, I spotted the command photos hanging there. Reason and judgment had long since gone home for the night, and I began to let out a series of expletives while trying to attack the photos of our ship's leaders.

It was admittedly not my finest moment, and if I had not earned the crew's respect, I'm sure the XO would have been called down, and I would have gone before the Captain for punishment. Thankfully, they covered for me, brought me to my stateroom, and put me to bed.

When I awoke with a hangover the next morning, I opened the curtains of my rack just as the Captain opened the door and entered the JO Stateroom. I froze like a deer in the headlights as the events of last night came flashing back, waiting for him to announce my fate. Instead, he handed me a *Playboy* one of the local suppliers had given him — a donation to the porn locker kept in our stateroom. He nodded his head and closed the door, leaving me confused and breathing a sigh of relief in the darkened stateroom. I'd truly dodged a bullet but knew my luck was due to run out.

After a port visit to Valetta, Malta, we soon entered the Dardanelles before passing through the Sea of Marmara and the Bosporus, transiting through Turkish waters on our way to the Black Sea. Having studied Constantinople — known today as Istanbul — in Western Civilization class back in college, I was disappointed that we wouldn't be making a port visit here and I was relegated to standing on deck admiring the Hagia Sophia as we cruised past in a moment of drive-by tourism.

We pulled into Varna, Bulgaria with a giant pirate flag flying from our mast. This was in fact our ship's battle flag, an ode to our namesake, Admiral Richard Ellington Hawes, who commanded a salvage vessel that saved several ships and submarines from destruction in the Philippines as the Japanese attacked on December 10, 1941. His ship's flag was shredded by enemy gunfire, so the crew sewed together a pirate flag out of scraps and proudly flew it from the ship's mast as the battle raged.

We were the only ship in the US — and probably any Navy — authorized to fly the pirate flag, and we took great pleasure in doing so when operating at sea. The problem was that we were now on what was essentially a diplomatic mission, steaming into a port that just 10 years ago was enemy territory, and we're flying a 30 x 50-foot Skull and Crossbones. Not the impression I'm sure Navy leaders were hoping to make.

It felt strange to sail past the Cold War-era, Soviet-made warships that comprised the Bulgarian Navy. It was almost like the final scene of period movie, where the war was over and we were entering as conquering heroes. I had been studying these ships and submarines for years, first as a kid fascinated by military hardware, and then as a Midshipman and Officer preparing for battle. I grew up expecting to fight these ships but now they were on our side, hoping to join NATO and fight not against us, but alongside.

I was excited to be in Eastern Europe, but liberty would have to wait as I had the first watch as OOD in-port, responsible for controlling access to the ship and rendering honors. Not long into the watch, a Bulgarian Naval Officer made his way towards the ship, and I immediately regretted not reviewing the rank insignia of the Bulgarian military the night before. He seemed to be in his 50s and wore a bushy mustache below the oversized Soviet-style officer's cover, but I couldn't figure out his rank and we hadn't received notice that any of their officers would be arriving for a visit.

I turned to the Petty Officer of the Watch in hopes that he had been more diligent than I was, but he just shrugged his shoulders. The officer made his way to the top of the gangway, saluted, and requested permission to come aboard.

With an expression of embarrassment, I asked, "Sir, what is your rank?"

"I am Admiral," he replied.

In fact, he was the head of the Bulgarian Navy. I ordered the Petty Officer to ring the bell six times and announce over the 1MC "ADMIRAL, BULGARIAN NAVY, ARRIVING." Seconds later, the Captain arrived on the quarterdeck, still buckling his belt, before greeting our unexpected guest.

Varna was one of my favorite port visits as it wasn't touristy, had some beautiful architecture, and we were warmly received by the locals. It was just a cool experience to be hanging out in a former Warsaw Pact country. Each city in Bulgaria had its own brewery, and the local beer, Zagorka, became a crew favorite, though we misread the Cyrillic writing on the label at first and mistakenly referred to it as "LaGorilla".

We'd been warned that in Bulgaria "No" literally does mean "Yes," specifically that a sideways head movement meant yes, and that an up-down movement meant no. I tried to keep this in mind as I asked a woman to dance with me and she shook her head from side to side. Thinking I was rejected, I turned to walk away as she said, "That means yes!"

It was at that same bar that I was hitting on a Russian woman who was doing a great job of ignoring me. I asked what she was drinking and thought she said "water," but she sternly corrected me and said "Wodka." Having grown tired of being ignored, I wished her a pleasant evening and was walking away when she grabbed me and said "Come, we dance!" It felt like a Bond film.

I had a fun evening but was tired and knew it would take a while to get back to the ship. I left the bar and hopped into an empty cab waiting nearby. Being from New York, I'd made sure that the meter hadn't been turned on until I entered the cab and as we arrived at the dark entrance to the port, I handed the driver the money listed on the meter plus a tip. He turned and demanded four times the amount listed, which I refused to pay.

He got on his radio and very quickly more drivers appeared as he insisted I pay four times the amount of the fare. I suggested we call the police and have them sort this out but of course he refused. I looked towards the entrance of the port and thought about making a run for it, but it was about a mile from the entrance to the Hawes and the space between was completely dark. The guard at the entrance seemed asleep in his booth, and even if awake, he didn't look like he would be of much help. After yelling back and forth with the driver for another 10 minutes, I realized I had no choice but to turn over the money.

I'd grown up in and around New York City and had never been robbed, so I couldn't believe that the first time I was mugged was by a cab driver in Bulgaria. I was able to communicate with the guard that I needed the police but when they finally showed up 20 minutes later in their broken-down, Soviet-era Lada Cruiser, they offered sympathy but no real assistance.

As I was wrapping up with the police, two of my fellow JOs arrived at the port entrance. Resigned to the fact that the money was gone and this crime would indeed go unpunished, I decided I wasn't going to let it ruin my time in Varna. Walking back to the ship we spotted a forklift approaching. We held out our thumbs hoping this international symbol had breached the iron curtain and to our surprise, the driver stopped and let us climb onboard. Hitchhiking back to the ship on a forklift in Bulgaria was definitely worth the price I had paid for admission.

Soon it was time to actually do some work and complete the mission that had brought us to Bulgaria in the first place, Operation Breeze 2000, where we would be training with the Navies of France, Greece, Turkey, Bulgaria, and Ukraine.

The Bulgarian Koni Class Frigate Smeli (F-11) was the flagship for Operation Breeze so as part of the exercise, all ships of our international task force prepared to file past and render honors. We once again had the Jolly Rogers flying high, but Commander Jones took it to a new level this time. He brought up a scimitar he had obtained during a previous deployment to the Persian Gulf and then had the ship's corpsman bring him an eye patch. In what should have been a dignified ceremony — one aimed at honoring Naval traditions and advancing international relations — our Captain stood perched on the bridge wing sporting an eye patch, waving a scimitar, and yelling like a mad man as the Bulgarian Admiral and his staff officers looked on in stunned confusion. Another 'face palm moment' for the Hawes and her crew.

We pulled back into Varna a few days later for a second port visit. Hawes hosted the final reception of Operation Breeze, which also coincided with my 27th Birthday. It was such a great experience to be able to socialize with the officers of the six nations taking part in the exercise, particularly the Bulgarians and Ukrainians whom ten years earlier we would have been training to fight against. Getting drunk with these guys, laughing, and telling stories — really drove home the point that we're not that different and if we were to fight each other, it would not be because of hate, but because of the failures of our leaders.

Catching up on work the next day, I opened up the torpedo magazine to check on the condition of the weapons stored inside. We were at max capacity, filled with MK-46 and MK-50 Torpedoes, AGM-119 Penguin anti-ship missiles, and AGM-114 Hellfire air-to-ground missiles.

I was staring at one of the torpedoes, contemplating how something just over 9' long could crack a ship open like an egg and kill hundreds in an instant. I'd seen the power of our Fleet's surface-to-air missiles while witnessing USS Donald Cooke (DDG-75) knock targets out of the sky with direct hits at a combined closing speed of almost five times the speed of sound. Earlier in the year, we'd had the opportunity to sink an old, decommissioned cruiser — USS Dale (CG-19) — as a target off the coast of Virginia, the nearby Destroyers' five-inch guns thundering in the background as our 76-millimeter cannon fired 80 rounds a minute, the force of each round such that you could literally feel the shock wave in your chest.

I both wondered at and wondered why we had developed such deadly efficiency, why we had become so skilled at killing quickly and accurately? Intellectually I knew the answer, knew that sometimes war was necessary, and that some men could only be kept from doing harm by the threat of even greater harm, but I wondered why we went to war so often. Our country had gone to war almost every 20 years throughout our history, mostly out of necessity but often out of choice. Even in those instances where it was necessary, was there not a possibility to find a diplomatic solution if the effort was made? We go to war too often, when instead of fighting we should just gather on the back of a ship somewhere and get drunk together as we laugh, and sing, and forget what we were arguing about.

I thought of myself as a pretty hardcore warrior, so this was a major course correction for me — an epiphany, if you will. When I joined the military just weeks after my 18th birthday, I not only wanted to be in combat, I wanted to be the first one charging up the hill and taking it to the enemy, but now I thought there had to be a better way. I recognized that this was a necessary evolution, that you need that 18-year-old kid who's fired up and ready to go to war, but you also need that more seasoned, mature leader to pull him back and only give the order to kill when absolutely necessary. It made sense that with more responsibility and authority would come the wisdom to know when to use force — and how to avoid ever having to.

I thought this revelation would be valuable to me in future commands, but also wondered if maybe it was time to get out, time to focus on more peaceful goals than being an expert at finding and killing enemy submarines — enemies only because both side's leaders said we were. It was a lot for a young Naval Officer to think about.

I'd have time to think as we crossed the Black Sea headed for Poti, Georgia. After first performing a Freedom of Navigation Operation (FONOP) off the coast of Romania — birthplace of my paternal grandmother — where we sailed along the 12 nautical mile limit to demonstrate that we did not recognize the extraterritorial claims of the Romanian government, things slowed down as we prepared for our next set of exercises with the Georgian Navy and Coast Guard.

We arrived off the coast of Poti at the Eastern end of the Black Sea on August 1, 2000. Being sailors, we of course started referring to it as "Port-o-Poti." Our orders were to dock pierside, so we could show the flag and demonstrate American military might to local Georgians. We were there to show our strength, but also to show our support for Georgia as she drifted away from Russian influence and fought a civil war to regain territory seized by what were essentially warlords.

Unfortunately, our Captain ignored our ship's motto "Ever Ready, Ever Fearless," choosing to anchor so far away from the port that, even with binoculars, we couldn't make out much of the city. His excuse was that the charts we had were old and dated back to the 1960s, but we watched large tankers and merchant ships with twice our draft sail in and out of port with ease. Our supply officer now had to scramble to hire boats to shuttle the crew back and forth. I had duty that first day but looked forward to taking the first boat out the next morning.

The seas were getting rough as a storm blew across the Black Sea. Getting into the liberty boat took careful calculation and timing, as the waves would force the Hawes into a trough while the smaller boat rose up on a swell. You had to time it just right to make it safely onboard. Waves continued to crash over the bow of the small boat as we headed towards Poti.

Finally on land, I took off my life jacket to hand back to the boat crew and noticed that the soaking I took from the waves had set off the dye marker. I went to the men's room to clean up, but there was no running water in the sinks. I bought several bottles of water and tried to wash the dye from my shirt, but it was hopeless, so I took the boat back to the ship to clean up and change shirts.

Unfortunately, that wound up being the last boat of the day and as the sea state further deteriorated, liberty was canceled. I hoped the storm would pass in the next day or two so that I could still get ashore, but it didn't look good. The Captain's lack of confidence in his own seamanship had left us bobbing off the coast and denied us the R&R we deserved. All except for a few sailors stranded onshore, including one of my Sonar Techs who had been the rescue swimmer in the boat and was now left with nothing to wear but a wetsuit, mask, and flippers. He was later spotted running around in a toga until arrangements were made to buy him some clothes.

The weather cleared, and we got our stranded shipmates back aboard, but the time for liberty had passed as we prepared to head back out to sea for exercises with the Georgians. They joined up in a mixed flotilla of Soviet-made patrol boats and an odd variety of Coast Guard vessels. Left destitute by their break from the Soviets, Georgia — once the jewel of the Soviet Empire and a popular retreat for Soviet elite — now had to take gas money from our government just to get underway for this exercise.

You could tell they hadn't been to sea in some time. They had difficulty keeping station, and you would occasionally hear what sounded like a small explosion, followed by black smoke, as one of the boats went dead in the water and fell behind. The exercises we ran through were really just basic seamanship, but at least it was a start and it also made for good press. I'd heard that our visit even made the papers in Moscow.

Soon the Georgians turned back, and we were on our own. As we headed west across the Black Sea, bound once again for the Mediterranean and then the Persian Gulf, message traffic brought word of a decision in my appeal to the Secretary of the Navy. Once again, I was denied. Once again they essentially said, "You were wronged, this never should have happened, but we're not putting you back into flight school." Once again, the organization I had longed to be a part of since childhood had let me down.

I read through Admiral Bucchi's final argument and focused on a line that compared the fact that I had been attrited with only one down to a habitual speeder only getting pulled over once by the cops. The fatal flaw with his logic was that the cop was riding with me in the back seat! It didn't matter, I had run out of appeals. Even the option to appeal to Congress seemed pointless now that it had been more than two years since I'd paid the price of honor.

Betrayed once again, I knew it was time to leave. I drafted my letter or resignation and waited for the right time. Since officers serve indefinitely, you had to resign your commission a year in advance to separate from the Navy. Having been denied justice at every level thus far, I had prepared for this moment, but it still felt like yet another crushing blow.

Serving under Commander Dixon and Lieutenant Commander Mahan had lifted me up, and I felt inspired enough that I was leaning towards staying in and pursuing a career as a Surface Warfare Officer, but then came Commander Jones and Lieutenant Commander Hill. I've always believed in leading by example and expected my leaders to do the same. Hill in particular, did not know how to lead, only how to threaten and punish. Leadership is about setting the example and inspiring members of a team to work together toward a common goal, but Hill never understood this.

The example set by these two men was not just uninspiring, it also demonstrated how easy it was for incompetent leaders to move up within a bureaucracy of mass promotion boards. I'd seen many of the officers I most respected leave the Navy, and knew it was now my time to join them. As an organization, the Navy no longer held a place of honor in my mind, it had lost its luster, the rose-colored glasses had fallen overboard.

CHAPTER THIRTEEN

A FAREWELL TO ARMS

After serving a few months under Commander Jones, I'd started thinking about what was next for me. In the culture of the Naval Officer Corps, a graduate degree is the expected next step after your first sea tour. If you stay in, you get a master's degree in International Relations, or Business Administration. If you get out, you are expected to earn a degree that leads to an esteemed profession, so that usually means business school, law school, or medical school. I knew my undergraduate grades in the sciences would keep me from medical school, so that was out. Having grown up in a blue-collar neighborhood where most kid's dads were cops, firefighters, transit, and utility workers, I didn't have any role models with an MBA. It meant 'Banker' to me, and I did not want to be a banker, so that left law school.

Fighting back against a system that wanted me gone was empowering. Researching the regulations violated by the very same officers that wrote and enacted those regulations allowed me to fight back, to not go quietly, to be heard! Though truly hollow, I did achieve victories all along the way, with those deciding my fate admitting that what happened to me was wrong and never should have been permitted.

Their refusal to reinstate me was due to the required loyalty down the chain to their subordinate commanders, upon whose shoulders rested their own performance evaluations. They admitted that an injustice had occurred but didn't possess the moral courage to stand up and do what was right. Quite simply, they were cowards!

The whole process had demonstrated both how broken the system was and how unwilling the Navy was to fix it. If the investigation and review had been conducted by someone outside the chain of command, I would still be flying. Maybe a legal career would enable me to become Secretary of the Navy someday and fix what was broken so that what happened to me would never happen again.

A career in the law seemed to hold the promise of a life spent helping others while also earning a good living in a prestigious profession. To be honest, it also seemed like a big FUCK YOU to the Navy and all of those that had abandoned me. I looked into the application process and when I would need to take the LSAT in order to start classes in August 2001. I'd be deployed until December 2000 so, looking at our schedule of port visits, I began the process of applying for a "Non-standard Test Site" in Bahrain so that I could take the exam that summer. One of the items I brought with me on deployment that June was an LSAT Review CD and I made no secret of the fact that I was thinking about getting out and going to law school the next year.

I'd been ready for the final step in my warfare qualifications since the day I'd earned my OOD Letter, but again, the command seemed to care little about developing their junior officers and preparing them for career milestones. I'd completed every required qualification leading up to my SWO Pin (the ship driver equivalent of a pilot's wings) in record time and drawn praise for my performance. I'd mastered the required skills and knowledge and all of the department heads agreed I was ready for my board. I reviewed regularly and waited, but it kept getting delayed and I wondered if the CO and XO would wait until we were back from deployment in December before giving me a chance to demonstrate my knowledge.

The OOD qualification was one thing since, on a small ship, you need officers to qualify and stand the watch so that the others aren't overburdened, but the SWO Pin was just that — a pin, an ornament you wore on your uniform. I knew I was getting out at this point so it didn't mean anything to me in terms of career advancement, but I had worked hard and I had earned it. All I needed was 30 minutes of the CO and XO's time to demonstrate my knowledge and have them sign off.

As we continued to transit across the Black Sea I looked nervously at the calendar. It was already the second week of August, and I was cutting it close if I intended to start law school next year. Sure, the Navy didn't always require a full year's notice, but it was the standard and I'd been screwed over so many times before so it wouldn't surprise me if they also screwed up my separation date, requiring me to put off law school for another year.

The only thing holding me back was the SWO board. The XO had shown himself to have a combination of thin skin and a mean streak, and I wanted to wait until after I'd received my pin to submit my letter of resignation, but when would that be? It had already been more than a month since my OOD board, and the SWO board usually happened just a week later.

I knew my resignation, at a time when officers were fleeing the Navy in droves, would reflect poorly on the CO and XO and worried that they, the XO in particular, would retaliate by denying me my SWO pin. This wouldn't be the end of the world, but again, I had worked hard to qualify faster than any officer on the ship and I had earned this insignia, or at least earned the right to stand before a board and prove why I deserved it.

With the decision made to leave the Navy, I now had to put my civilian career ahead of a gold-colored piece of plastic that I would never again wear after getting out. I submitted my letter of resignation somewhere in the western portion of the Black Sea, and just days before we arrived in Limassol, Cyprus for a port visit. I wanted to send one last message to Navy leadership and wrote that;

> "I have resigned my commission in the United States Navy because I have not found the Navy to be the professional organization I was looking for. I was attrited from the aviation community for doing the right thing and standing up for what is right. Because I reported an unsafe instructor pilot, I was kicked out of doing the thing I love most, flying strike aircraft. This is something I will never forgive the Navy for. I have appealed this decision and it took more than two years to have my appeal adjudicated. I believe this is a clear example of the inefficiency that plagues the Navy and I'm tired of dealing with it.
>
> After being attrited from aviation, I selected Surface Warfare as my first choice. I was motivated to still be a warrior and serve my country, but again what I found did not come close to my expectations. I expected to find a collection of professional warrior leaders, but what I found amongst my peers was instead a group of timid immature managers. I have found the Navy to be an organization that is not open to change or innovation, does not allow Junior Officers the opportunity to take risks, and is not interested in knowing what is wrong. **The Navy will not let new ideas and new talent get in the way of two hundred years of tradition** and I feel that in the civilian world I will be given more freedom to use my mind to come up with solutions to problems."

As you can imagine It didn't go well after that and I knew it probably wouldn't, but I'd just stopped caring about the egos of small men in high places. I planned to complete the deployment and continue to serve onboard Hawes until June or July, when I hoped to take some time off before classes started in early August. Instead, I faced a meltdown from the CO and XO and was ordered home almost immediately. The same command that just weeks earlier wrote that I was "rapidly becoming outstanding surface divo. Fleeting him up to 2nd tour divo job (ORDO) will catch him up to his SWO peers", now wrote:

> "LTJG ROSENBERG HAS SINCE SUBMITTED A LETTER OF RESIGNATION. BASED UPON PERFORMANCE OF SNM AND WARDROOM COHESION HAWES SUPPORTS THIS RESIGNATION AND HAS DECIDED TO SEND LTJG ROSENBERG TO RSG NORFOLK TO AWAIT SEPARATION. THIS ACTION GAPS THE ORDINANCE OFFICER BILLET."

They were not only sending me home out of spite, they were also hurting themselves and the mission to do so. Hawes would now enter the potentially dangerous waters of the Persian Gulf without an Ordinance Officer and with one less trained Boarding Officer and qualified Officer of the Deck. I was also told that there would be no SWO Board for as the XO put it, "If you don't want to be a member of this community then you don't deserve to wear the symbol of this community!" I argued that I'd earned the symbol of this community and deserved a board, but my appeal once again fell on deaf ears.

The other JOs were pissed about the command sending me home early, not because of warm feelings for me, but because this now meant a ton of extra work for them on top of the near sleepless schedules they already tried to manage. Things turned petty during a small-arms shoot when I was about to practice with the .50 cal machine gun, until the XO approached and said that he didn't want to waste ammo training someone that would not finish the deployment.

The tone for the remainder of my time onboard was set. I'd immediately gone from "Golden Child" to "Redheaded Stepchild." This treatment of course served to reaffirm my decision to submit my letter of resignation and eliminated any remaining doubts I'd held onto. I would have preferred to complete the deployment, not because I loved life on the Hawes but because I'd been working with my sailors for over a year to be ready for action should it come, and I believe in following through on my commitments. The decision was out of my hands and was final. I wasn't going to write my congressman to complain about being sent home by incompetent leaders. Sent home to where I would enjoy a few months of busy work while still getting paid. It was final — I would depart in three weeks, just after we arrived in Bahrain.

It felt great to arrive in Limassol, Cyprus for a port visit, knowing that I no longer had much to worry about. I was still the Wardroom Mess Treasurer, which, among other things, meant that I was responsible for securing a hotel room in each port city that could be used as an "Admin", a place where the officers could go to relax, take a nap, clean up, or just drop a few things while touring the city. I was concerned that the room we were given was too small, so I only paid for the first night while waiting for the other officers to check it out and give their opinion, but once this duty was complete, I was free for the day.

I met up with the sailors of my division, wanting to celebrate the first night of my last port visit with them rather than the members of the wardroom. Though "Fraternization" —Officer hanging out with Enlisted — is against the rules in the Navy, I always thought this was a misguided rule intended to protect weak officers. The idea was that if your men saw you drunk and stupid one night, they wouldn't follow your orders the next day. I didn't have this fear, and I was confident enough to know that I could drink with my men and know that they would still obey my commands.

We started early and moved amongst Limassol's finest drinking establishments. I wanted to thank them for all of the hard work they had put in and for putting up with my constant drive to train. We were seated at an outdoor table of one bar when I noticed a cigar shop nearby. I bought them out of Cuban cigars (Montecristo and Cohiba) and handed them out to my sailors and the other Hawesmen nearby. I don't even smoke, but I wanted to celebrate in style.

As day turned to night our crew thinned out as sailors spread throughout the city. We arrived at a Karaoke club and took over a section of the bar. I was flirting with one of the waitresses who said she like my singing, which either meant that I sing better when I'm drunk or she was hard of hearing. Our flirting intensified, and we made plans for after she got off work when the bar closed. I didn't want to make anyone else wait around so I told the rest of our crew that I was fine and would head back solo. Though the buddy policy was in place for port visits in the Mediterranean, it generally wasn't applied towards officers as long as you didn't come back to the ship drunk or in handcuffs.

Her name was Danijeela, and she had come to Cyprus from Serbia to escape the war — a war that had taken her brother's life. She was a beauty, her curly hair dyed blonde, her skin tanned by the Mediterranean sun. We walked the streets of Limassol holding hands and talking about our lives, our hopes, and our dreams. We decided to spend the night together and rented a room at a nearby hotel. It felt so good to hold her and to sleep in a real bed for once.

We woke up early from our evening of romance. She had to get ready for work and I had to get back to the ship. Liberty expired at 0930, so with more than two hours to go, I figured I had plenty of time to make it back. We made plans to meet up again that night so I walked her home and then looked for a taxi back to the harbor. With no cabs in sight, I headed towards what seemed like a main street but there was little to no traffic this early in the morning — and not a cab in sight. I didn't have a map with me, so I headed in the direction I thought would take me to the harbor but couldn't be sure.

I must have walked for 45 minutes, head on a swivel searching for a taxi before I found not a taxi but the offices of a taxi company! I ran inside and requested a ride to the pier. They were lounging around drinking coffee and smoking cigarettes, surprised to have a fare this early. I arrived back at ship around 0915, on time, completely sober, and not in handcuffs!

I was all smiles as I walked up the gangway and requested permission to come aboard. The OOD informed me that XO had ordered him to take my ID and instruct me to head straight to the XO's stateroom. Confused, I did as instructed. Upon entering the XO's stateroom I was informed that I had been put in "hack," confined to the ship for the rest of the port visit because I had violated the buddy policy and returned to the ship alone.

I knew that this was Hill's way at getting back at me for my letter, for making him and the Captain look bad, but I was way past caring. It was common for officers on our ship to arrive back from liberty on their own and had never been an issue, let alone a reason to be restricted to the ship. Besides, the night was totally worth it, and I would have done it again. The only thing I cared about was letting Danijeela know that I had not ditched her. This was before cell phones were common, so I tried calling her at home and at work, but to no avail. I couldn't make her feel like she had been stood up; I had to let her know somehow but how do you get off of a Navy warship when the command doesn't want you to?

That's when I remembered that I had only paid for one night of the officers' Admin room and only I could sign the check to pay for the remaining nights. I went to XO and explained the situation, never allowing that I could sign the check on the ship and simply have another officer bring it to the hotel. After speaking with the Captain, Hill acquiesced and issued an exception to my confinement, allowing me to head back into to Limassol to take care of the hotel bill as long as I had an escort — a brand-new Ensign named Mike — and as long as I went straight to the hotel and came right back. "Of course," I said and left to prepare.

The mission took on a whole new level of humor as we were given the keys to the Captain's rental car and I told the young Ensign, "I'm driving!" When we pulled into the parking lot of a different hotel and parked by the exterior wall of the parking lot, Mike asked, "What are we doing?" "Don't worry about it," I replied, "I have something to take care of first."

There had apparently been a big fight between members of our crew and some locals the night before, so the area around the karaoke bar was off limits to us and the entrances were guarded by shore patrol. I scaled the wall, squatting for a second to see if I had been spotted before running for cover. As I darted between buildings avoiding the watchful eyes of the shore patrol, I was thankful for all that Sergeant Major Briere and Master Sergeant Anderson had taught me about Individual Movement Techniques (IMT) back in Army ROTC Ranger training.

All that was left was to make it across a plaza like area. I had about 100 feet to go, but it was fully illuminated in the sunlight with nothing to hide behind as I sprinted across. I scanned for shore patrol and then made my move, running full speed across the plaza and crashing through the old west style swinging doors at the bar's entrance. As I burst in, I surprised not only Danijeela but everyone in the bar. I quickly explained what happened, how I'd gotten in trouble and wouldn't be able to see her that night, but didn't want her to think I was standing her up. We exchanged contact information, and I hoped we'd meet again once I was out of the Navy. I stood by the door, making sure the coast was clear and readied myself to once again evade Shore Patrol and not add to my list of woes.

Dropping back down into the hotel parking lot, I was glad to see Mike was still there. Some of the other JOs would have driven off to alert the XO and score some brownie points for themselves. Mike would be a fine officer! "How'd it go?" he asked. "Good," I replied, still catching my breath from the sprint. "This isn't the right hotel," I said, looking around before driving off. I took care of the hotel bill for the rest of our port visit, and we headed back to the Hawes. To his credit, Mike never mentioned a word of our trip to anyone and forever earned my respect as Naval Officer and as a man.

We were now leaving the white sand beaches and welcoming people of the Eastern Mediterranean for the heat of the Persian Gulf, a place where no one liked us. The Command may have been angry about my letter of resignation, but they still recognized me as one of the best OODs onboard, so Lieutenant Brewer and I swapped off the watch during our transit of the Suez Canal. I was also in command of the bridge as we sailed into Aden, Yemen for a BSF (Brief Stop for Fuel).

Aden was an ominous place. Something seemed off — you could just sense it. We arrived in the company of the USS Donald Cooke (DDG-75) and decided that while one ship was refueling, the other would sail near the entrance, weapons ready, in case we had to shoot our way out of port. We weren't even allowed off the ship and pulled not up to a pier, but a refueling dolphin, which is basically an offshore platform. In charge of the bridge as the OOD, I noticed that crowds of people had watched us sail in, but none had waved. We weren't welcome here. The only other vessels in Aden at the time were two half-submerged, capsized wrecks, and around a dozen Iraqi merchant vessels impounded due to United Nations Sanctions.

For most of the cold war, Yemen was an ally of the Soviet Union; U.S. Naval vessels were not welcome in its ports. To improve our relations with Yemen and to remind them how powerful we were, we now stopped in Yemen for fuel. So, while Soviet made fighter planes flew overhead, we made a significant contribution to the local economy and topped off our tanks for the trip to Bahrain. Donald Cooke was next to refuel, and when she was done, around two in the morning, we both got underway, leaving Aden amid a starry Arabian summer night.

I was once again chosen to be the OOD during a critical operation, passing through the narrow Straits of Hormuz within anti-ship missile range of the Iranian coast. Iran had been increasing its harassment of both US warships and neutral shipping traffic in recent months, and, as I mentioned earlier, there was real concern of an attack by a swarm of Iranian "go fasts." For someone on the outs with the command, they sure were putting a lot of trust and confidence in me!

We passed through the Straights at night to lower the possibility of conflict and to do what we could to conceal our presence. No need to announce our arrival; they'd find out soon enough we were here if they caused problems. I got off watch in the middle of the night and realized that it was evening back in New York. I hadn't called home in weeks, so I used the phone card operated satellite phone to check in with Mom. Operational Security (OPSEC) still applied so when Mom picked up all, I could tell here was that "I'm in a really cool place but I can't tell you where it is. I'll be in port in a few days and will have more time to talk then. I'll be flying back to the States soon. Not too worry, I'm okay and look forward to seeing you and Craig."

We arrived in Bahrain on August 26, 2000 and moored at the end of a long pier where some of our Minesweepers were tied up, as well as a former US Frigate of our same 'Perry Class' that now belonged to the Bahranian Navy. Most of my stuff was already packed, so I was able to spend time at the club on base.

Enjoying beer and burgers while 80s music videos played on a big screen TV, I bid farewell to my fellow JOs. We toured the city for a while before meeting up at the house of a 5th Fleet Staff officer who was hosting a 'Rug Flop' that evening, sort of a Tupperware party but for Persian Rugs. The city of Manama was the Las Vegas of the Middle East, a place where wealthy Saudis left the strict rules of their home country behind to binge drink, gamble, and engage in debauchery in Bahrain. Even with that in mind, I was still surprised when the rug merchant served us beer as he ran through his collection.

If you saw a rug you liked, you would point at it, and the merchants would set it aside so that you could settle on a price later in the evening — after more beer. I found three that I liked — one for my mom, one for my brother, and one for me. These would be the ultimate souvenirs of this deployment as they were hand-crafted beauties that would last and could be handed down through generations. We headed back to the ship and I found a place for them in my luggage.

My last night in Bahrain featured a 'Hail and Farewell' for both the Combat Systems Officer and me. As a departing officer, you are given the chance to roast and be roasted, and I took on this challenge with enthusiasm. I reserved my best lines for the XO who had come to us from the pre-commissioning crew of USS Benfold (DDG-65) and never stopped talking about. I told the officers in attendance how his nonstop talk about USS "Last Ship" always made me think of the movie 'American Pie', with the XO saying, "and one time on Benfold...." as laughter erupted in the room. I took my good share of ribbing as well, most of it deserved, and was glad I'd had the opportunity to bid farewell to the members of the wardroom.

The next evening it was time to depart. Hawes would be getting underway in the morning, headed to the Northern Arabian Gulf (NAG) to perform the boarding mission for which I had trained up two teams. Though I wouldn't be leading them, I knew they were prepared. I was confident that they were ready, and in that I took great pride. With our driver waiting on the pier, we made our way out to the quarterdeck as they gonged us ashore with two bells, then, "Lieutenant Junior Grade Rosenberg, United States Navy, Departing." Driving down the long pier, I looked back with no regrets as my service on the Hawes came to an end.

In Norfolk, I wound up being assigned to the Command JAG office at NAS Oceana in Virginia Beach. Reporting to the Lieutenant in charge was an odd experience as he was sporting the high and tight haircut of a Marine Infantryman and had a large, framed picture of Admiral Nimitz hanging on the wall behind him when a Supreme Court Justice seemed more appropriate. He was obviously fired up about serving in the Navy, yet he hadn't been anywhere or done anything and was serving in a position where he would never get close to combat, let alone danger. I'd come straight from deployment and I was nowhere near as motivated as he was.

I'd thought about going JAG and letting the Navy pay for law school but that would have meant that, after serving more than four years before law school, I would owe the Navy another six after three years in law school, so the earliest I'd be able to get out of the Navy would be after almost fourteen years of service. With less than six years to go until retirement, you obviously stick it out and collect the pension so serving in the JAG Corps would essentially be a 16-year commitment for me, and I was ready to leave.

To be honest, I couldn't stand wearing the uniform anymore, walking around on base in polyester clothing, aka "Certified Navy Twill" like it was the leisure suit days of the 1970s. I hated how I could tell what someone did for their job, how long they'd been in, and where they'd served, not from talking to them but just from looking at their uniform. After all the disappointments and letdowns I'd faced over the past four years, my morale was at an all-time low. When I woke in the morning, I dreaded not going to work but going to work in uniform.

Still, this was my assignment for the last few months of my time in the Navy so I tried to make the best of it, hoping to learn a few things that could be of use in law school. I was excited when one of the prosecuting attorneys asked if I wanted to come observe him in Federal Court. I jumped at the chance, only to learn it was Federal Traffic Court. Since the Federal Government has jurisdiction over Naval installations, all traffic infractions are handled by a Federal Magistrate Judge.

I kept in touch with several JOs still on the HAWES and it seemed like they were going to have a rough deployment. In an email sent just weeks after I had departed, one of the more senior JOs wrote, "Of course the Hawes-asylum hasn't changed significantly. The XO has only become more pompous, more difficult, and less willing to accept reason. Oh, and not to mention the micromanagement issues. The CO, well, do we really need to go there?" And the Navy wondered why so many JOs were leaving for civilian careers!

I had essentially already checked out and become a civilian in my mind, but still needed to go through the formalities, one of which was TAP class, or the 'Transition Assistance Program,' which teaches soon to be former servicemembers how to be civilians. For a week, we sat through lectures about how to wear a suit, write a resume, come across professionally at a job interview, as well as what VA benefits we were now entitled to. Much of the course was devoted to translating "I'm really good at killing people and blowing shit up" into the language of the civilian workforce, "I'm a highly organized self-starter who works tasks through to completion and makes sure the job is done right the first time!" The suit class was probably the most useful.

October 12, 2000

I'd only been back in Norfolk for about a month when the USS Cole (DDG-67) was attacked in Yemen. "That was my battle group. Fuck, I know those guys!" And in Aden, I was just there and if it had been the Hawes — a much smaller and lightly armored warship — we would have been split in half. It seemed like an ominous place when we were there in August, and now I knew why.

COLE was a late deployer; her departure staggered so that there would be overlapping coverage in the Persian Gulf while waiting for the next battle group to arrive. As such, she was on her own as she entered the port of Aden. It just as easily could have been us, so I wondered if maybe it was the fact that HAWES and DONALD COOK arrived together that gave the attackers pause and caused them to wait until the next big gray warship with a US Flag arrived in October.

Though their Captain, Commander Kirk Lippold, was unfairly blamed and became a scapegoat for the failings of Naval Intelligence and senior leadership, there was nothing he or the crew could have done to prevent the attack without advanced warning. In fact, Commander Lippold was regarded as the best Captain in our Destroyer Squadron and we all would have literally jumped ship to serve under his command if the opportunity arose.

The attackers used a small boat, about the size of a bass boat, loaded with explosives concealed in the hull while pretending to provide services to the ship before detonating their hidden cargo right up against the armored hull of the COLE. We'd been serviced by the same type of boats, and it just as easily could have been us. The attack was just as unexpected as someone flying two planes into the World Trade Center was almost a year later.

HAWES had been on her way home and was already in the Red Sea, ready to transit through the Suez Canal, when the COLE was attacked. She arrived in Aden the day after the attack — the first reinforcements to relieve the beleaguered sailors on the COLE. This left me proud, sad, angry, and with a feeling of regret — all at the same time.

I was proud that it was HAWES coming to the rescue, for I knew that the men of the HAWES would take care of their fellow sailors and do what needed to be done in spite of the inept leadership team of Commander Jones and Lieutenant Commander Hill.

I was sad, knowing that 17 sailors had paid the ultimate price for our freedom and I thought about how scary it must have been for the crew to be alone and isolated for 24 hours after their ship had been attacked in an inhospitable port in one of the most dangerous areas of the world.

I was angry that the CO and XO had ordered me home early after submitting my letter of resignation. I'd served honorably and until I resigned, they were setting me up for a career track to Admiral. Why should the fact that I wanted to get out after fulfilling my commitment change how I was treated? I knew I could do better than most in a situation such as this, where leadership and innovation were required but lacking amongst many in the HAWES wardroom.

I also felt regret about submitting my letter of resignation when I did. Much of it was due to the emotions felt after receiving the final decision of my appeal and wanting to give a big middle finger to the Navy. If I had waited a few more weeks I'd be there now. I'd be back in Aden able to lend a hand to my fellow sailors and protect them while they tended to their wounded and mourned their dead. Instead, I was working in the office of a lawyer/wannabe warrior, investigating claims against the Navy, such as the woman in North Carolina who insisted that the shock wave from a Navy bombing range had cracked the glass on her stereo case.

I attended the memorial service at Naval Station Norfolk later that month and listened to President Clinton speak as he eloquently honored the sacrifice of those men and women. The attacks of 9/11 nearly a year later overshadowed the attack on the COLE and many have forgotten about it, but those who served in the Navy at that time will never forget that these brave sailors died not going to work, as did the victims of the 9/11 attacks, but so that others could.

Though working with the JAG office, I was still technically assigned to the HAWES so I met the ship as she arrived back from deployment in December in order to complete my separation paperwork and check out of the command. I was then on leave, using up the vacation days I'd been unable to enjoy while assigned to a class of ship (FFG) that technically stood for 'Fast Frigate Guided-missile,' but which we all understood to really mean 'Forever Fucking Gone'.

As I walked down the pier, past the ship and back to my Cherry Red Jeep Wrangler in the parking lot, I turned back and stared at the Hawes for a moment, thinking, "Wow, I'm a Veteran now!" I'd done my duty, served my country at a time when few had, and I'd done so out of a sense of duty and patriotism that endured despite all the slights and setbacks. I was proud of what I had accomplished! I was proud and relieved that it was all over. I was ready for a new adventure.

Commander Jones would go on to make Admiral, mostly because he was in the right place at the right time. He had always lucked out by having enough good officers serving under him to make him look competent and being the first ship to arrive in Aden after the attack on the COLE brought him out of anonymity and into the limelight. All he had to do was make sure the COLE didn't get attacked again, and he would be rewarded. No longer able to hide behind more competent subordinates, Admiral Jones was relieved of his command of Expeditionary Strike Group 7 in Okinawa Japan in May of 2012 and forced into retirement. He now works in sales, hawking cruise missiles to foreign governments on behalf of Boeing.

With a blizzard moving up the East Coast, I raced out of Norfolk and sped along I-95 hoping to beat the worst of the storm, arriving back on Long Island around 2 in the morning. I had been planning to leave the next day but worried about being trapped by the storm and didn't want to spend another day in Norfolk than was necessary. I flew across the Chesapeake Bay Bridge with Norfolk DJ's 'Tommy and Rumble's' version of the Ramone's classic *'I Want to be Sedated'* playing in my head.

"20, 20, 24 hours to go, oh oh, I wanna be a civilian,
Gonna call up the skipper and tell him that he blows,
I wanna be a civilian,
……Oh hurry tomorrow I wish it'd get here fast,
So I can tell the Navy that they can kiss my ass,
Oh, oh, oh, oh, oh, ohhhhhh"

CHAPTER FOURTEEN

ARE THERE REALLY ANGELS AMONG US?

January 2015

A storm was forecast to hit towards the end of the snowshoe hike I was leading up Slide Mountain, but I was more worried about it affecting the drive back to Brooklyn than the hike itself. A bitter wind blew drifting snow on the summit of Slide, the highest peak in New York's Catskill Mountains, so we took shelter amongst the trees while eating lunch. The folks in the group were coming together well and seemed to be enjoying each other's company over sandwiches and small talk.

I must have led over a hundred hikes up Slide, so it can get a bit old but hiking up to the summit in winter is always enjoyable, even when the temps dip down to -20 Fahrenheit., my lower limit for taking clients — and then only if they had the right clothing. Normally a glacially-carved, rock-filled trail, winter snowfall fills in the gaps and creates a white ramp that is perfect for running down in snowshoes.

The storm picked up as we headed east on Hwy 28 towards Kingston and the New York State Thruway. Passing Phoenicia, we were brought to a halt after a driver skidded down a hill and struck a snowplow, knocking the plow off the truck before overturning. Thankfully, no one was seriously injured, but the way everything landed completely blocked the two-lane road. We must have sat there for at least an hour until the state troopers diverted traffic back west and through a detour around the accident scene.

The topics of conversation in the van started out light as folks began sharing stories of favorite hikes and adventures, but then the conversation somehow drifted to the financial crisis. Riding shotgun that day was Steven Rosenblum, a former Goldman Sachs investment banker and current hedge fund manager who lived just a few blocks away from my shop in Park Slope.

Personal views aside, I was there as a mountain guide and not to debate "too big to fail," the government bailout, or whether those bankers responsible for the crash of '08 should have gone to prison — they should have! I kept my mouth shut and tried to stay out of it until finally forced to join with a question directed at me and the state of my business. I didn't want Steven to feel uncomfortable or ganged up on, so I just focused on how I was affected by the crash. How the banks that received bailouts wouldn't consider lending me money and ignored the "Patriot Express" program with its 90 percent guarantee from the federal government.

I continued, explaining that I had the demand for more products and a bigger shop, but couldn't get the financing needed to meet that demand. My shop had been honored by the Outdoor Industry Association and I had appeared on ABC's *Nightline* and the Science Channel's *All-American Makers*, but I was stuck in a 225-square-foot shop because I couldn't get a loan, and angel investors only seemed to be interested in tech companies.

Hours later, when we finally pulled up in front of the shop in Brooklyn, Steven asked me to send him my business plan. I was surprised, but had no reason to be excited or expect anything to come out of this interaction, as I'd been through this before. A wealthy guy stuck in the '*Groundhog Day*' routine of Wall Street and family life gets inspired by my story or his desire to get back to his wilderness roots and starts talking investment and growth, only to tell me in the end that there's just not enough of a reward in retail.

Having met with several angel investors over the past few years, I already had a well thought out business plan that analyzed the state of the market using data from the Outdoor Industry Association (OIA), taking into account both local and national competition as well as the threat posed by online shopping. The Executive Summary section really laid out my vision for the larger shop.

> "As you stroll along 7th Avenue, you notice what looks like a backwoods cabin right on the avenue. Approaching the main entrance, you look up to see Gear To Go Outfitters' logo engraved on a hand painted wooden sign above the store. Seeing the lone backpacker staring off into the sunset against the mountain backdrop makes you dream about leaving the city for an adventure in the wilderness.
>
> You notice the window display of a fully decked-out backpacker, and you realize it's been too long since you've had some adventure in your life. It makes you wonder when you last tested yourself in the mountains. You need to refresh that wild feeling living deep within us

all, that spirit of self-reliance and adventure that we sometime suppress in order to deal with working out of a cubicle and living within a city. You long to relive your experiences of prior trips when you relished the fact that nothing else mattered except food, water, and shelter.

As you enter the store, you notice the rows of backpacks to your left and climbing gear on your right. You start thinking about what you need to upgrade. You are greeted by the friendly staff, who inform you that a free backpacking gear lecture will begin in 15 minutes. You strike up a conversation and mention how you are thinking about upgrading your gear and learn that Gear To Go Outfitters rents gear as well as sells it, and they even apply 50 percent of your rental fee towards the purchase of a new item.

The salesperson also tells you about the other events they have planned that month, like a reading from an author who has hiked the entire Appalachian Trail barefoot. Near the register, you stop to check out the latest in GPS units, altimeter watches, binoculars and personal locator beacons. You turn around to glance at the rows of sleeping bags and wonder if it's time to make the switch from a synthetic bag to a down bag. You decide to pay particular attention to that part of the lecture.

As you walk further into the store, you head up onto the mezzanine to check out the latest in outdoor apparel. It's starting to get chilly this month, and you wonder if now is the time to buy that lightweight down jacket you've been thinking about. The friendly staff member strikes up a conversation, and after hearing what you are looking for, and for which activities you expect to use your new jacket for, comes up with a few suggestions for you to consider. You go over the variety of insulation materials available and grill the salesperson about the pros & cons of goose down, duck down, and primaloft. He thoroughly and patiently answers your questions and even tells you about the variety of new waterproof, treated down insulation now available. "Wow, this store has it all," you think, "And the staff is so knowledgeable and friendly."

You want to check out the rest of the store before the gear lecture, so you decide to come back later for your jacket. You head downstairs and browse the latest in lightweight backpacking and camping tents. You're amazed at how roomy, yet light they have become. You think back to those camping trips with your dad and wonder how heavy that old *tent must have been! As you reminisce, you hear a voice from the main showroom announcing that the gear lecture is about to begin.*

You head over and take a seat amongst people from all over NYC. Some are experienced adventurers looking to learn about the latest innovations in outdoor gear, others are novices looking to get into backpacking and seeking to learn what they need to carry in order to have a safe and enjoyable adventure. The salesperson giving the lecture tells the audience that they are also a licensed guide. You wonder why the other outfitters in New York do any business at all and you make it a point to tell your friends about your new favorite outfitter, Gear To Go Outfitters."

I emailed Steven the business plan that night and figured, with his background in finance, at the very least I might gain some insight into whether my projections made sense, and whether my plan was viable. The response was favorable, and we discussed meeting for coffee in the neighborhood to discuss things further. He had a packed schedule and I'm sure investing in an outfitter wasn't top of mind for him, so it wasn't until May 22, 2015 that we finally got together at Café Dada on the corner of 7th Ave and Lincoln Place.

Steven seemed to be legitimately interested in investing in Gear To Go Outfitters, but without a background in finance or experience in dealing with investors, I couldn't answer and truly didn't understand many of his questions. I knew gear better than just about anyone in the country and was the most experienced guide in the region, but financial projections, accounting methods, and securities regulations were a mystery to me.

Worried that the opportunity to finally have a larger shop would disappear, I consulted a friend from the neighborhood, David Henritze, and asked him to help answer Steven's questions and address his concerns. I knew David from my street stand days when he would stop by the stand to chat while on his way home from work or while running errands in the neighborhood on weekends. A native of Atlanta, David had moved to New York in the 80's and worked in finance. He was a fan of the business and had both an MBA and decades of experience, so he was the natural choice to guide me through this process.

At first, David was essentially an interpreter, translating finance speak into plain English and breathing new life into a deal that seemed doomed to failure simply because Steven and I weren't speaking the same language. We operated on an informal basis at first, with David giving advice the way I would help someone plan their upcoming backpacking trip, but as Steven understandably asked more detailed and complex questions requiring spreadsheets, calculations, and forecasts, David came onboard as a paid advisor and representative of the company. He soon joined the meetings with Steven and me, where I felt like I was watching a tennis match as the two went back and forth on the numbers.

We reached a deal that July that would finally give me the resources needed to open a larger shop and included plans for a second and third shop a year later, so long as we hit our sales projections. Gear To Go Outfitters was valued at $1,000,000 based on the sales and goodwill of the small shop on Garfield Place, as well as the potential that the new, larger shop held.

Growth in the original shop was constrained by the size of the space, but with a larger shop on a prime corner and written commitments to finance two more locations, it seemed like we were poised to dominate the outdoor retail market in the Tri-State area. We signed the agreement on August 3, 2015 and I immediately got to work making sure we opened as scheduled on April 16, 2016, exactly five years after the opening of the small shop on Garfield Place.

Being honest about your strengths and weaknesses was an important part of being a Naval Officer. It's important to work on your weaknesses and capitalize on your strengths, but you also need to delegate or otherwise share responsibilities. Though many entrepreneurs try, you simply can't do it all — at least not well — so if someone on your team has expertise in your area of weakness, it's best to delegate responsibility for that area of the business.

Accounting and financial planning were those areas for me. With Steven's background and success in the world of finance, I let him choose our bookkeeper and accountant, entrusting financial oversight to Steven and his expertise. Frankly, I knew that I was too ADD to deal with it and was happy to concentrate on creating the new space, hiring and training more staff, and searching for the latest, greatest, most innovative outdoor gear. The new shop was going to be a work of art — my masterpiece!

I took a moment to reflect. Six years ago, I'd taken a $20,000 loan to start a business in my living room that almost failed within the first year. Street vending saved the business and after persevering through two record cold winters and one scorching hot summer, I was able to open a tiny shop on a side street with little foot traffic. Hard work and a dedication to customer service had elevated what should have been a forgotten business into the national spotlight and established Gear To Go Outfitters as the premier outfitter in NYC. I'd been working pretty much seven days a week since 2009, but it was satisfying to see the $1,000,000 value assigned to what I had built through hard work and determination.

CHAPTER FIFTEEN

HOW DID I END UP IN LAW SCHOOL?

This is a question many law students ask themselves after agreeing to spend the price of house on an education, hoping to then pass the bar exam and go on to a lucrative career. This question usually pops up after the significance of the debt has had time to sink in and before you know it, you are stuck — a prisoner to debt and a captive of the legal profession.

For me, inertia and the traditions of the officer corps culture I had just left, had a lot to do with my decision. I saw becoming a highly paid lawyer as a big FU to the Navy, and frankly, as the youngest sibling, I'd developed a lifelong interest in the fight for justice and what was fair. As I prepared to leave the Navy, I wavered between moving to Alaska and becoming a bush pilot or moving back to New York and becoming a lawyer. Clearly, I fucked up!

Though I had submitted my letter of resignation in August of 2000, which meant I planned to leave the Navy in July of 2001 and take terminal leave through August, Commander Jones and Lieutenant Commander Hill were so incensed by my decision to leave the Navy that they forced me out in December 2000, which marked the end of my active-duty obligation. This left me with more than seven months of free time which I used to hike and experience jobs I would normally not be able to take.

I worked as a waiter at TGI Fridays to get the experience, and I can back up the idea that everyone should work as a server at some point in their lives as it gives you valuable perspective on how to treat people. Next, I spent a few weeks hiking the Appalachian Trail, where I met folks that I am still friends with to this day. Returning to New York, I soon became the First Mate/Engineer on The Water's Edge restaurant's yacht — Marika — until I grew tired of my paychecks bouncing.

The camp experience was next. I took a job running the zip line and ropes course at West Hills Day Camp on Long Island. It was a bit of a surreal experience arriving on the first day of camp as "Ravioli, I love ravioli…" blared from speakers near the camp's entrance. Just a few years ago in ROTC, we'd be singing "Kill, kill, kill, blood makes the grass grow," but now I was listening to songs about ravioli. I was definitely in the civilian world now.

With the mass exodus of talented officers leaving the military in the late 90s, I expected to be one of many veterans in my class of first-years at Benjamin N. Cardozo School of Law, but as the Dean of Admissions announced, "And we have 'a' Naval Officer," I knew I was alone. In fact, I'd say that over 90 percent of my classmates were straight out of undergrad. Though I had only graduated 4.5 years before them, it felt like a lifetime and the experiences and opportunities afforded me as a Naval Officer seemed to equal a career for most people.

For me, one of the greatest experiences of law school was simply getting to know people without a connection to the military, to sit in the student lounge and just share ideas and debate politics. Most of my friends in undergrad were in ROTC or had some connection to the military and immediately upon graduating, I was on active duty. This was the first real chance I had to meet and learn from educated people with no connection to the military.

As the only veteran in the class, for the other students, of course I was 'the military,' but that was also a good thing; it gave me the opportunity to dispel myths and stereotypes and explain what military life is really like. It was truly refreshing to be completely out of the military and its culture. I even let my hair grow out about half an inch and occasionally skipped shaving as I adapted to life as a dirty hippy.

I was living in Manhattan now, 16th Street just west of 6th Ave, so there was no need to own a car. I loved my '97 Jeep Wrangler, but it was time to let her go. I'd been trying to find a buyer since early August but had failed to attract any serious offers. It was now the second week of September, and I was getting nervous, so when a buyer called asking to test drive the Jeep, I agreed to meet him that same night. I took the train out to Long Island after class and picked up the Jeep from my Mom's house. It was only my third week of law school, and I worried that I would now fall behind, but I needed to sell this thing already. I'd just have to wake up early and study before my morning class.

The next morning, I got up around 5:30 or 6 a.m. and figured if I was going to be up this early, at least I would treat myself to my favorite breakfast: egg and cheese on a toasted everything bagel. The streets were empty as I turned the corner onto 6th Ave and looked right to see the Twin Towers illuminated by the rising sun. Walking up 6th Ave to the bagel shop, I studied the Empire State Building and thought how cool it was to be able to see both iconic buildings from my corner. It was good to be back in New York!

I left my apartment around 8:35 am for the 15-minute walk to Cardozo on the corner of 5th Ave and 12th Street. I preferred taking 15th St because it was quiet, but about midway to 5th Ave I heard what sounded like a fighter jet approaching at mil thrust — the highest throttle setting just below afterburner — and it sounded fairly low. I looked up, expecting to see an F-14 Tomcat or an F-15 Eagle, but was surprised when it was an airliner. It seemed to be flying at pattern altitude — around 800 feet — which was strange. When you're dealing with an in-flight emergency, you want to get clear of other traffic while you troubleshoot, so I figured maybe LaGuardia or JFK had diverted him over Manhattan. My next thought was about how cool it must be for those passengers to get such a great view of Manhattan.

Walking east along the south side of the street, I continued in relative silence, my thoughts undisturbed on the nearly empty street. It was still pretty warm and I wondered when fall would arrive and the leaves would change. I hadn't experienced a real fall since 1990, but it has always been my favorite season. As I approached the corner, I noticed a homeless man — a regular — standing up from his broken desk chair, his gaze focused on something down 5th Avenue, but I was too far away to see what he was looking at. I made the corner and looked south to see what had caught his attention, flames and smoke billowing out of the North Tower!

I couldn't believe that the plane I had just seen, which had just flown over my head, had seconds later crashed into the World Trade Center. I wondered if the emergency they had was 'smoke in the cockpit.' In the T-2, we could just blow the canopy if we couldn't see, but all you could do in an airliner was open a few windows. Plus, their controls were fly-by-wire, so the chances of an electrical fire were much higher. I wondered if the pilot thought he was out of the usual traffic pattern and higher than any obstacles and the one thing that he'd missed was the height of the World Trade Center!

Maybe it was a military thing but since I couldn't do anything to help, I didn't see the point in hanging around on the street gawking and I still had class at 9 a.m. As I walked through the 5th Avenue entrance, I turned to watch several fire trucks responding to the growing crisis. These were some of the first to respond, and I am sure some of the first up the stairs in the towers. I don't know why, but I concentrated on their faces as they stretched out of the open windows to see what they were facing.

I remember walking up the stairs to the fourth floor as fellow students were racing down to see for themselves as news of the crash spread. What I remember most was smiles on their faces and their giggles, the human urge to "rubberneck," and the visual manifestations of schadenfreude.

Professor Newman arrived for class and hadn't yet heard about the crash, as it hadn't even been 15 minutes since impact. She excused those that needed to check on friends and relatives working in the area. A few students — some near tears — left at once. For the rest of us, it was on with the mission of studying the law.

Just fifteen minutes into class, one of our classmates, Lev Kransler, burst in, and without pause, announced that a second plane had hit the South Tower. It was now obvious that this was an act of terror. Having experienced the increased level of alert in Bahrain as Bin Laden threatened US servicemembers, and closely following the investigation into the attack on the COLE, the obvious culprit was Al Qaeda, but the method of attack seemed straight out of Tom Clancy's novel *Debt of Honor*. Though most Americans hadn't heard the name Bin Laden, he'd been on our radar since the embassy bombings in Kenya and Tanzania back in '98. As Professor Newman announced that class was canceled, I thought, "So much for law school," as I expected to be recalled to active duty the very next day.

Upon reaching the street I saw that both towers were on fire now, with steady streams of thick black smoke billowing skyward. This was truly an unbelievable sight, but we all thought that this was as bad as it was going to get. I even remarked at how strong the towers were to have withstood the impact of two airliners. Surely, the firefighters would be able to put out the flames. Surely, they would rescue the office workers. Surely the towers would remain standing. Just then, an Air Force F-15 streaked down from the heavens and circled the towers as if looking for the culprit of the crime, and finding none, climbed back up to its perch high above Manhattan. It was too late.

Traffic had long since ceased, and the remaining motorists parked along the curb were blasting the news from their car radios as we crowded around, starving for information. We heard a rumor, which obviously turned out to be true, that the Pentagon had been attacked, but we also heard that the White House was attacked. Rumors were everywhere. Although we were eyewitnesses to history, we were cut off from the rest of the world and the big picture about what was happening.

A few minutes later, it happened. It started with just a few puffs of smoke from the top floors. I whispered "No!" I couldn't believe it.

Seconds later the South Tower began to collapse. I am not sure how long it took, but it seemed like slow motion. First the puffs of smoke, then the actual collapse of the building, followed by a cloud of gray dust. And then there was one!

People all around me were screaming, some collapsing to the pavement in disbelief while others took pictures to record history. It was surreal, almost like being in a movie. It was then that I remembered that my brother was flying back to New York that day from a business trip in Toronto. Not knowing where the planes had originated I feared that I might have just watched him die. My emotions turned to anger, not just about what had happened, but because there was nothing I could do about it. We all stood there for another half an hour just staring. Staring at the smoke, staring at the endless stream of fire trucks, staring at the people covered in dust making their way north, staring at each other.

With the North Tower still standing, and not knowing if my brother was alive, I headed home to find out. A friend offered to buy me a drink, but I declined, I needed to know. I entered my apartment and turned on the television just in time to see the North Tower collapse. That was it, it was over. I thought of the thousands of people who had just died in an instant and how the city where I grew up would forever be changed, forever scarred.

I called my brother's company and was transferred around to different people, but no one had any information. I was finally able to get through to his friend Mike, who thankfully informed me that his plane was not scheduled to depart until later that afternoon. Thank God! Next, I called my mother to let her know that I was all right and that Craig was still in Canada.

While fighter planes flew combat air patrol overhead, a friend and I rushed from hospital to hospital trying to donate blood, but they were all overloaded. Later that night, around midnight, I thought I had found a way to help. Though I had been out of the Navy for about nine months now and was not part of the drilling reserves, I was still listed as a reservist and I still carried a military ID.

I called the closest National Guard Armory and informed them of my status. Trained in shipboard firefighting, I asked if I could help out and was told that they could indeed use my skills. With only a patchwork of busses and subway trains running, I managed to make it to the armory in less than an hour, but when I arrived, I was told that the officer I had spoken with had just left for home and that there was nothing I could do to help out. I left with the same feeling of helplessness that I had been filled with earlier in the day.

Two days later, I tried to simply walk to 'the site' to volunteer my services, but was stopped at the barricades set up along Houston Street. I was told that they were taking volunteers at the Javits Convention Center in midtown and that they were shuttling people from the West Side Highway. I walked towards the Hudson River and waited around for fifteen minutes for a ride before noticing what appeared to be a Reserve Center. I walked in, showed my ID, and once again volunteered my services. After waiting around for another hour, I was told that they could not use me; they were only using people from their units.

Still determined to help, I walked along the Hudson to the Javits Center and joined the line of thousands of volunteers. FEMA was taking applications inside, but the process was very slow. No one complained. After several hours of standing in line, there was an announcement that no more applications would be taken that day. We were all heartbroken. This scene was repeated all over the city.

There simply was no one to rescue, no need for volunteers, no way to help, and that was yet another tragedy.

Our city and our country had been attacked, and there was nothing we could do now to help. There was nothing to do but grieve for those who were lost and hope for a miracle at the site. I still remember the missing posters covering downtown as family and friends of the victims held out hope. For those of us who fortunate enough to not lose anyone that day, as we walked among the posters of the missing our pain was in not being able to help — not being able to come to the rescue. It may have been a selfish pain, but it was pain nonetheless. Thankfully, this was the only pain I suffered on 9/11 as I began my new life.

Eventually classes would resume, and life would return to a new normal, but I still wondered what I was doing there? What was I doing in law school? Is this really want I want to do with my life? Returning for my second year, I gained entrance into a prestigious civil litigation clinic where I had real cases and real clients whom I represented under the supervision of an actual attorney.

This was what I thought I wanted to do, or what I thought I was supposed to do, but I was miserable. I couldn't see spending the rest of my life in an office doing research and writing memos. I realized I'd made a huge mistake, but I was trapped. Trapped not only by the mountain of debt I'd already accrued, but also by the military mindset of "I started it, I have to finish it!" Global events and failed leadership would soon give me some time away from school to think things through.

CHAPTER SIXTEEN

BREAKING GROUND, LITERALLY!

We took over the adjacent and much larger corner store that had been home to Palma Chemists for decades. Peter, our landlord, also ran the pharmacy, but with insurance companies now often requiring their customers to receive their prescriptions by mail, he couldn't afford to remain in business and our expansion promised a steady stream of revenue. Peter didn't want to make the announcement to his customers, or even his staff, until just a few weeks before closing, so having the architect and contractor develop a plan for renovations required early morning covert site visits with my staff sworn to secrecy.

Nothing had changed since the 1970s, and the condition of the floor was a mystery, hidden under well-worn carpeting for at least a generation. The basement, however, was no mystery. The walls were made of stone, which was common for the area as most of the buildings were built between the end of the Civil War and the early 1890s. There was no concrete — only dirt for a floor — and the pipes, their seals filled with oakum, often flooded in a storm. There was a dumbwaiter for some reason, though I don't think the building was ever home to a single family, and a coal chute that had fed the building's furnace back in the day. It was dark and dirty, with random chains attached to the wall, making it look like the perfect set for a low-budget horror movie.

On the outside, iron columns had been covered in layers of yellow paint, and the exterior mounted heavy-duty security gates, added in the 1980s as crime took over the neighborhood, made it look more like a fortress than a welcoming local shop. For decades, no effort had been made to encourage passersby to stop in and of course, as a pharmacy they didn't need to. With our new store located on what was arguably the busiest retail corner in Park Slope, I wanted to both draw in customers and also add to the feel of the neighborhood. We had a lot of work to do!

As a lifelong student of history, I looked forward to what we would find as we peeled back the layers. On the main floor, we pulled down the partial drop ceiling and restored the tin ceiling where it had been damaged by years of flooding. Having spent years living in Arizona, I wanted to add copper to the atmosphere so, once restored, the ceiling was painted to look as if it was copper, not tin. On walls hidden behind display fixtures for generations, we found old wallpaper that probably dated back to the '20s or '30s, a section painted with a floral print, and a remnant of tin wall covering, which I'd never seen before. We exposed the bricks on that wall but preserved the tin-covered section.

The best find was on the wall that ran along Garfield Place, where we uncovered a door that had been hidden from view. The outside of the doorway had been bricked over long ago, but they'd never bothered to remove the door itself. As the current renovator, we did the same, and it is now hidden behind a layer of slatwall.

The floor was the big problem. It had rotted away in places and needed to be replaced, which added significantly to our budget. You can't just throw down laminate flooring in a high traffic retail space, and I didn't want to have to shut down in a few years to replace the flooring again, so we went with solid oak that would last.

We were also moving the stairs, since we actually had to use them frequently to grab products from the basement. The rickety staircase with a section of barely attached conduit pipe for a railing simply wouldn't do. I'd hoped this would be towards the back of the shop, but the location of the building's heating and water supply pipes necessitated a more central location. The old stairwell entrance became a broom closet.

Wanting to retain elements of the store's legacy, which had been a pharmacy since it was built, we kept the upper sections of the windows that said "Drugs." It had been covered up by the most recent tenant but was found when we opened up the window boxes. We restored everything we could and incorporated these elements into the design.

On the outside of the shop, I wanted to make it look reminiscent of a cabin in the mountains and really set the mood for a customer before they even walked through our door. We used reclaimed wood to make shingles for the exterior and mounted carved wooden signs displaying our logo, which we illuminated with goose neck lights. We removed the layers of yellow paint and brought the iron columns down to the metal. The prison-like exterior security gates were removed and new see-through ones were installed inside the windows, where they could roll up out of sight during the day.

What threatened to really delay the project was the basement. The landlord agreed to pay to install new pipes so that we weren't counting on hemp soaked in tar to keep water out, but the project start was delayed. We were further delayed when we found ourselves waiting on the cement truck, as our one truck order was considered insignificant, and we often got bumped for larger jobs. When the truck finally came, it was exciting to watch the torrent of gray pour in and cover the dirt floor.

I bought large flat files at auction from the city and used two of them to build a map table, which would be the focal point of our adventure planning center. Surrounded by books and maps of the area, the center would be a space to help folks plan their trips or leave room for them to explore options on their own. I had to buy 14 file cabinets and worked the phone to unload the rest before having to return the rental truck, unsure of what I would have done if I had to store them in the still unfinished shop.

Finally, we added ceiling fans and a large screen door to complete the cabin look, and constructed fixtures out of reclaimed wood from an old building in Manhattan. The centerpiece was of course the sales counter. It was custom made and was covered with a layer of copper that was a quarter-inch thick.

It was a challenge to dream big yet stay within our budget. I had so many ideas for the shop, and for me, it had to not only be a functional retail space, but a work of art as well. I'd long had a vision of what an outfitter should look like and how it should feel when you walked in, transporting you out of the city and into the mountains.

We held onto the small adjacent shop as well, knocking out a doorway in the basement so that staff would be able to move back and forth. Our old shop would house our rental fleet and would be where pickup and drop-off would take place. The old shop would also serve as our workshop, providing space to take care of maintenance and cleaning in between rentals. To draw attention to the shop and also let folks know that we offered rentals, I hired an old graffiti artist to paint a mural on the large brick wall that included the words 'Sales' and 'Rentals' with arrows pointing to the appropriate shop.

I'm not sure I slept much in the months leading up to opening day, as I had to not only run the current store, but also plan for a new one, adding new brands and categories and placing orders for a 500 percent increase in retail space. It was difficult to plan for such a leap and my inclination was to be conservative, which meant ordering what we could afford to pay for in advance, accepting that we risked not being able to get product in that season if sales took off.

I felt pressure from Steven to not just break even that first year, but to hit it out of the park as soon as we opened. He was used to investments in companies with rapid growth and big returns, and I wanted him to be rewarded for believing in me and my dream. When I sent Steven my orders for review, he asked if we were ordering enough to put up the numbers we were forecasting. I questioned my own judgment and ordered more, ensuring that we would have enough product in stock early on to fuel the growth we expected and to meet the numbers we had agreed upon in order to secure financing for a second shop in 2017.

In aviation, we were taught the importance of being on target, on time, and I applied this discipline to the new shop, pushing the contractors to stay on schedule. Opening day would be Saturday, April 16, and it was important to open up on time, not just for my ego, but to take advantage of the upcoming summer season. Over the years, I'd found that folks browse in April as they emerge from their winter isolation, and then buy in May and June as they prepare for summer adventures. July and August are still strong sales months, but people are more likely to rent during these months, viewing the summer as "almost over" by the second week of July.

As guests arrived for our pre-opening celebration on the evening of the 15th the construction crew was wrapping up a few final tasks on the façade. I was proud of how the shop looked and all that I had accomplished in just a few years. Through the window of my masterpiece, I could look across the street and silently observe the spot where I'd first set up a folding table on a cold December evening in 2009. Family and friends joined in the celebration as the staff and I began a new adventure.

Opening day was filled with excitement, and crowds of customers poured in as soon as we opened our door. Even with four guides helping out that day it was an exhaustive pace. Everything seemed to come together, and at the end of the day I proudly reported our sales figures to Steven, our angel investor.

CHAPTER SEVENTEEN

WHO'S PLAYING IN THE SANDBOX?

The Naval Reserve Officer recruiter for the New York Region had been calling me ever since I'd gotten out and my answer was always essentially: "No way in hell."

I'd fully expected to be recalled the day after the 9/11 attacks but that call never came, as the Bush Administration decided to put minimal effort into fighting Al Qaeda, holding back the bulk of our forces for their planned invasion of Iraq.

In law school debates at the time, I expressed the opinion, "Okay, but why are we invading?" Saddam Hussein had used Weapons of Mass Destruction (WMD) in the past so he could not be trusted to possess them now, but we had demonstrated our ability to take out Iraq's WMD sites as recently as 1998's Operation Desert Fox. We had demonstrated that a combination of air strikes and special forces could eliminate the threat, so why were we invading? I faced the difficult personal choice of protesting against my country's government for the first time in my life.

I remembered back to the Fall of 1990 and how strongly I'd felt about the protestors gathered outside of the armed forces recruiting center in Hempstead, New York to voice their opposition to Operation Desert Shield. I saw them as traitors back then, but now I felt it was my patriotic duty to protest what would be an unnecessary — if not illegal — war. I had made the commitment to lay down my life for my country if need be, but it had better be for a damned good reason. My comrades deserved the same respect. I couldn't accept that brave men had to die so that a few draft-dodging cowards in the White House could feel like big men.

I spoke out against the war when I had the opportunity and joined protests to show my support. It was an uncomfortable feeling, but I knew it was right. Eventually, it seemed like war was inevitable. The White House was determined, and in the wake of the legitimate bloodlust that followed 9/11, the Democrats were left too weak to stop it.

In the military, we are taught that it's okay to have a political opinion but once the order comes down, those opinions go away, and it's time to focus on the mission. I called up the recruiter and asked, "Who's going to play in the Sandbox?" a reference to what we called the Persian Gulf.

I may not have agreed with the war, but having recently gotten out of the military, and with friends preparing to serve on the front lines, I wasn't going to sit back and just watch it happen. I wanted to do my part, and besides, how could I tell my kids that there was a war going on, but I couldn't go because I was in law school? I wanted to not only return to active duty but deploy in theater and join the fight.

A reserve coastal warfare unit in the Bronx, MIUWU-203 (Mobile Inshore Undersea Warfare Unit) had an opening for a surface/sub-surface officer, which seemed like a perfect fit for my background. These units were originally developed to provide coastal ASW protection, making sure submarines didn't sneak into protected harbors, but since the attack on the COLE, they had been evolving into more of a surface-based force protection unit.

I met with the CO and XO in late November of 2002 and quickly joined the unit with the expectation that we would soon deploy to Kuwait and then help the Marines take over the Iraqi port city of Umm Qasr. I was ready to go to war, not because I believed in the cause, but because my country had decided we would.

My first experience with the Reserves, I was surprised at how little time there was to actually train to perform our mission. Drill weekends were spent filling out required paperwork or sitting through lectures on things like sexual harassment or substance abuse. Since I no longer owned a car, I'd have to leave my house at 5 a.m. in order to be on time for quarters at 7. I'd first stop at the Hollywood Diner on the corner of 6th Avenue and 16th Street — the only place open at that time to grab a cup of coffee — and would chuckle at the reactions my camouflage uniform would evoke among the crowd of gay men from the Heaven nightclub across the street, who were wrapping up their night with a visit to the diner. It seemed to be a mix of fear that I was some sort of right-wing vigilante set against visions of a Village People music video.

I'd grab my coffee and walk to Union Square to catch an uptown Lexington Ave express train to 125th Street, where I'd have to transfer to the local for the Westchester Square/East Tremont Ave stop. Once at Westchester Square, I'd wait 15-30 minutes for the bus to arrive, which I would then ride to Fort Schuyler — the end of the line — where both the Naval Reserve Center and SUNY Maritime were located. I hoped we would deploy soon just so I didn't have to keep up this commute!

It was early morning on a weekday in late January when the phone rang. I was sleeping next to my girlfriend, Allison, cuddled up together in the lofted queen-sized bed of my tiny Chelsea studio. Abruptly brought out of my peaceful slumber, I hurried down the ladder, hoping to reach the phone before Allison woke up. Hearing my department head on the line, I immediately knew what this call was about, we'd gotten our orders and would soon be deployed. There was a lot to get done before we left, and I was taking notes, trying to be as quiet as possible while Allison slept.

I hung up the phone and still barely awake, climbed up the ladder to rejoin Allison in the loft. I tried not to wake her as I crawled along the mattress to her side, but soon realized she was awake, she'd heard it all. Her eyes were filled with tears as I held her close and assured her it would be alright. Allison was a grad student as well, working on her Master of Social Work (MSW) degree at Yeshiva University. We'd met while working together at the Bet Tzedek Legal Services clinic at Cardozo, where law students and social work grad students teamed up to address the needs of our clients.

Both of us knew this day was coming, but I guess the reality of it hit home for her with that phone call. We'd started dating in late fall and were still in the honeymoon phase. This was now her day, so we blew off class and went to her favorite dessert spot in Forest Hills for chocolate cake.

The reality of it hit home for me as I realized there was a chance that I wouldn't be coming back. It was still early in our relationship, but if Allison was this distraught over me going to war, I worried how she would handle things if I didn't return. I didn't want the first time she met my family to be at my funeral, so I arranged for everyone to meet over dinner on Long Island before I deployed.

We started packing up our gear, going through the checklist of tasks we needed to complete before heading overseas. We were still expecting to fly into Kuwait but hadn't yet received desert camo uniforms and were initially issued Vietnam-era body armor before more modern gear arrived just in time.

I hadn't fired a weapon since early 2000 and had to requalify on pistol and rifle. I've always been a pretty good shot and held the Navy's 'Expert Rifle' medal and 'Sharpshooter Pistol' ribbon, but without any practice in almost three years, I was a bit worried about how well I'd do. One element of the qualification requires you to draw your weapon out of a holster and fire something like five accurately aimed rounds in three seconds. At the command to fire, I drew my weapon as fast as I could, staring at the target as I brought the pistol up to meet my gaze, and pulled the trigger five times. It looked like a scene straight out of a Western as my quick-draw was followed by bullets tracing up towards the target, kicking up sand in a neat line of progression.

"Um, can I go again?" I asked.

Once I received my orders, I let the administration at Cardozo know that I had been recalled to active duty and would be putting my studies on hold. I was told that Dean Rudenstine was planning to send a message to both students and faculty, making note of the fact that, not only was I going to war, but that I was the first Cardozo student to do so. Of course, this never happened, and Cardozo essentially abandoned me since the war was controversial and I was out of sight and out of mind.

Now on active duty, I was making the long commute to the Reserve Center five days a week. On the way home one night, I stopped by the Dunkin Donuts on 6th Ave and 14th Street. As I entered, two aging hippies stopped what they were doing and just stared at me as I walked towards the counter dressed in my Service Dress Blues and Bridge Coat. With coffee in hand, I headed for the exit, when they suddenly jumped in front of me, blocking the door.

"We're against the war," they said.

I smiled and said, "Me too."

I walked around them and exited, leaving them in confused silence.

Our orders came in, and it was not what I had expected. We would not be heading to the Sandbox; we would not be playing in the big game. Instead, we were relegated to the minor leagues, guarding ships coming in and out of Souda Bay — a NATO base on the Greek island of Crete.

Since the overwhelming majority of the equipment needed for an operation such as 'Iraqi Freedom' goes over by ship, Souda Bay was an important refueling port for the cargo ships and warships headed for the Persian Gulf. Many of the tomahawk missile and carrier-based air strikes would actually launch from the Eastern Mediterranean, so those ships and submarines would be coming back in to resupply and rearm throughout the early days of the offensive.

Staring out the window while we waited for our charter flight to take off from McGuire AFB, I started thinking, "What am I doing?"

I was out. I'd done my time and served my country. Why did I leave law school and volunteer to serve in a war I didn't even believe in? I didn't have any good answers other than pride and patriotism, which didn't satisfy my questioning voice, but as we sped down the runway, it was too late for doubts.

Our setup at Souda Bay was a bit chaotic. We were housed at NAMFI (NATO Missile Firing Installation), working at a Marathi Piers, and eating meals at NSA Souda Bay. Once we arrived, we teamed up with 3 IBUs (Inshore Boat Units), IBU-24, IBU-25, and IBU-26, whose boats were basically small patrol craft with a machine gun mounted on the bow. We would provide surveillance and command and control for the boats to ensure that allied ships were protected and any threats identified could be neutralized.

Commander Mike Bartlett was our CO. A detective on Long Island who had served on a supply ship during his time on active duty, he ran the unit as if it was a college fraternity, and he was chapter president. On our first night in Souda Bay, when he should have been focused on making sure we were prepared to perform our mission, Mike was instead getting drunk with the enlisted sailors in the hallway of our barracks. How can you expect anyone to work when the commanding officer is acting like we're on vacation?

I caught a ride down to Marathi Piers to set up our Tactical Operations Center (TOC). With the Captain's party going on all night, I couldn't get the help necessary to be ready to go the next day, so I pulled an all-nighter to make sure we met our mission requirements. Set up inside of a field tent, the TOC was where we were supposed to run our operations and manage the battle space if faced with a threat.

Instead of operating from our TOC and having a liaison officer standing watch with the Greek forces, Commander Bartlett set up shop alongside the Greeks in the air-conditioned comfort of what became the Joint Tactical Operations Center (JTOC). This decision often caused confusion among our forces, who were reporting to one command center but receiving orders from another, and risked operational security, as intelligence reports marked "NOFORN" (No Foreign Nationals) were often read in the JTOC.

Our unit was primarily made up of NYPD officers who joined the Reserves mostly because they could "double dip", continuing to earn their NYPD salary while also being paid by the Navy on deployment. They were also earning two pensions with the Naval Reserve pension kicking in at age 65 if they completed 20 years in the Reserves. Many seemed to look at our deployment not as wartime duty but as a chance to get away for a while. Few took our mission seriously, which I found surprising, given that the attack on the USS Cole happened just over two years earlier and we were here to prevent a repeat.

Commander Bartlett's two favorite JOs, Lieutenants Kucharsky and McCormick, had never actually served on active duty and had barely been in the Reserves. They'd graduated from the United States Merchant Marine Academy, which meant they were commissioned as Ensigns in the Naval Reserves upon graduation, but didn't need to actually serve in the Navy or join a Reserve unit, which neither did.

Their only requirement was to work in the maritime industry for five years. LT Kucharski worked in maritime insurance, and LT McCormick, after sailing for a time on a cargo ship, had recently become an air marshal. Promotions from Ensign to Lieutenant Junior Grade and then Lieutenant occur automatically every two years, as long as you don't do something stupid like get a DWI, so after four years of not being in the Navy, both were automatically promoted to the rank of Lieutenant and then at that point chose to join the drilling reserves. The problem with this system is that they had the knowledge of brand-new Ensigns but held the rank and corresponding authority of more experienced Lieutenants.

We finally stood up the unit and were performing our mission as ships carrying the tanks, armored personnel carriers, artillery, and support vehicles for the 3rd Infantry Division stopped in to resupply before making their way to Kuwait. I got along very well with the officers from the IBUs, and after witnessing the leadership style of Commander Bartlett and his cronies, they often joked about adopting me into one of their units.

I was soon tasked with taking over responsibilities as the unit's Intelligence Officer in addition to my regular duties. I hadn't received any training for this, so I visited the local NCIS (Naval Criminal Investigative Service) to get some pointers, as they were the closest thing to Naval Intelligence that we had at Souda Bay. I was given an interim Top Secret clearance, granting me access to the Defense Department's Top Secret websites, which I scanned for relevant information and put together a daily report each morning.

We became the focus of the anti-war protest movement in Greece and could match the start and end time for student protests by checking the ferry schedule for Athens. After they left, we'd find graffiti outside the base labelling us as "NATO Bastards." A California Air National Guard unit whose enlisted men shared our barracks, had money allocated to establish a lounge on the base. I know what you veterans are thinking: "An Air Force unit with extra money for recreation facilities, how strange!" They invited us to join them, and the name chosen for our new hangout was, of course: "NATO Bastards."

In mid-March, before combat operations had even commenced in Iraq, Commander Bartlett put us on Force Protection Condition Delta, which according to Department of Defense regulations, is ONLY to be used when a terrorist attack has occurred or in response to a threat that is deemed imminent. Neither requirement was met, and I should know, as I was the intelligence officer for the unit! Everyone was now walking around in full body armor and carrying weapons locked and loaded. We all had to sleep on the pier, hot racking in cots, since we only had enough for about ten percent of the unit. We were kept on alert for days, amusing the Greeks who went about business as usual knowing that there was no threat.

The alert did coincide with another of the regularly scheduled student protests but we had no reason to be concerned about students cursing us out and venting their anger about an unjust war. What was concerning was a group of Reservists with little-to-no training walking around heavily armed while suffering from sleep deprivation.

For some unknown reason Bartlett tasked LT Kucharski, the Vehicle Maintenance Officer, with observing the protestors, even though we weren't responsible for perimeter security on the Greek base, and the Greeks hadn't asked for our assistance. I was on watch in the TOC during the protest when Kucharski got on the radio and in a panicked voice yelled, "WE'RE BEING GASSED, WE'RE BEING GASSED!" Given a credible worldwide threat that Al Qaeda might use nerve gas against US forces, we all took this warning as the first stage of an actual attack and donned our gas masks, inserting new filter cartridges into the respirator. "That went sideways fast" I said as I screwed in the cartridge.

Next, we heard Kucharski yell, "THEY'RE COMING TROUGH THE GATES, THEY'RE COMING THROUGH THE GATES!" Unclear if he meant protestors or terrorists, it didn't matter, since we had only one tool to deal with either: deadly force. We weren't equipped with less-than-lethal weapons and had encrypted communications equipment, sensors, and weapons that could not be allowed to fall into the hands of terrorists, or even protestors, for that matter. We set up a few firing positions for M-60s while the rest of us got ready with M-16s and 9mm pistols.

Of course, the onslaught Kucharski warned about never came. In need of extra manpower to deal with the protest that day, the Greeks had called in police cadets to help out. They weren't equipped with gas masks, so when the police fired tear gas, unfortunately upwind of their own position, it blew back on the cadets. Choked by the gas, the cadets ran back towards the entrance of the base, which is what Kucharski witnessed and saw as a nerve gas attack. I gave him the callsign 'Fear' after that and was thankful that no one got shot, especially a protestor exercising their rights in the birthplace of democracy.

Things got worse in the early morning hours of March 17th. I was on watch in the TOC when I started receiving reports that Commander Bartlett was drunk and causing problems in the Argonaut, which was the recreation center and snack bar on base. The first reports I received were from members of a Coast Guard Port Security Unit that was augmenting us. I was informed that Bartlett was not only drunk, but also yelling at everyone inside and trying to pick fights with his own sailors. This was especially alarming given that everyone was carrying weapons and live ammo since we were still at Delta.

Bartlett focused his rage on the unit supply officer, the only African American officer in the unit, grabbing him out of a chair by his shirt collar and pinning him up against the wall while screaming insults at him. When Lieutenant Johnson, the Coast Guard officer in charge of the detachment, tried to intervene, Commander Bartlett turned his attention to the Coasties, many of whom were also police officers, making aggressive moves that convinced them they were about to be attacked. Still armed, they prepared to defend themselves. They told me that Bartlett's actions would have resulted in his arrest in the civilian world.

The Argonaut, the one place on base where sailors could go to relax while crowded together at Condition Delta, was cleared out by Bartlett's actions. Most sailors left to find a place to sleep, but not our fearless commanding officer, whose rampage was just getting started. He next added 'Driving While Intoxicated' to his list of accomplishments for the night, driving his government vehicle to one of the tents where sailors were sleeping and then stumbling through, crashing into things, screaming in a drunken rage, and waking up the entire unit.

This, too, would not satisfy Bartlett's mission to demonstrate how unfit he was for command. He would now take things international by drunk driving over to the JTOC where those on watch noted that he was visibly intoxicated. His conduct scared the Greeks on duty and caused the Watch Officer, Lieutenant Commander Miller, USCG, to write "drunk and disorderly" in his logbook and to note that "Commander Bartlett smelled of alcohol."

But wait, there's more! It's now about 0230, and I've been following this trail of destruction to investigate and pick up the pieces for at least an hour when he calls me directly and unleashes a screaming, rambling, incomprehensible stream of words. After several attempts to understand what he was saying, I was able to ascertain that our Commanding Officer now wished to rearrange the entire watch team deployed around the harbor. He wanted all of the senior experienced sailors to be grouped together at one site and all of the new, inexperienced junior sailors to be grouped together at another. I tried to reason with him, but had no choice but to carry out his orders.

In light of the reports I had received, my first thought was "My God, this guy's armed!" As the officer on watch, it would be up to me to disarm him, which, given his state of intoxication, could be very dangerous. I had the gunners mates check the logbook, and thankfully, he had not checked out a weapon. This was a huge relief, but his conduct that night was the last straw for me.

I'd had enough of the disorganized, thug-like conduct of Mike Bartlett. While on active duty, I had served in professional units. They may have been occasionally led by incompetent officers, but it was nothing like this shitshow. I had joined this Reserve Unit fully aware of the upcoming wartime deployment and had voluntarily left law school to serve my country. I was willing to put up with brutal conditions and even lay down my life for my country, but I was not willing to serve under an officer who ran his command as if it was his own street gang. Still wishing to serve my country in its time of need, I requested a transfer to another unit, preferably in Kuwait, but my request was denied and I was stuck.

Following complaints by the Coast Guard personnel and possibly even from within our unit, Captain MacCormick, the commanding officer of our parent command Naval Coastal Warfare Group 2 (NCWG2), was sent to investigate the incident. In anticipation of MacCormick's arrival in Souda Bay, Commander Bartlett organized a dinner party for all the officers to meet and greet the Captain. Coincidentally, this event was scheduled for when I would be on watch and thus unable to attend.

Though ready and willing to discuss what I had witnessed, Captain MacCormick never asked to interview me, and I was cautioned not to approach him on my own because he and Bartlett were old friends. I was warned that if I said anything about the incident, nothing would happen to Commander Bartlett, but that I would suffer as a result. Isolated and trapped within this unit, I was intimidated into silence.

Immediately before the Captain's arrival, an all-hands meeting was held where the CO made clear that no one was to say anything to Captain MacCormick or his staff. Bartlett told the troops that the unit's motto was now "No Complaints!" The command may have been in full cover up mode, but they were assisted by an investigating command that had no interest in an investigation. Nothing ever became of Captain MacCormick's "investigation," and based on my active-duty experience, I wasn't surprised.

A few days later, Commander Bartlett decided that he wanted to put a third coastal surveillance site on the far side of Souda Bay, an area that was off base and unsecured. My watch team was tasked with making it happen, and as usual with this unit, there was no advanced warning. Nevertheless, we were getting everything organized when the question of weapons accountability came up.

Because the Greek government didn't want us travelling through their cities with weapons, those watchstanders on duty at the new unsecure coastal surveillance site were told they would turn over their weapons to the sailor relieving them in what is known as "watch to watch turnover." While this may be fine for a set of binoculars or sound-powered phones, it was not okay with weapons which require direct accountability. Essentially, someone has to sign for and be responsible for each weapon.

Thinking this was just an oversight, I called the JTOC Watch Officer to find out what the plan was for weapons accountability. My query was met by stunned silence so I explained that someone had to sign for the weapons, and it wasn't right to have two enlisted men accountable for weapons that they would have no control over. If they were to go missing or were mishandled, they would be financially responsible for the loss as well as subject to court martial for violating the Uniform Code of Military Justice (UCMJ).

I explained that I was not going to allow members of my watch team to sign for the weapons, and that, since I had control of neither the weapons nor the armory, I would not sign for them either. I asked the watch officer who was going to sign for the weapons and expected him to say that Commander Bartlett would take on that responsibility since it was his order. There was a pause while the watch officer discussed the issue with Bartlett, and the response was "You're relieved!" "You're relieving me for following Navy regulations?" I asked in disbelief. "Yes, the duty driver will be there to pick you up."

I'm not sure many of the officers in this unit had even knew what regulations were. As I mentioned before, one of my concerns about the JTOC being used as the primary command center was due to the risk of an intelligence leak. One morning, while I was in the TOC preparing the daily Intel brief, I received a call from my department head, Lieutenant Commander Murphy, who was on duty in the JTOC. He asked me to bring the daily brief to him for review, but I politely explained to him that it was classified as SECRET/NOFORN, which meant it could not be distributed to foreign nationals.

This level of classification is not uncommon and means that anyone who views the material must possess a Secret-level clearance, be a U.S. citizen, and have a need to know the information. Such material can only be viewed in a secure space with access controlled to allow only those with a Secret or higher level of clearance entrance into the space. The TOC, which was such a space, was also the location of all available unit intelligence, and was a 10-minute walk from the JTOC. I explained to Murphy that since the brief was classified as SECRET/NOFORN, he would have to come to the TOC to view the brief.

Murphy replied that he needed to see the brief and would not leave the JTOC. I explained that this was not a flexible rule and could not be bent to accommodate him. His response was "Lieutenant, I am giving you a direct order to bring the Intel brief to me!" I explained that he could not order me to violate that laws of the United States and that his order was an unlawful one which I would not follow. He repeated his order and after another minute of trying to bully me into breaking the law, hung up the phone.

In order to protect classified information and sensitive equipment, as TOC Watch Officer, one of my duties was to ensure that the operations area was secure. After several incidents of unauthorized Greek civilian personnel walking into the TOC, seemingly out of curiosity, I went to investigate and realized that there wasn't a security checkpoint in place as required.

The sailors on duty at the armory were tasked with providing security, but were routinely hanging out in an area flooded with bright lights while the entrance was completely dark. Once, I even found them huddled together in a shipping container watching a movie on someone's portable DVD player. This left not only the TOC, but the rest of our equipment and the IBU boats unprotected, unwatched, and vulnerable. To remedy this situation and properly carry out my duties as watch officer, I ordered them to post a sentry at the entrance, and to have that sentry stand watch outside of the bright flood lights that would rob them of their night vision.

The watch was posted on the night I gave the order, but on subsequent watches, I found that there was no sentry in place. I also learned that the armory/security watchstanders were routinely abandoning their posts at their leisure with no consequences or accountability. I discovered this when one of our more remote Mobile Sensor Platform (MSP) locations was being flooded out during a severe storm and was in danger of being washed over a cliff. I called the armory to send the security force in their Humvee to help out, but the response I received after a long pause, was that members of the watchteam had taken the

Humvees to grab lunch at another base that was 30 minutes away, having done so without permission from me, the watch officer.

On the morning of March 29, 2003, after repeatedly finding that my orders were not being followed, I gathered the armory/security watchstanders. I reminded them that the reason we had all of these weapons here was not to protect the weapons, but to protect our sensor platforms and the patrol boats. I'd run out of patience and warned them that if I ever found that the sailor assigned to stand sentry duty was not at his post, he would be sent to Captain's Mast (non-judicial punishment) no questions asked.

Soon after announcing my warning, I received a call from their new to the Navy Division Officer, Lieutenant McCormick. I suspected that he had been telling his sailors to ignore my orders because he didn't understand that they were his sailors for administrative purposes, but while on watch, they worked for me as the Watch Officer. He asked if we could meet with the officer on duty in the JTOC, Lieutenant Commander Goutink, to discuss the matter. Knowing that he was inexperienced and hadn't been trained on this concept, I agreed, expecting that an adult conversation would resolve what should never have even been a dispute. McCormick instead threw a tantrum, complained about me ordering his men around, and got his way. There would be no sentry!

I was still responsible for ensuring our operating area was secure, but after McCormick's tantrum, I couldn't give the orders necessary to actually make it so. Frustrated and angry, I called McCormick and asked, "How is everything with PN1?", referring to a well-known rumor about an affair between Lieutenant McCormick and PN1 Crawford. Within minutes, I was approached by both my department head, Lieutenant Commander Murphy, and McCormick's department head Lieutenant Commander Kruger. Once again, I was informed that I was relieved. I was then ordered to turn in my weapon and informed that I was barred from the armory.

I soon found out that the rumor was true, and that, fearing that I had reported his affair with PN1 Crawford — an enlisted female who was also rumored to be sleeping with Commander Bartlett — Lieutenant McCormick tried to cover up his crime by claiming that I had threatened to kill him. Without any investigation into whether this was true, I was relieved. Upon my insistence, the Executive Officer, Lieutenant Commander Rufo, conducted a cursory investigation into McCormick's claim. Though this investigation was by no means thorough, it soon became obvious to everyone that Lieutenant McCormick's claim was a lie — a fairytale created to distract from his very real crimes.

Realizing that the CO's campaign to intimidate me into silence was escalating and finally becoming fed up with being prevented from doing the job I had been asked to do, I directly informed Commander Bartlett that I would no longer work for him. He could transfer me or send me home, but I would not put up with his antics any longer. Looking worried, he agreed.

Fearing that I would report his juvenile and dishonorable conduct up the chain of command once out of Souda bay and out of his control, Bartlett attempted to discredit me by attacking my character. The day after I demanded a transfer, he announced to the rest of the unit's officers that I had suffered a mental breakdown and would be sent home. Though obviously untrue and based on no medical evidence or examination, Commander Bartlett continued to spread this rumor outside of our unit and among my intelligence contacts on base, including NCIS Agents and Base Security Officers.

I first learned of this vicious attack when I stopped by NCIS to say farewell to the agents who had assisted me in keeping the unit appraised of the current intel situation. Their reaction was, "What are you doing here? Aren't you supposed to be in the hospital?" When I asked why they thought I should be in the hospital I was told that Bartlett had informed them that I had suffered a mental breakdown.

I was informed that there was no way for me to be transferred, but that I would be sent back to the U.S. and demobilized (released from active duty). I was told that if I submitted a letter or resignation that the process would only take days. Fearing further retaliation, I complied and promptly submitted my letter. I was then exiled to our barracks for several weeks as I waited for my flight home. They kept making excuses until I threatened to send a letter to my Congressman, at which point, I was booked on a flight the next day.

As I was checking out and heading to the airfield, Commander Bartlett threatened that if I wrote a letter to any representatives or reported his misconduct to the Navy, no one would believe me, and I would suffer payback. I was then told that I was not to show my face at the Reserve center, and it was only after I agreed to these conditions that I was given my orders and plane ticket and allowed to proceed to the airfield.

Though told that I was heading home that day with only a stopover in Sicily, and with my family expecting me back in the States, I arrived in Sicily to learn that I would be further delayed on the island for no apparent reason, other than to prevent word from getting out about the outrageous misconduct of Commander Mike Bartlett. I was not given accommodation in the Bachelor Officers Quarters as is customary, assigned instead to the Bachelor Enlisted Quarters by Captain MacCormick and the staff at NCWG2 then based at NAS Sigonella.

Every day, I was told to check in and see if I was flying home and every day I was told there was a delay. After three days of hanging around the base, I rented a little Fiat and set off to explore Sicily. This was the true silver lining of my deployment as I visited Enna, Agrigento, Syracuse, Taormina, Messina, and more, all while getting paid full salary plus per diem and having no responsibilities other than to check in each night to see if I was flying out the next day.

It seemed like I was being kept on the island in an attempt to keep me quiet, but by now, you know me well enough to realize this was a huge mistake on their part. I contacted Senator Schumer by both email and post, detailing how I had tried to report gross misconduct and violations of Navy regulations as well as of the Uniform Code of Military Justice. I also detailed the retaliation I had suffered, including being exiled to this Mediterranean island as if I was an overthrown dictator. I ended my letter with the following statement:

> *"I regret that it has come to this. In my time on Active Duty, I never felt compelled to write a letter to an elected official concerning the performance of a fellow officer, however, in this case I feel that failure to report this conduct would be a violation of my duty. My duty to my country, my service, and my subordinates. Cdr Bartlett must never again be allowed to command troops. He has demonstrated that he is unworthy of the distinction, "Commissioned Officer, United States Naval Reserve." For the good of the United States, the Navy, and all those who may serve under Cdr Bartlett, I ask that he be stripped of his command and his commission."*

I assumed that, as with my attrition from flight school, nothing would come of this, and the Navy would once again cover it up, but at least it might finally allow me to return home. I truly enjoyed my Italian vacation but touring a place by yourself gets old after three weeks.

I arrived back in the United States on April 24, 2003, and cut the yellow ribbon that my Mom had tied around a tree in our front yard. Though she put on a brave face when we spoke on the phone, the truth was that she was a wreck. Neighbors couldn't even mention the war without her breaking out in tears. I thought she was used to me serving by now, but she said this time was different because I told her that I didn't believe in the war. She had accepted the possibility of me dying for a cause I believed in or doing what I loved, flying jets, but she couldn't accept the possibility that I might die for this war — for a cause I considered unjust.

The extra money I had made while on vacation in Sicily paid for another vacation. Allison and I flew out to San Diego and spent a few days with my flight school buddy Steve Bury, who was now based at NAS North Island. We then drove up the Pacific Coast Highway to visit my old flight instructor, Jon Sherman, in Port Hueneme, before touring Monterrey and San Francisco.

It was good to be a civilian once again, and I was now certain of one thing: I would never again work for the federal government. All I'd ever wanted to do was simply serve my country but I seemed destined to be placed in situations where my sense of honor and morals compelled me to take action. I took no joy in this and wished it had been someone else for once.

In flight school, I spoke up to save lives. On the Hawes, it was incompetence, not misconduct, that convinced me it was time to get out. With MIUWU-203, I witnessed real crimes being committed by a commanding officer and had to choose between reporting these crimes or joining the cover-up and being just as guilty. Others may have acted differently in any or all of these situations, but guided by my moral code, I saw no other choice. Though I acted out of a sense of honor and duty, I would have much preferred to be able to just do my job and not have to take a stand. It seemed that God, the universe, or whatever higher power you believe in, had assigned me the role of 'moral compass officer' and I had reluctantly accepted those duties and responsibilities.

Returning to law school in August 2003 was a bit strange, and I was surprised at how insulated the student body was from the war. Whether they agreed with the war or not, men and women were fighting and dying on their behalf. I felt disillusioned by both my wartime service and the apathy I encountered at home.

I applied to resume my GI Bill Benefits but the VA treated my resumption of benefits paperwork as a new application, applying a new policy put in place by the Bush Administration — in the midst of a war — that denied GI Bill benefits to anyone that had received even a partial ROTC Scholarship. I appealed all the way up to the DC Circuit Court of Appeals but lost every battle along the way. In fact, the VA and the Justice Department spent more money fighting me than it would have cost to simply pay me the benefits I was promised

What angered me most about this was that if I had not volunteered to serve in a war I didn't agree with, I would have continued to receive the benefits I had earned. I was being penalized for serving my country a second time despite no obligation to do so. This really opened my eyes as to how America treats its veterans.

In the middle of that first fall Semester back in school, I received a phone call from an investigator at the JAG office in Norfolk. It turns out the Navy was actually investigating Commander Bartlett and had found enough damning evidence to file charges against him. I enthusiastically offered to testify and even offered to pay my own way down to Norfolk if necessary.

Commander Bartlett was indicted and stood trial, but he hired a civilian criminal defense attorney and beat the charges. I was never called to testify because the inexperienced prosecutor in the case worried that I might appear biased because of the actions Bartlett took against me. Instead, the prosecutor relied on the testimony of Lieutenant McCormick and PN1 Crawford.

McCormick and Crawford had fallen out with Bartlett over Crawford's decision to end their love triangle, choosing McCormick over Bartlett. LT McCormick and PN1 Crawford now lived together, and both testified against Commander Bartlett at trial. The problem was that their testimony was impeachable as both had admitted to crimes of their own, the least of which were fraternization and adultery. Bartlett was guilty as sin, but a skilled lawyer got him off. What should have been a slam dunk case was lost because of a botched prosecution.

Bartlett even got promoted to Captain and continued to command troops. I took solace in the fact that at least he went to trial, and hoped this had scared him enough so that he wouldn't behave the same way in the future, but who knows? I had done what I could to achieve justice in the matter, done what I thought was right. I was a civilian now, and this was no longer my concern.

Coming home from class one night in December of '04, I had a bit of a scare when I found a manila envelope leaning up against my mailbox marked "Department of the Navy." "Fuck," I thought, was I being recalled again? I angrily tore open the envelope, expecting to find a set of orders, but was relieved when I realized it contained not orders but my 'Certificate of Honorable Discharge.' This meant my eight-year obligation to the Navy was over and I could no longer be recalled. "Whew!" I sighed, glad to close that chapter in my life.

CHAPTER EIGHTEEN

LIVING THE DREAM!

The new shop quickly grew in popularity, drawing outdoor enthusiasts from all over the tri-state area. They came not for a huge selection — Campmor was just across the river with around 100,000 sq ft of showroom space — but, instead, they came for our expertise and our tailored recommendations. I was still doing all of the buying and one of the rules I applied to choosing the best products was that it had to do the job and do it well, regardless of whether it was a budget-friendly product or a high-end one with lots of cool features. I wanted customers to feel confident in our advice and know they were getting the right product for their adventure. Expertise was what set us apart from the competition.

The customer service motto that I emphasized with the staff was "Never sell a customer something they don't need!" I didn't want staff trying to pump up sales by telling inexperienced customers that they needed something just to have them spend more. I believed that by being honest and upfront with our customers, we would build trust and loyalty that would benefit us in the long term as well as satisfy my code of ethics. I called it "Doing business with honor!"

When I hired someone, I would personally run them through every single item that we sold in the shop, explaining why we carried this product over another and what it was best used for. My goal was that every employee could present three facts and a story for every product. It didn't even have to be your own story, but it had to be true. This applied for everything from super expensive 850-fill down sleeping bags to a travel-sized roll of duct tape.

I trained my staff to ask questions and have a conversation with the customer, to find out their plans and level of experience so that we could give them the best advice. For example, many new adventurers assumed a sleeping pads' purpose was cushion and comfort, which is a nice side benefit, but the main purpose is actually insulation from the ground. Without an insulated pad underneath your sleeping bag, you're likely to get cold. For someone just getting into the outdoors, I wanted my staff to bring up the idea of renting gear first — an option that many didn't even know was available.

I actually preferred that those new to outdoor adventure rent first and offered a "try before you buy" program, where we would apply half of the rental fee towards the purchase of a new item in the same category (tent, sleeping bag, stove, etc.) within 30 days of the end of their rental. This gave folks the opportunity to see if the outdoors was really for them before they spent a few thousand on a complete set of gear. It also let them try out somewhat higher-end products to see what they got for their money if they chose to spend a bit more.

Though many shops in New York would raise their prices to account for high rents and labor costs, we sold everything at MSRP — and usually for the same price as you could find online. This often shocked customers who would tell me that they had just bought an item online because they assumed our price would be higher. We were fighting the perception that buying outdoor gear online was cheaper when it was generally the exact same price.

I was focused on building relationships with our customers, not worrying about profits in the near term. I knew that the money would come with time. I'd already established myself as the local outdoor expert and was the go-to-guy for local journalists doing a story on the outdoors so I hoped that folks would value my expertise and choose to buy from my shop rather than a large chain. In New York City, everyone "knows a guy" for something, and if it dealt with the outdoors, my customers would say "I've got a guy."

This was the New York I knew. The New York I'd grown up in, where businesses lasted for generations and personal relationships were everything. If a business owner didn't build trust and become a part of the community, they were done for. That's all changed over the last two decades as people now view New York as a place to live for just a few years. They want to get the "New York experience" before moving back home and buying a ranch house in the suburbs.

New York has always welcomed immigrants from abroad, but most of these immigrants stayed, establishing businesses and building their lives in the city. With this new cycle of temporary domestic immigration, new arrivals were willing to pay whatever it cost for a few years of the experience, knowing that they would then be going back to more affordable cities and towns. They pushed out longtime residents who couldn't afford the artificially inflated rents and altered the character of many neighborhoods as family-owned businesses were forced to close. These new arrivals then left as even newer arrivals came to replace them in turn.

Relationships now mattered less, but as a native New Yorker, that's how I knew to conduct business. Sure, we offered convenience as well, delivering rental gear throughout the city for free and staying open late so that folks would be able to stop by on their way home from work, but I tried to build the business based on relationships and integrity. I believe in serving the community and giving back, so we offered free skills classes, storytelling events, lectures, and movie nights, but business now seemed to be worn down to how cheaply could you sell something and how fast could you get it to the customer.

I found myself often working from home, since we were so overloaded with merchandise there wasn't even room for a desk. I tried to work at the register counter, but my passion for helping customers would always draw me away. I realized that with the new shop open and my staff trained, I didn't have to live in Brooklyn any longer, I could finally move out of the city. The lease for my apartment was up at the end of May, and after my landlord passed away, his daughter wanted to raise the rent by 30 percent. It was time to leave, and I was excited be closer to the mountains.

I would be gone most of the summer leading trips, so I did the math and realized it would be cheaper to rent a hotel room when back in Brooklyn, than it would be to rent an apartment for the summer. I moved out at the end of May and officially became a vagabond. Much of June was spent on the Big Island of Hawaii preparing for and then leading a trip for the United Nations International School (UNIS) as part of their 'Duke of Edinburgh' program. July took me back to Iceland to lead that year's journey on the Laugavegur Trek. After a short period back in Brooklyn to check on the shop, I was off to Denmark and then Greenland, leading trips there in August followed by Norway for yet another adventure before returning to the States in early September.

I was truly living the dream! The shop was doing well, and my managers had things under control. Our international trips were becoming more popular than ever, allowing me to travel from one country to the next leading adventures. Though many people would long for home after a few weeks, I really loved life on the road and found joy in the wandering life. I'd check on the shop when back in Brooklyn, handle any matters that required my attention, and then leave for the next adventure. This was how I had envisioned my life when I started Gear To Go back in 2009: making the buying and hiring decisions but leaving day-to-day operations to my staff while I led folks on the adventure of a lifetime.

I arrived back in Brooklyn shortly after Labor Day and moved into a rented house about two hours north of the city in Beacon, New York. Beacon was a compromise for me. I'd dreamed of moving up to the Adirondacks or the White

Mountains of New Hampshire but still needed to be able to get down to the city, so Beacon would have to do. There was some good hiking in and around Beacon, and it was a nice small town with a solid arts scene. Beacon was an old factory town that had been pretty depressed for decades until the arrival of the DIA art museum sparked a renaissance that drew many artists and work-from-home professionals out of the city and into the Hudson Valley.

It was nice to have space for once. I set up a home office where I could work without distraction and enjoyed cooking meals at home in the first spacious kitchen I'd had since moving back to New York in 2000. The commute down to the city was a pain but I only needed to get down there two, maybe three times a week. Technology allowed me to keep an eye on things remotely with access to cameras and real-time sale figures. I was happy living up in the Highlands and dreamed of someday being able to move even further away.

Just over a week after moving up to Beacon, I was in the shower when I sneezed and my back went out. I'd herniated a disc back in college but after treatment and physical therapy, I'd had no further issues throughout my 20s. In my 30s, I started to have back spasms every year or two that would leave me in pain for a few days but would then disappear. This one was different. I'd never felt so much pain from a spasm before. It left me limping and often barely able to move without pain shooting through my body.

This began a long battle with the Department of Veterans Affairs for treatment other than another shot of pain killer. A battle that would last seven months and result in surgery, but I'll get to that later.

The commute down to the city caused nerve pain to shoot down my leg and often required me to pull over in order to straighten my back and get some relief. I was in agony but I did it, limping to the shop after finding parking and working a full day before the long, painful drive home. Physically, I felt a bit broken, but I was still excited to have made the shop of my dreams a reality.

CHAPTER NINETEEN

A SEA CHANGE

Sales were solid over the summer, but as expected, things slowed down dramatically in September. With kids back in school and folks back at work, there's always a few weeks where all we sell are water bottles and back-to-school packs as we wait for the crisp autumn weather to arrive and bring with it the magic of fall foliage.

We stocked up in October for the winter season, knowing that the first cold day in the city brings in customers looking for a new coat, warm hat, or pair of gloves. But winter came late, and we experienced record-high temperatures that fall with highs reaching into the 70s in November and the low 60s in December. This was the second fall-winter season in a row with record warmth. Climate change was making it impossible to plan for the future.

As we approached the holidays, the bills were already coming in for cold weather gear that should have sold by now. Many of the folks that did come in, tried on a few jackets, and left saying, "I'll think about it." Retail workers know this really means, "Now that I know my size, I'm going to buy this jacket online." We started to see this more than ever in 2016 as a dramatic shift in shopping habits occurred. Folks started to not only do more of their shopping online; they also started buying most of their clothing and footwear online as well.

We were selling lots of last-minute items such as gas canisters and water bottles, but not nearly as many backpacks, tents, and sleeping bags as expected. More and more customers seemed to be "showrooming" us, coming in to ask questions, get advice, and check out a product in person but never buying anything. Some didn't even hide the fact that they intended to buy online.

I started to worry about the growing threat of e-commerce, but since we were in an industry where most of our customers don't have the knowledge to pick the right product without expert advice, I figured that as long as we established that, WE were in fact the very best, industry-recognized experts, customers would recognize the value of what we offered. They would appreciate our expertise and choose to shop with us instead of buying online.

Instead, interactions such as the following became more common.

It's 7:50 p.m. on a Friday night in October when a customer rushes through the door, panicked and scanning the aisles and walls with wild eyes. I've seen this look before and calmly ask her, "Are you looking for anything in particular?" Yes, she has a list. There's always a list when it's a few minutes to closing time!

She tells me that she'd ordered everything she needed online but is leaving for a trip early in the morning, and the package still hasn't arrived. She's panicked because she's been dreaming about this trip for a long time and spent her travel budget for the year on non-refundable airfare, lodging, and tours.

We're closing in ten minutes, but I tell her not to worry, we'll take care of her. I look over her packing list and happily report that we have everything she needs. I add that it's probably even the same price as she paid online — it usually is — and that if she keeps buying online, eventually, we won't be around to help her like this. A lightbulb turns on in her head, but I wonder how long it will stay illuminated.

We lock the doors at 8 but stick around until 8:45 p.m., waiting until she's tried everything on and has all the items she needs for her trip. Three weeks later, we see her again and ask her how her trip was. She says that she had a great time but that she needs to return a few things she didn't end up using. The more likely truth is that her package arrived after she returned from her trip and either she can't return them to the web only store or maybe they undercut us by 10 percent on the price. We honor our return policy, take back the items, and issue a refund.

A man walks into the shop wearing a new-looking backpack that is obviously too small for his frame. He says he's looking to get into backpacking, starting with a weekend adventure in the nearby Catskill Mountains, but he's not sure where. He's worn the pack on a few days hikes and weighed it down with whatever he had on hand to help him train for the jump from day hikes to overnight trips.

I ask, "You have shoulder pain, don't you?"

His response: "Yeah, how did you know?"

"Because that pack is too small for you," I answer, "and all of the weight is being borne on your shoulders, not your hips where it belongs!" I pull down the same model backpack, but in the correct size, and adjust it to fit his body. He tries it on, and I teach him how to adjust all of the straps that will enable the pack's suspension system to properly support the weight of the gear he'll put inside. I add sandbags and ask how it feels.

"How much weight did you put in there?" he asks incredulously.

"Twenty pounds," I answer.

"That's amazing — I don't feel the weight on my shoulders. It feels great!

He needs some time to think about buying another pack, so we move on to the other gear he'll need and then we start working on his trip. He figures he can do twenty miles a day, so without telling him he's wrong, I remind him that the Catskills can be pretty tough, with lots of rocks and straight up and downs that will wear out even the fittest adventurer. Besides, isn't the whole point to get out and commune with nature? Eight to ten miles a day will allow you to see some beautiful country while also allowing you to relax in camp, enjoy a warm dinner, and still have time to sit around in the morning enjoying a cup of coffee or two. He comes around to my way of thinking, and we map out his route.

He leaves, only purchasing the map we used to plan his trip. I've spent about an hour and a half with him but he tells me he'll think about the pack and heads out the door. A few weeks later he comes back and tells me that he found the same pack online for 40 percent off and asks me if I can match it. I tell him that that's pretty much the price I pay for the packs, and that though it might be cheaper online, I did spend an hour and half with him, helped him choose the right pack for his body, and planned his trip for him. His response: "It's still money!"

Let me give you some insight into what goes into running an outfitter. First off, we're a bit like farmers in that our success or failure is largely affected by the weather. When making decisions about what and how much to order/plant, we're trying to predict the weather through the end of the growing season.

Almost without exception, manufacturers require us to place our orders almost a year in advance. They might offer some small discount or free shipping, but they basically outsource their forecasting to retailers. If a retailer chooses not to play this game and waits to see how they season turns out, chances are there won't be any product left to buy.

We also need to have sufficient inventory on hand — like a farmer fills a grain silo — so that when the customer comes in for the that first big snowstorm of the season, for example, we have all of the hats, gloves, wools socks, shell pants, and long underwear they need. If we haven't ordered enough a year in advance, we'll likely be unable to get the inventory we need for the season and will lose customers because the manufacturers have already run out of product.

This system worked in the decades before the internet, when folks shopped at their local outfitter for what they needed and a bad season or two could be endured and made up for in future years. With an exponential increase in the number of folks doing most of their shopping online, local outfitters are losing what I'd call "planned purchases" — such as a new tent or high-end sleeping bag — but are still expected to be fully stocked for emergencies and last-minute items.

With low overhead — and without the need to hire knowledgeable employees — web-only stores can easily afford to fill their warehouse, and if the season doesn't turn out as planned, they can simply dump the product on the market at a deep discount, still making a profit based on volume.

There are Minimum Advertised Price (MAP) policies that are supposed to protect small brick & mortar retailers from this practice, but they are rarely enforced by the manufacturers. When I found a nearby retailer advertising a steep discount on a water bottle brand I was carrying, the response from the manufacturer was, "Well, they buy a lot of bottles!"

Basically, a small local outfitter is bearing the risk of a bad season for both itself and the manufacturer. It then must compete with a giant warehouse-based web store that can blow it away on price due to low operating costs and minimal customer service requirements. To make matters worse, in the last few years, these same manufacturers that require outfitters to figure out how much they should produce, are now selling against them with direct and often discounted sales from their own websites.

Now you may be thinking that this situation is just progress and that efficiency in business and cost cutting is to be rewarded.

I agree, but I believe we're leaving a few things out of the equation. There is value that a neighborhood outfitter offers that cannot be provided by a website and that value cannot be made up with a 10 or 20 percent discount.

First, there's money wasted when a customer goes online and buys the wrong product for their needs. It might be an ill-fitting backpack, a canister stove that won't work in below freezing conditions, or a really comfy sleeping pad that has no insulation for cold weather trips. Second, there's the education that comes not just from interactions with employees but also from the free classes and lectures that most local outfitters provide.

Finally, there's the sense of community! At my shop, we hosted outdoor-themed movie nights, invited speakers and authors in for lectures and book signings, hosted a storytelling event called "Trail Tales," led day hikes and weekend backpacking trips in the nearby mountains, and even organized a shuttle service to make sure folks could get to the wilderness without a car.

When natural disasters such as Hurricane Sandy hit with just a few days' notice, and without time to order supplies online and have them shipped, we had everything folks needed to get through the storm. We also offered our rental gear to those who needed it without charge, collected and delivered relief supplies to hard hit areas, and even shuttled relief workers to where they needed to go. These are areas where a website cannot compete, and it is this value that is being overlooked by consumers.

As for manufacturers, I believe their refusal to enforce MAP pricing, their eagerness to increase sales by selling direct to consumers, and their practice of offering steep discounts to large-volume, warehouse-based webstores, will only end up hurting them in the end.

Online sales are essentially a race to the bottom, with only price determining where a customer buys what they need.

The problem is that most consumers won't recognize the difference between an $80 tent that might be sold in Wal-Mart, and a $300 tent that might be sold in an outfitter. They won't know that if they purchase the $80 tent and it rains or the wind blows, they're likely to wind up wet, with broken poles and a collapsed tent. It takes a knowledgeable employee to educate the consumer and then guide them through the decision-making process, so that the value and advantages of a product are understood beyond simply looking at its price.

Let's revisit that customer with the ill-fitting backpack. If I hadn't told him that it was too small for him, he might have decided that the manufacturer just makes poorly designed backpacks that don't support the weight properly and hurt his shoulders. He might mistakenly blame the manufacturer and vow never to buy one of their products ever again or he might even give up on backpacking altogether, thinking it's simply not for him. What will happen when there's not a knowledgeable employee around to fit him properly?

In the future, when that package doesn't arrive on time and your trip is the next day where will you go after your local outfitter has shut down? When that storm warning is broadcast and there's not enough time to have supplies shipped, where will you find the emergency supplies needed to ride out a storm and its aftermath? When you want to get inspiration for a new adventure, share stories from your last, or just see what's new in gear, where will you go?

Finally, when you drive past rows of empty storefronts and long for the unique mom & pop shops that drew you to your neighborhood or made your hometown special, who will you blame?

CHAPTER TWENTY

CIVIL WAR

By the middle of Fall 2016 I realized that we were in trouble. We hadn't seen the increase in sales that would normally occur with the autumn dip in temperatures, and with campgrounds closing for the season, we wouldn't see much rental business until the spring. By itself, the warm temperatures would mean that we would break even or turn a smaller-than- expected profit. When combined with the dramatic rise in e-commerce sales, it became obvious that our ship was in trouble. We were headed for the rocks and I needed to take action.

I essentially ran the ship aground to avoid a much worse fate, halting payments on the line of credit Steven had extended to us to purchase the initial inventory, followed by a reduction in staff hours. I delayed any payment I could as I worked to repair the damage. We weren't sinking but we weren't making way either. The long-range weather forecast became an obsession of mine, and I checked it often, looking for a hopeful sign that cold weather would soon arrive and bring with it a flood tide to lift our humble vessel. We needed the winter to be an actual winter but at least the holidays were approaching, and that should help keep us afloat.

Steven came in unannounced one day in mid-November and asked to speak with me. He opened the conversation with a demand that I give him a larger percentage of ownership. I was surprised but open to the idea of selling him part of my interest, but this wasn't what he wanted. Steven made clear that he didn't want to buy a larger interest; he just wanted me to give him more because the business wasn't performing as we both had expected.

I stayed calm and explained that we had negotiated and signed a contract that spelled out the ownership interest, so why would I just give up mine? He grew angrier as the conversation went on and was essentially demanding that I give him a majority ownership interest, surrendering control of the company I had worked so hard to build. Of course, I refused, and this sent him into a rage. He stormed out yelling, "You'll hear from my lawyers!" as he slammed the door. Walking back to the counter and the stunned employees, I said, "That went well." So, now, on top of all our debts, I'd have to hire lawyers to represent the interests of the company instead of using that money to keep us in business.

We were really gambling on winter and the holiday season to bring in enough revenue to pay off our debts and keep us afloat until things picked up in May. If we could just make it to May I knew we could pull through. I'd have to cut back on inventory and invest more in marketing and advertising, but I knew that if we could just make it to May, the summer would bring in the cash we needed and even provide a reserve. We just needed our winter bet to pay off so we could make it that far.

I ordered more of the products I knew would sell, so that when winter finally did arrive, we'd be able to profit from it and get back on track. The largest order was with Mountain Hardwear, and as the ship date approached, I sent in a few last-minute revisions only to learn that the order had been canceled. Panicked, I called our sales rep and found out that, after our contentious conversation in November, Steven had not only called his lawyers but had also called our vendors and canceled our orders. He stated that he was the sole source of financial backing for Gear To Go Outfitters and that he was pulling out, demanding that no further product be shipped to Gear To Go.

Steven had no authority to do this, and I was surprised that a company like Mountain Hardwear would allow someone, who wasn't listed as a buyer or a corporate officer, to simply call up and cancel orders. When I explained that Steven had no authority to change or cancel anything they agreed to reinstate the order but most of the best-selling items had already been snatched up by other retailers. We would make do with what we could get, but it would now be even harder to catch up this winter.

By calling our suppliers and not only canceling our orders, but also bad mouthing us to these companies, Steven did real damage to relationships that I had spent years building. It was now harder to get orders shipped on credit, and many of the items we wanted were instead sold elsewhere. Steven caused damage not only the company but also to his own interests, as it was now even more difficult for us to bring in the revenue needed to pay back his line of credit and grow the company.

Our lawyers were already arguing back and forth about the future of Gear To Go as well as who was at fault for our failure to meet financial expectations. I was really fed up and if this was how it would be going forward, I was fine with leaving the company as long as I got paid. For his part, Steven refused to pay anything and demanded that I simply leave and surrender my majority interest to him. This insane demand grew out of his ego as a banker. He believed that because he'd had success in picking stocks and choosing investments, that this would naturally translate into success at running a business.

Steven then claimed that he had no idea that the business was in trouble and that I had failed to update him on the financial status. To clarify, he claimed this until I produced the email where he asked if he could take over the financial side of things including choosing whom to hire as a bookkeeper and accountant. I valued his expertise in these matters and recognized that this was a weakness for me, so I consented and granted him the authority to choose whomever he wanted. The email put an end to that part of our dispute but things were still escalating.

I thought back to law school contracts class and recognized that Steven's conduct in taking it upon himself to call our suppliers, cancel our orders, and damage our reputation, constituted 'Tortious Interference with a Contract.' I asked our lawyer to raise the issue with Steven's counsel and to look into filing suit. Steven's team of lawyers dismissed our claim, arguing that he had only informed our suppliers that he was no longer guaranteeing the orders, and that he had a right to do so. I had hoped that raising this issue would help Steven see that he was doing damage to both the company and his own interests, but it didn't work.

We filed suit against Steven, which caused one of his lawyers to go into a rage, essentially throwing a tantrum by email as he made wild threats against both Gear To Go's attorney and me personally. My goal was really just to end the dispute, but I also wanted to show that I was not powerless to fight back against what was essentially a hostile takeover. Steven was trying to take the company out of my hands for something that neither of us had foreseen and that neither of us could control.

I told our lawyer, "If he thinks he's such a great businessman, then let him buy me out." We seemed close to a deal where I would get some money and carry on with the rental business and guide service while he would take over the retail store. I even gave him an idea of how best to proceed with his new business.

I'd seen the shift in demand to last-minute items and suggested he focus on these types of products. I'd also noticed that many of the millennials living in the city were really into products that made them look outdoorsy, even if they wouldn't necessarily function well in the mountains. I suggested that a combined focus on these two areas would likely be more successful in the current retail climate than the expertise-based model that I had been operating.

We seemed close to a deal — until the issue of who would own the name 'Gear To Go Outfitters' came up. I needed to take the brand with me if I had any chance of the rental business succeeding and assumed Steven would want to rebrand the shop with a new focus. I was wrong. The deal fell apart over Steven insisting that he get to keep the brand name without paying anything extra for it. We were locked in a stalemate as the situation grew more dire.

CHAPTER TWENTY ONE

"CRY OF THE VULTURES"

I cut back on everything I could and soon we were operating with just two employees per shift, down from four or five when we opened. I would occasionally cover the shop by myself, which risked not only theft, but also the loss of waiting, impatient customers. On Christmas Eve, it was just me in the shop, and I stayed open until around 9 p.m. That night, as I totaled up the sales for the holiday season, it looked like there was hope that we might be able to hang on if winter would just get here already. I noted that most of our sales had come in the last week as people shopped for last minute gifts and worried about online orders arriving in time.

As January temperatures climbed into the 60s, I knew on some level that we weren't going to make it, but I was too stubborn to admit it. The clearance sale that would normally run in March, started just after the new year, and I focused on paying the bills that were the longest past due. I held off on paying rent to make sure I had enough money to bring in spring products and meet payroll. We were dropping out of the sky, but I didn't want to give up. Like a good Navy pilot, I would try A, try B, try C, and keep going, hoping I'd find the solution and not wanting to admit that it was time to bail out.

I flew out to Salt Lake City in early January for the Outdoor Retailer winter show. I was the feature story in Outdoor Retailer Magazine. Copies of my blown-up image on the cover were distributed throughout the convention center and displayed prominently on the show floor. I went there with an attitude that had soured as our sales failed to meet expectations. I was angry that manufacturers were not only allowing their products to be blown out at discount prices on Amazon but were now also selling against us with direct discounted sales on their websites.

I tried to use the publicity I had received to raise these issues with the executives of several leading brands but failed to find a receptive ear. The brick & mortar ship had already sailed. Though they wouldn't announce it publicly, at least not at a show called "Outdoor Retailer", they all knew it and were planning accordingly. I advocated for the importance of expert knowledge to help customers choose their products over cheaper, but less capable options, but they weren't interested in hearing it. It felt great to be recognized for all the creativity and hard work I had put into growing my business in the past, but instead of this honor being a harbinger of good things to come, I began to realize it was a sign that the end was near. Sort of like receiving a gold watch as a retirement gift after serving a company for 30-plus years.

Sometimes you have no other choice but to eject, and towards the end of February, with temperatures 60 degrees above average, I admitted to myself that it was time to pull the handle. I had our lawyers let Steven know that it was over. If he wanted to buy me out, the time was now. He said he wouldn't agree to shutting down, but we simply didn't have a choice. We were already two months behind on rent, owed nearly all of our vendors, could barely meet payroll every two weeks, and there was no indication that things would get better.

By making the decision now and selling off our remaining inventory on clearance, we could at least pay most of what we owed and minimize the damage. We probably could have held on for another year or two, but then we would just crash and burn, causing more collateral damage to our suppliers. Shutting down the retail shop would provide money to settle our debts and allow us stay in business as a rental outfitter and guide service. Due to the new preference for online shopping, the rental service now would be run out of a warehouse, gear shipped to your door with no in-person interaction.

I called a staff meeting at the end of February for those that remained and broke the news to them. I wanted to give them plenty of notice so they could find other jobs and wouldn't be caught without a paycheck unexpectedly. For some, I was even able to find new jobs from within the network of small business owners I knew.

The public announcement came a few weeks later in the form of a 'Moving Sale' sign in the main window and a farewell note to the community that was posted on the door. I'd been seeing more and more of these notes recently and knew that many of my fellow shop owners in the neighborhood were struggling, so I decided to use this opportunity to draw attention to the issue and hopefully encourage folks to shop local.

WE'RE MOVING
STORE CLOSING 4/15/17

AFTER 8 YEARS IN PARK SLOPE, FROM STREET STAND TO STOREFRONT, WE'VE DECIDED TO CLOSE OUR RETAIL STORE AND MOVE OUR OPERATIONS TO THE HUDSON VALLEY

Unfortunately, two record warm Winters piled onto a dramatic shift in how folks shop has made it impossible to maintain a brick & mortar location in Park Slope. We will be focusing our efforts on the areas of our business that made us the most unique, rental gear, adventure travel, and guided trips. **YOU WILL STILL BE ABLE TO RENT GEAR FROM US OR JOIN US FOR THE ADVENTURE OF A LIFETIME.** Rental gear will be shipped to you with just 1-day transit time. This shift in focus will also allow us to add more trips to our schedule. Look for more options in Iceland and elsewhere overseas, plus the addition of trips out West. We also expect to add more rental items to our inventory as we work to grow our business nationwide.

By now you've read way too many of these letters and sadly it looks like there are more coming soon. I hope you will look at our shop closing as the proverbial "canary in the coalmine" and shift your shopping habits back to shopping in your own neighborhood. I've heard way too many people talk about how much they love the "Mom & Pop" shops of Park Slope only to talk about the great deal they got online in the very next sentence. Put down your phone and shop at the great local businesses that are available to you now but are struggling. If your life becomes all about your phone, so will your neighborhood and soon all that will be left will be real estate offices, nail salons, and banks.

We've all enjoyed being a part of the local community and especially loved hearing about your adventures around the world. All of us here at Gear To Go Outfitters hope that we were able to be a small part of what made those trips possible. Thanks for all the support over the years and I hope to see you on the trail!

Very Truly Yours,
Kevin J. Rosenberg

The 'Cry of the Vultures' soon began as folks we had never seen before flooded in to take advantage of our misfortune. Everything was 30 percent off, and even then, folks said they would come back at the end when prices dropped. I told them there would be no further discounts and anything leftover would be liquidated online, but some still showed up in April, only to be disappointed.

I paid off the smallest businesses first, paying them in full and then working to settle debts with our larger suppliers. Most were understanding, and I'm sure they'd been seeing the same story play out around the country, collateral damage from the rise of e-commerce.

I let our landlord Peter know that we couldn't hang on any longer and would be moving out by the end of May. We were breaking our lease, but Peter would benefit from the valuable improvements we had made to the shop. Our rent was overdue, and I had intended to prioritize paying our back rent just as I had with our small business suppliers, but then I was served with an eviction notice. Peter and I had been on good terms for years and I found this to be an unnecessary personal insult. I immediately called Peter and left a message on his voicemail asking him, "Why would you hire a lawyer and pay court fees to achieve the same result you had already achieved without them?" He never responded.

I worked out an agreement with his lawyer where, in exchange for the back rent being forgiven, we would consent to the eviction if we had not vacated by May 1. I was angry that Peter felt it necessary to kick me when I was already down, and as a result, we never did pay that back rent, using that remaining money to pay more to our suppliers.

Gear To Go's last day as a retail store was April 9, 2017. I wanted to have a farewell party on April 15th and needed to time box up the remaining merchandise, sell off the store fixtures, and clear the floor. To tell you the truth, I was relieved that it was almost over; this would be the last day I would ever have to work in retail. I felt let down by the community that I had loyally supported over the years — a community where I now saw an increasing number of Amazon boxes deposited on front stoops and in apartment building vestibules.

Though I was obviously paying a financial price, I actually felt bad for the neighborhood. No one was coming to replace us. Our departure meant that there would never again be an outdoor store in Park Slope. When the next blizzard hit, they'd have to trudge into Manhattan for a new pair of waterproof gloves or warm socks until those stores closed as well. When the next hurricane hit and they needed last-minute items to keep their family safe, what would they do after delivery services were shut down due to the storm? When they forgot a few things before their big summer camping adventure, would they now postpone the trip while waiting for their order to be delivered?

We were busy that last day as folks came looking for one final bargain. I enjoyed watching those that had expected us to offer a greater discount be disappointed to find the prices were the same, or even better, that the item they were hoping to pick up for next to nothing had already been purchased by someone less greedy.

As we closed for the last time, I was glad it was over and looked forward to new adventures to come. Sales were just under $1,000,000 for that first year, but with the cost of operating in the city, our break-even point had been $1,200,000. I knew I'd made the right call as the outlook for brick & mortar retail wasn't getting any better, and most of the neighboring shop owners quietly told me about their own exit strategies. I drove back to Beacon that night feeling at peace.

The following Saturday, we invited the community to join us in celebrating eight years in Park Slope. The floor was wide open with plenty of room. My friend Kari Groff, who played fiddle with the band 'Calamity Janes,' brought along some friends who performed for us, the sounds of bluegrass and old-time music bringing people in from street. Longtime customers dropped by with pizza and beer to help fuel the celebration, and my brother even drove down from Connecticut with my nephew to join in. It was the perfect way to say goodbye to the neighborhood — just the way I wanted it. Farewell to 'The Slope' and good riddance to retail!

CHAPTER TWENTY TWO

A ROUGH TRANSITION

The movers delivered everything to our new home in Buchanan, New York. We were now based in an old factory complex that lay only one nervous mile from the troubled Indian Point Nuclear Power Plant. I quickly hired and trained a new staff, set up the warehouse, and updated the website, all in just over a week. It was the first week of May and I was on a tight schedule. After battling the VA for nearly a year, I was finally having the back surgery I needed. The surgery was scheduled for May 9, 2017 and I would be incapacitated in the weeks that followed while I recovered. The timing wasn't ideal, but I had been in agony for months, and didn't want to put it off.

I remember laying on the stretcher in a cold dark room, laying there by myself as I waited to be wheeled into surgery. I was there for maybe 30 or 40 minutes, just staring at the ceiling and taking stock of my life. I was now free of the anchor that the retail shop had become, and though I was proud of all that I had accomplished, I wasn't happy. I silently asked, "Now what?" What did I want out of my life now that I had achieved so many goals? In the cold, stark loneliness of the room, I thought about a new adventure. "Maybe it was time for a wife and family?"

I had earned a commission as a Naval Officer, flown jets, served in two conflicts, earned a law degree, been admitted to the bar in two states, established myself as an internationally known guide, built a street stand into a million-dollar company, and created my dream outfitter. I had devoted almost all of the last eight years to creating and growing Gear To Go Outfitters, but maybe now, at 43, it was time to focus on more humble goals. For those eight years, I had essentially been living in a bubble, too focused on my mission to even recognize what I was missing out on. I do acknowledge the irony of my midlife crisis; that at a time when most men feel like they sacrificed a life of adventure for their family, I had been living a life of adventure and dreamed of having a family. An adventurous family — or at least an understanding wife.

The surgery went well, but there were some complications. It turned out my disc was herniated not once but twice, with one of the herniations having wrapped around the nerve and calcified. In the process of removing that herniation, the surgeons accidentally nicked my spinal cord, causing a leak of spinal fluid which then required that I lay completely flat for 24 hours. Though I had initially been told that there was a chance I would be able to go home that same night or the next day, the complications resulted in a five-day stay at the Manhattan VA Hospital.

I was really lonely, and though I had a few visitors, I realized that I had sacrificed so much for Gear To Go — not just time and effort, but also friendships and relationships that fell by the wayside as I focused on the business and put these necessities of life off until later. I was thrilled to leave that Friday and spent the next week with my brother and his family. I was in an incredible amount of pain but knew this was a new beginning for me, acknowledging that maybe I needed to be sidelined with a back injury to figure out what was next.

Recovery took a long time and it was probably August before I was able to work in the warehouse. Full recovery took almost a year, but I was motivated and started while in the hospital, walking up and down the hallway doing laps as soon as I was given the green light. My first day hike was a big milestone and I made sure to hike or walk every day, dreaming of when I could once again guide trips.

I worried that being out of sight meant out of mind, and that proved to be true, as we received calls almost daily from customers that were pleasantly surprised to find that we were still in business. "I thought you guys closed," they would say, and I would explain that we had just moved and were no longer offering retail sales. Even Google did us in, listing us as "Permanently Closed" for months until my persistence finally got that corrected.

There was an increase in the amount of national business we did, but we saw a simultaneous drop-off in local rentals as the option to place a same-day order was now unavailable. With a spike in orders from the West Coast, I thought about adding a warehouse in Reno where we could ship quickly to California while also avoiding the high tax rates of the Golden State.

The rental business was making a profit, but nothing like retail had brought in. I'd had to cancel the summer's adventure travel vacations since recovery from my surgery was going slower than I had expected, and at the time, I didn't have any guides that knew the routes well enough to take over. My income dropped rapidly as I tried once again to reinvent both my business and my life.

Working alone in the warehouse that fall, as I packed orders to be sent around the country and cleaned gear that had been returned, I realized that I was becoming depressed. I loved interacting with people, helping them prepare for adventures or leading them on bucket-list trips. Now I found myself simply working in a warehouse packing boxes and scrubbing sleeping pads. I decided it was time to sell Gear To Go and start a new company that would focus exclusively on adventure travel.

I reached out to the major competitors, one based in Colorado and one based in Arizona. I was losing orders on the West Coast that I couldn't ship in time, and I was sure they were losing orders on the East Coast for the same reason. I pitched our 1-2-day shipping time for Northeast Corridor cities as the main selling point and soon heard back from both companies, but they were in no rush and the process dragged on for months.

As my income dropped precipitously, my student loan debt became an even bigger problem than before. I still had the private lender's judgement on my credit report but had worked out a payment arrangement with them and was paying back $500 per month at the time. Navient, the servicer for my Federal loans, was even harder to work with. I had been paying back the loan under an income-based repayment program, which amounted to a significant payment when the shop was doing well and I was earning $100,000 in salary, but now that Gear To Go had collapsed, I was bringing in barely a third of my prior income.

Navient refused to accept evidence of my current income and insisted that I pay over $1,300 per month, basing that figure on tax filings from the prior year. I told them that this amount was impossible, especially given that I was also making payments on my private loans, but they wouldn't budge, demanding that I find a way to make the payments or else!

Unable to pay back my loans and even falling behind on rent while my business continued to struggle along, I looked into bankruptcy. I was tired of being an indentured servant, beholden to these student loan companies that tacked on fees and interest while pushing me into programs that added interest to the principal, forcing me to pay interest on interest. Loans taken out for undergrad and law school that totaled less than $200,000, had artificially snowballed to almost $400,000 in less than 14 years.

I learned that, contrary to popular belief, student loans are in fact dischargeable in bankruptcy, but the process has been made more difficult over the years due to Reagan-era "welfare queen" like propaganda that promoted the false narrative about an epidemic of doctors graduating from medical school and then immediately declaring bankruptcy. The bar was very high but not unreachable in my mind and required a debtor to essentially file a civil lawsuit against the lenders in what is known as an adversary proceeding.

I was left with the choice of living life as an indentured servant, never able to own a home, support a family, or live anything more than a subsistence life, working tirelessly for the lenders and dying still in debt, or I could file for bankruptcy and possibly get a second chance at life.

I chose bankruptcy and feeling simultaneously demoralized and defiant, I walked into the Federal courthouse in Poughkeepsie, New York and filed for Chapter 7 in March 2018. I was done! I'd leave the country if I had to, but I would no longer be a slave!

Though I had graduated from law school 14 years earlier, I'd only practiced law for 2.5 months and didn't really know how to be a lawyer. I met with several attorneys but was quoted unaffordable retainers of between $25,000 - $40,000. I thought, "If I could afford that much in legal fees, I wouldn't need to declare bankruptcy!" I'd have to represent myself in this complex matter and just do my best to both outline the standard for discharge and demonstrate how I met it.

I tried to settle with both Access Group, the private lender, and ECMC, a quasi-governmental collection agency representing the federally guaranteed lender. I offered an amount that I felt I could afford to pay off within five years, but both lenders rejected my offer without consideration. They weren't interested in negotiating, confident that they would prevail and keep me in servitude.

Part of my argument was that the private loans weren't actually student loans after all. My federal loans covered tuition, books, and fees, so I had used the money from the private loans to pay for living expenses such as food, shelter, clothing, and utilities. Since these were general consumer purchases, not educational ones, the debt was best categorized as consumer debt, which is easily wiped out in bankruptcy.

The lawyers for Access Group dismissed my argument until Judge Cecilia Morris, the Chief Judge of the Bankruptcy Court for the Southern District of New York, seemed to indicate that the argument was reasonable and she would consider it. Access Group changed its tune soon after and was suddenly very interested in settling, worried about what it would mean for its other cases if I were to prevail in my argument. We settled for what I consider to be very favorable terms, but which I cannot detail due to a non-disclosure agreement I signed as part of the process.

ECMC was another matter, they simply would not budge and showed no interest in settling. During 'discovery' — the process where each side provides documents and testimony to their adversary — I had requested not only the loan promissory notes but also an accounting of my loan payment history as well as a communication log. I needed these documents to show that I had in fact, been making payments when I could, and communicating with Navient to make arrangements when I could not. I also wanted to show that in the months before being placed into default, I had made several attempts to work out a reasonable payment that I could afford, only to have Navient insist once more on $1,300.

ECMC stood in the shoes of Navient as well as CitiBank and Sallie Mae — the lenders that had come before them. As such, ECMC was required to produce the requested documents but initially refused, arguing that they didn't have access or that it was too burdensome. When the judge ordered them to comply, they sent me a data dump of more than 100 pages of coded text that was practically indecipherable. I had given them every document they requested, been interviewed by their expert witness, and sat through an hours-long deposition where I answered every question they could think of, but instead of extending me the same courtesy as the law requires, ECMC was playing games.

Judge Morris once again ordered them to turn over the requested documents, and I was still waiting for them to comply when I filed for summary judgment on August 24, 2019. In plain English: summary judgment essentially means that the facts are not in dispute and both the law and facts weigh so heavily on the moving party's side that judge should rule in their favor without the need for a costly trial.

I argued that my income, assets, and debts were not in dispute and then outlined how I met the standards to have my student loan debt discharged as set forth in the landmark case of In re Brunner (46 B.R. 752 (S.D.N.Y. 1985)), known thereafter as the "Brunner Test." Even the testimony of ECMC's expert witness was more supportive of my position than it was for theirs, so in their response to my motion, ECMC attempted to lure the judge away from the facts and law, which I pointed out in my reply brief.

> "Defendant, through its lengthy brief, attempts to distract this court with gaslighting and shiny objects because it has no real argument. As Senator Moynihan famously said, 'You're entitled to your own opinion and not your own facts!' Here the facts are undisputed."

I didn't expect to win my motion, but we were taught in law school that it would be legal malpractice not to give summary judgment a shot. Besides, the worst thing that would happen if I lost was that there would be a trial — a trial at which I could still prevail after having the opportunity to provide a more detailed argument.

With ECMC still refusing to comply with my discovery requests, a hearing on the motion was scheduled for December 17, 2019. A few days before the hearing, Judge Morris' law clerk emailed me to let me know that the hearing had been canceled and that the judge planned to issue her decision in the coming weeks. Though unexpected, it seemed like a good sign since I was arguing that there was no need for further hearings and that the judge should simply rule in my favor.

I knew that no decision would come until after the holidays so, once the New Year came, I anxiously awaited word from the court. On the evening of January 7th, I was quietly working at home, catching up on email and planning new trips for the following year.

I then received a surprising email from a reporter at *The Wall Street Journal*.

"I am reaching out to you because I am working on a story about a decision today by a bankruptcy judge at the US Bankruptcy Court Southern District of New York to discharge your student loan debt because it 'imposes an undue hardship on the petitioner and is discharged'."

This was the first I had heard of my victory, so it took a moment to process. I felt relief, knowing that I was out from under the crushing burden of debt I could never repay, but then felt a bit panicked, knowing that my story was now going to be in the *The Wall Street Journal* and shared with the world. I tried to argue with the reporter that I was not a public figure and didn't see why my name had to be a part of the story but they were going to print it anyway and were offering me the chance to make a statement. I figured that ECMC would once again attempt to distort the truth, so I accepted the offer as a chance to at least frame the argument, writing:

"The tide is turning against the idea that student loans should not be dischargeable in bankruptcy. This creation of the banking industry has done harm to many hard working Americans that are simply down on their luck and looking for a second chance. Putting up extra hurdles just because the debt that's crushing them is student loan debt is arbitrary and should not be tolerated. The news today leaves me with a feeling of relief, not celebration. I'm thankful that I get to recover from a crushing financial blow and have a chance to get up, dust myself off, and keep going."

This victory was noteworthy not because I had represented myself, but because I had achieved what just about every bankruptcy lawyer in the country believed was impossible. Over the years, many judges had tacked on a standard that was never included in the Brunner decision: "the certainty of hopelessness" standard. Under this standard, student loans are never dischargeable because you have to prove that you have no hope of ever being able to pay back your loans in the future — even though bankruptcy is supposed to look at the present conditions. One judge even ruled against a debtor because he opined that she might win the lottery someday.

This piece of judicial fiction became the standard, not because an appellate court had affirmed it, but simply because ECMC kept arguing for it and many judges bought in. It was never established as precedent, yet somehow gained the same weight as a Supreme Court decision. It brings to mind the old saying, "repeat a lie often enough and it becomes the truth." Since I was looking at 'Brunner' for the standard, I never considered 'certainty of hopelessness' to apply and never realized how hard it was supposed to be. I just looked at the standard and knew that I met it.

A flood of reporters contacted me as news of the case spread quickly and made national news. Initially, I gave the same statement to every reporter, not wishing to become the face of student loan bankruptcy and hoping to go back to being just a mountain guide, but then I started getting emails from folks in desperate situations that seemed even bleaker than my own. My case had given them hope, hope that they too would be given a second chance to live free from the sentence of student loan debt. I shared my pleadings with them and offered advice on how to obtain legal representation at low or no-cost, but this also made me realize I had the chance to really help people. Sure, it would be humiliating, but I was okay with humiliating myself if by doing so I could help others.

I got back in contact with the reporters that had reached out and agreed to be interviewed. My story was out there and of course the critics tried to distract from what the case stood for by focusing on my decision not to practice law as the cause of my bankruptcy. Focused on this distraction, even though the two events had nothing to do with each other and were separated by 14 years. I'd made more money as an entrepreneur than I ever had as a lawyer, but that didn't fit the narrative about student loan debtors they were trying to spin. It was frustrating to see my case twisted into something it was not, but that just showed how desperate they were, desperate to intimidate others from seeking relief.

My victory against the student loan industry has given hope to hundreds of thousands of Americans being steamrolled by an industry that never thought it could lose. Courts around the nation have already cited the case, while ECMC has appealed the judge's decision and the case will likely make its way to the Supreme Court. The law, the facts, justice, and public policy are all on my side and I'm confident that my attorney, Austin Smith, and I will be victorious, paving a new road for Americans down on their luck to get a much needed second chance.

The issue of student loan bankruptcy is even more pressing given the impact of the COVID-19 pandemic. Millions are out of work and countless businesses will be unable to survive. All of our lives have been upended by this worldwide emergency, but some of us will need more help to get back on our feet than others. Isn't that the point of bankruptcy — to give a second chance to fellow Americans that have been knocked down?

CHAPTER TWENTY THREE

TRAIL BETA - LESSONS LEARNED

Do one thing

My vision of a full-service outfitter may have been too much. I wanted customers to be able to get everything they needed from my shop, whether buying or renting the gear they needed, getting expert advice to plan their trip, and even joining a guided trip. My goal was to make it as easy as possible for folks with busy lives to get out of the city and experience the restorative power of the mountains, but I now realize that it was too much — on many levels.

In business as a retail store, rental outfitter, and guide service, I was essentially running three separate companies, which sounds like a smart idea if you can handle the workload, but after being in business for a while, I realized how this actually hurt all three operations, PARTNERSHIPS!

The outdoor industry in the metropolitan New York region is limited, but there are some great companies in business there, or at least there *were* before retail collapsed in 2017. The problem was that I was competing with everybody!

I couldn't partner with an outfitter to offer classes and presentations in their shop because I was competing against them. I couldn't partner with a guide service to send customers to my outfitter for gear because I was also a guide service. I couldn't offer rental services to either an outfitter or a guide service because, again, I was competing with both. A hard lesson learned: when you're a small business owner, the opportunity to partner with related businesses — ones that you're not directly competing with — makes growing both businesses a whole lot easier.

There's also the exhaustion factor. You hear many folks legitimately complain about how exhausting it is to run one business as an entrepreneur; now imagine running three! I had no time for a social life and sacrificed years of my life, obsessed with growing my business and creating my dream outfitter. It wasn't until I had fulfilled my dream that I realized how exhausted I was. Any one of these businesses could have provided a fulfilling and lucrative career, but I challenged myself to run all three and paid the price. It was a mistake that I know I won't repeat, and I hope you won't either.

When you focus on one thing it's easier to establish yourself as an expert in that field. It's also easier to team up with other businesses to grow your business faster while also enjoying a better quality of life. Do one thing, do it well, and enjoy life!

Don't do it alone

Though it's nice to get all of the glory when things go well, running a business by yourself can be exhausting. You're always on call and when no one else is around to deal with an emergency, you are the one that must drop your plans and miss important family or social occasions to handle things.

As a small business owner, you also need to be a jack of all trades, even if your skills in an area are lacking. Working with a partner may divide the glory, but it also divides the work.

I would, however, recommend that you choose your partner based not just on friendship. Look for a business partner whose strengths complement your weaknesses. You definitely want to find someone you enjoy being around, because you're going to be spending a lot of time together, but you also have to make sure they can do the job. When the Blue Angels pick a new team member, their decision is not based on which candidate is the best pilot, though they obviously must be competent aviators, they look for the one that they best get along with, because they're on the road together for most of the year and spend more time with their teammates than their own families.

Having a partner with a different background or work experience than you is also valuable when making important decisions about the future of your business. You might fall into that 'Field of Dreams' mentality I discussed in Chapter 2, and it may take your partner to help you snap out of it. We all believe that our ideas are based on solid reasoning and logic, but sometimes we're just daydreaming. Though businesses are built on dreams, calculated risk-taking and well-thought-out decisions are required to grow them and keep them afloat.

Avoid Angel Investors

An angel investor will never care about your business the same way that you — the owner — will. They are, by definition, focused on profits and nothing else.

Getting involved with an angel investor may often mean sacrificing your dream for a slightly bigger profit, which for an entrepreneur is like sacrificing your soul. Though they may be called 'Angel Investors,' you really are making a deal with the devil!

Look first for bank loans and other sources of financing if possible. You may have slower growth, but you'll be happier and to me, being an entrepreneur is about more than just profits, it's about dreams and visions, it's about creativity. Entrepreneurs are artists painting on the canvas of commerce and hoping the world appreciates the beauty they've created.

It's still good to be the king

Even if your kingdom is small, or even a street stand, it's still good to be the king. It's a great feeling to walk up to your business in the morning knowing, "I created this!" It feels great to know that you are adding to your community and helping folks out in some small way. You don't need to be the CEO of a fortune 500 company or the profile of a magazine cover to feel this way, it's all about building your dreams. Whatever the size of your business it's still yours and naturally reflects your personality, as well as that of your partners, with whom I hope you are jointly ruling.

Create, don't imitate!

If you're going to start a business, make sure you're adding something and not just imitating another company. It may be that you found a better, more efficient way to do something, or you've created a new and improved product, but whatever it is, make sure you are adding something to the community. If you're drawn to an industry, study it thoroughly and figure out where improvement is needed. Don't just copy someone else and dilute that industry, work to make your industry better; add something to it!

What I've learned

Being an entrepreneur is such a personal thing that it takes a lot of self-reflection to do well. In ROTC we memorized leadership principles, and the one that has always stuck with me was, "Know yourself and seek self-improvement." I've tried to always keep this in mind and the most challenging part has been to "know yourself," to admit who you are, who you want to be, and what you need to do to become that better version of yourself. Be honest and admit your faults and failures while humbly celebrating your victories and strengths.

As a creative person, I've learned that I grow bored by the day-to-day operations of running a business such as a retail store. Though I looked at my creation with immense pride, I'd also started to look at it as an anchor, holding me back from my next adventure. I'm now focused on providing adventures for my clients, so I'm truly in my element, but it took a while to admit that to myself, to admit that I didn't want to run a retail store anymore and that I really didn't want to live in New York City.

I wanted to spend as much time as I could overseas meeting new people and sharing the magic of a wilderness adventure with them. I wanted to help people achieve something they thought was beyond their reach. Just as I couldn't handle the thought of spending my working life in a law office, the thought of spending it in a retail store wasn't much more appealing.

I was diagnosed with ADHD as a kid and always had to do things my way. Once I learned how to adapt, ADHD has been a blessing to me, opening up my creative side, allowing for new experiences and new ideas.

That's what my adventures are after all, a creative expression of how I would like to present a destination, which sites to visit, which mountains to explore, and the order in which to experience them. Sure, I could make more money in a different field, but being a guide is where I belong. As a guide, I can use my talents, express my creativity, and share beauty with the world.

What good did I do?
As I said before, there's no point in starting a business if you aren't adding something to the community, so what did I add, and what good did it do? I believe that I was able to help many New Yorkers overcome their fear of the outdoors and learn to truly enjoy the wilderness. I believe I made it easier for busy city dwellers to escape to the mountains and find some sanity. I believe my outdoor education programs instilled a spirit of adventure in the children I taught and, hopefully, even some of the adults. I believe I established a home, though temporary, for New York's outdoor community and loved how folks would stop in just to tell me about their latest adventure with childlike excitement.

In the end, it doesn't matter what I believe I added — it's really up to the community I served to decide that, but I know that I tried to make things better, and I am satisfied with that.

CHAPTER TWENTY FOUR

"TWO ROADS CONVERGED IN THE WOODS..."

I've always been a fan of the Robert Frost poem "The Road Not Taken" and when deciding on a motto for Gear To Go Outfitters, the choice seemed obvious: "Helping you journey the road less traveled."

Two roads diverged in a yellow wood,
And sorry I could not travel both
And be one traveler, long I stood
And looked down one as far as I could
To where it bent in the undergrowth;

I went to law school because I was following the road I thought I had to. I left that path to start Gear To Go, and grew it from a humble street stand into a million-dollar company, but it wasn't until after I had moved the business out of Brooklyn and undergone back surgery that I finally had time to think about where I was headed. I was burned out from years of running three businesses by myself, but also knew that I couldn't go back to working for someone else. The thought of being able to live where I pleased was exciting, no longer tied down by a brick & mortar business. I was at a crossroads and it was time for a change.

Then took the other, as just as fair,
And having perhaps the better claim,
Because it was grassy and wanted wear;
Though as for that the passing there
Had worn them really about the same

I parted ways with Gear To Go Outfitters at the end of 2018, coming to another spot where "two roads diverged in the woods", selling to a competitor in Arizona and choosing to follow a new and untraveled road where I hoped to find the life I had been searching for as I launched International Adventure Guides in 2019. My path is untrodden and its destination unknown, but it feels like I'm finally headed in the right direction.

> *And both that morning equally lay*
> *In leaves no step had trodden black.*
> *Oh, I kept the first for another day!*
> *Yet knowing how way leads on to way,*
> *I doubted if I should ever come back.*

Gear To Go Outfitters lives on, following the path of its new owner and I feel that for once I am on the right path as well and don't think I'll ever look back. My road is uncertain, but adventures always are, and I feel free to wander the earth in search of where I truly belong.

> *I shall be telling this with a sigh*
> *Somewhere ages and ages hence:*
> *Two roads diverged in a wood, and I—*
> *I took the one less traveled by,*
> *And that has made all the difference.*

Ready for a new adventure, I had planned to move to Norway in the spring of 2020, but the pandemic put those plans on hold for now and I've been travelling around out west while working on this book. I hope to make it over there in spring, to begin a new adventure as an expat.

Life is all about exploration and adventure, or at least it should be. When we challenge ourselves to go beyond our comfort zone, we learn about ourselves and about life. I hope my story will inspire you to reach out for your own goals and dreams, taking risks and occasionally stumbling but always finding a path forward that is uniquely yours. LIVE TO EXPLORE!

Since I started this chapter with another man's poem, I feel it's appropriate to end it with one of my own, thus concluding my story with some final insight into who I am and how I got here.

I'M AN EXPLORER

I'm an explorer, restless, untethered
Driven by wanderlust, ungrounded and weathered
My pack on my back, I'll set off on the trails
Or maybe hop a freight and just ride the rails

Adventure is what guides me, often alone
But still longing to have someone waiting for me at home
Crossing mountains and rivers with skill and with ease
But after decades of wandering, it's now with pain in my knees

I've seen more than most, traveled near and afar
Never satisfied, always curious about what's under the stars
No I can't settle down, just work nine to five
Not knowing what's ahead is what keeps me alive

I've crossed oceans through hurricanes to see what was there
Soared high up in the clouds and floated on air
I've roared with the rapids and sailed calm bays
I pray this is how I get to live out my days

Always dreaming of the next one, never satisfied
Knowing when I fail that at least I tried
Though sometimes pushed back, my spirit is unbroken
I'll be back the next morning as soon as I've woken

It's the spirit within us, we live to explore
Like Franklin, and Amundsen, and all those before
So lace up your boots, go find your glory
Buy me a beer and I'll tell you a story.

ACKNOWLEDGEMENTS

Though my story is the epitome of bootstrapping, that concept is a bit flawed, since I, like everyone else with such a label, had lots of help along the way. To list everyone individually would fill an entire book, so please forgive me if I failed to list your name, and know that I am grateful for all that you have done to help me by giving advice, lending a sympathetic ear, or just being there when I needed you. In the interest of brevity I've focused on those that helped me write this book and share my story with the world.

To my mom Sharon: Thanks for guiding me in my early years and providing me with the courage and inspiration to seek out new challenges and overcome seemingly insurmountable obstacles. I know how much you sacrificed and can only hope that this book serves as a fitting tribute to all that you have done for Craig and me. You passed on a love for books and a passion for writing, and without you this story would never be told.

To my brother Craig: Thanks for always having my back, letting me tag along when you were a teenager, supporting my crazy adventures, and for being strong enough to make peace when we fought. You've always put family first and everyone in your life is better for having known you. Over the process of writing this book we both relived old memories — some painful, some joyous — but I appreciate you taking the journey with me.

To my sister-in-law Mary Ann: Thanks for the support and kindness over the years, for driving me around after my back surgery, for the amazing home-cooked meals, and especially for the birthday pies.

Steve Bury: Thanks for always having my back, sharing the adventure of learning to fly, and helping me start Gear To Go Outfitters. You were with me for many of the stories detailed in this book and I hope we share some epic adventures in the future.

Julie Safran: Thanks for being there for me after my surgery, for offering a rational perspective on my crazy ideas, and for listening with a sympathetic ear when I just needed to vent.

Tracy Ross: Thanks for inspiring me to write my story and helping me to get started. I look forward to reading about your next adventure.

Jon Glaser: Thanks for stopping into my shop to talk gear and for writing the foreword to this book. I hope your future projects allow you to combine your passion for the outdoors with your passion for making people laugh.

Dan Hudson: Thanks for taking the time to serve as a mentor with the Veterans Writing Project, helping me navigate the publishing process, and most importantly, for offering valuable feedback and straightforward advice.

Anne Kniggendorf: Thanks for taking the time to serve as a mentor with the Veterans Writing Project and for helping me navigate the publishing process.

To Jayne Turner, Fred Dobro, Misty Huggins, Luke Norris, Catherine Borgia, and Jen Doebler: Thanks for reading through rough drafts and providing valuable, honest, feedback.

Neil Napolitan: Thanks for taking the time to read through early drafts and for serving as my "Senior Advisor," always ready to help out with shop repairs and tangled fishing lines.

Niv Novak: Thanks for the generous gift of a new laptop after mine broke in the midst of writing my manuscript, literally making this book possible.

Thanks to my fellow shop owners of Park Slope, especially the folks at D'Vine Taste, Community Bookstore, and Tony Fanning Realty. Thanks for the encouragement, inspiration, and most of all, your friendship.

To my former employees: Thanks for sharing this adventure with me. For a brief time we worked as a team to operate the only authentic outdoor shop New York City has ever known, and I couldn't be prouder. We shared victory and defeat together, but no other business has come close to reaching the heights to which we soared.

Thanks to the loyal customers who frequented my street stand and later my shop. I hope my staff and I inspired you to spend more time seeking adventure and less time seeking fortune. Life is short, so live to explore!